D0482745

"Sandra Day O'Connor and her brother, H. Alan Day, have taken all the themes of the conventional Western narrative—the roundup, the wild horses, cattle and cattle stampedes, the rattlesnakes, the natural disasters like flash floods, and the colorful figures of cowboys—and transposed them from the usual narrative of the isolated, rootless male figure of the Western into the story of three generations of a family and their relationship to an arid and beautiful expanse of land on the border between Arizona and New Mexico. It's a story of what the land taught them and what it takes to survive under extremes of drought and distance. This is a book for every reader, whether interested in conservation, history, family dynamics, education, or just plain adventure." —JILL KER CONWAY

"A loving but clear-eyed portrait of a distinctive and vanished American way of life." —*The New York Times Book Review*

"There is a line in this book that says it all: 'The dust didn't settle on the ranch road for days after the wedding.' The wedding was that of Sandra Day O'Connor, and the road led to a ranch and a life called the Lazy B. This beautifully told story of the Lazy B will eventually settle on the reader and, like a magic dust of smiles and pleasures, stay there forever." —JIM LEHRER

"A charming memoir about growing up as sturdy cowboys and cowgirls in a time now past." —*USA Today*

"Though O'Connor's name initially conjures images of austere black robes and the halls of justice, a very different person emerges from the childhood recalled here. . . . [A] clear picture of the American Southwest during the early to mid-twentieth century." —*Publishers Weekly*

"[An] affectionate portrait of life on a desert ranch in the years before WWII." —*Kirkus Reviews*

PHOTO COURTESY OF MARGARET PLUNKETT LORD

SANDRA DAY O'CONNOR was born in El Paso, Texas, and attended college and law school at Stanford University. She has been married to John O'Connor since 1952, and they have three sons. She was an Arizona state senator from 1969 to 1975, and she served on the Arizona Court of Appeals from 1979 to 1981. Nominated by President Reagan as associate justice of the United States Supreme Court, she took the oath of office on September 25, 1981, the first woman to do so.

H. ALAN DAY is a lifelong rancher who, after graduation from the University of Arizona, managed the Day ranch, the Lazy B, for thirty years. He also purchased and ran ranches in Nebraska and South Dakota, where he established a wild horse sanctuary that cared for fifteen hundred wild horses under contract with the U.S. government. He lives in Tucson.

Lazy B

SANDRA DAY O'CONNOR

AND H. ALAN DAY

Lazy B

Growing Up on a Cattle Ranch
in the American Southwest

RANDOM HOUSE TRADE PAPERBACKS

NEW YORK

2003 Random House Trade Paperback Edition

Copyright © 2002 by Sandra Day O'Connor and H. Alan Day

All rights reserved under International and Pan-American
Copyright Conventions. Published in the United States by
Random House Trade Paperbacks, an imprint of The Random
House Publishing Group, a division of Random House, Inc.,
New York, and simultaneously in Canada by Random House
of Canada Limited, Toronto.

RANDOM HOUSE TRADE PAPERBACKS and colophon are
trademarks of Random House, Inc.

This work was originally published in hardcover by Random
House, an imprint of The Random House Publishing Group,
a division of Random House, Inc., in 2002.

All photographs, unless indicated otherwise, are courtesy of
the Day family.

Maps on page vi by Jackie Aher

Library of Congress Cataloging-in-Publication Data

O'Connor, Sandra Day
     Lazy B / Sandra Day O'Connor and H. Alan Day.
        p.   cm.
     ISBN 0-8129-6673-2
        1. O'Connor, Sandra Day, 1930– 2. United States.
Supreme Court—Biography. 3. Judges—United States—
Biography. 4. Ranch Life—Arizona. I. Day, H. Alan.
II. Title.

KF8745.O25 A35 2002   347.73'2634—dc21   2001041751
[B]

Printed in the United States of America
Random House website address: www.atrandom.com

9 8

Book design by Barbara M. Bachman

This is in memory of our parents,

Ada Mae and Harry Day

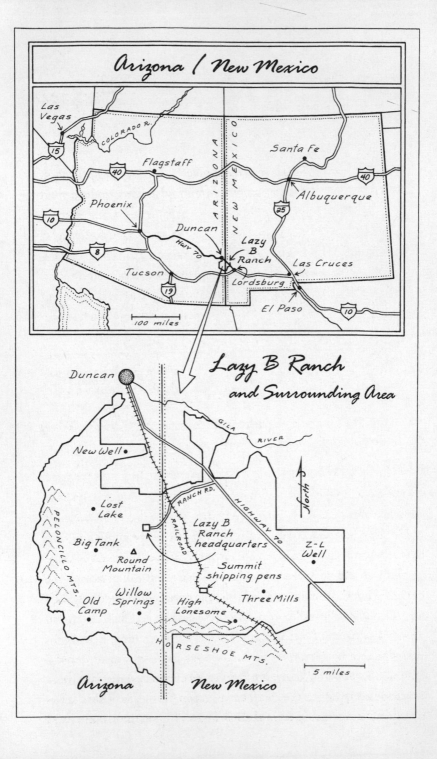

Preface

> There is something about living in big empty space,
> where people are few and distant, under a great
> sky that is alternately serene and furious, exposed
> to sun from four in the morning till nine at night,
> and to a wind that never seems to rest—there is
> something about exposure to that big country that
> not only tells an individual how small he is, but
> steadily tells him who he is.
>
> WALLACE STEGNER,
> "FINDING THE PLACE:
> A MIGRANT CHILDHOOD"

MOST ANY PLACE PROVIDES BETTER GRAZING THAN THE sparse, open high desert country south of the Gila River on the border of Arizona and New Mexico. The rainfall averages ten inches a year or less. There are semiarid mesas ringed on the south and west by volcanic hills littered with boulders and rocks of vesicular basalt—angry black and dark red rocks that are heavy but full of holes. The bubbling liquid from an ancient volcanic core cooled suddenly, before the bubbles burst. To the north is the Gila River, small and timid most of the year. It flows from the nation's first national wilderness area—the Gila Wilderness—and runs across all of Arizona to join the Colorado River below Yuma. For thousands of years prehistoric Indians made camps along the river, as well as on the mesas, where occasionally the rains would form shallow lakes. Around these lakes lived

an impressive array of animals, reptiles, and birds: deer, rabbits, antelope, javelinas, coyotes, bobcats, quail, ducks, doves, rattlesnakes, bull
snakes, Gila monsters, desert tortoises, and a wide variety of insects. It
was no country for sissies, then or now. Making a living there takes a great
deal of hard work and considerable luck. Our family stayed there for 113
years.

H. C. Day, our grandfather, was a New Englander—shrewd, conservative, careful with his money, intelligent, not afraid to tackle new ventures.
He was named for Henry Clay, whose Whig politics were popular in New
England before the Civil War. H. C. Day worked on the family farm in
Coventry, Vermont, until 1865, when he turned twenty-one. Then, a free
man, he opened a general merchandise store on the Canadian border,
some ten miles north of Coventry. He made a nest egg and moved west to
Wichita, Kansas, a central hub in the westward expansion. There he
opened a building-supply business, furnishing materials for the rapid
expansion of that city after Congress abruptly appropriated lands claimed
by several Indian tribes. He acquired a cattle ranch outside of Wichita, as
well as various other properties. In 1879, at age thirty-five, he married
Alice Edith Hilton, the eighteen-year-old daughter of John Price Hilton
of England, the rector and founder of St. John's Episcopal Church in
Wichita.

The following year our grandfather decided to take advantage of the
availability of public lands for the grazing of livestock in the New Mexico
Territory, in the area covered by the Gadsden Purchase from Mexico. All
one needed was a herd of cattle and a few people to watch over them; God
and the free market would do the rest. H.C. bought a herd of cattle in
Mexico and put them on a parcel of land. He hired Lane Fisher, the son of
a Wichita judge, to run the ranch operations. The Mexican cattle were
branded on the left hip with a B lying down flat. A brand lying down is
called "lazy." Lazy B Ranch it became, and so it remained.

In 1880 the cattle business looked good enough to attract even some
canny investors from Scotland and England to the western United States.
Once the mother cows were purchased, they would produce calves, which

could be sold a year later at a handsome profit. Demand for beef cattle was strong. The grazing on the public domain was essentially free for the taking. Some of these investors put cattle in Montana and Wyoming and later learned to their sorrow how the excessive snow and severe cold weather could destroy the herds. In the Gadsden Purchase area, snow was virtually unknown, and the chances were better that the cattle could forage for grass year-round. Only an occasional Apache raid or a summer drought would cut down the herd.

The problem in the Arizona–New Mexico area was water. Water was scarce and limited the use of the land. Wells could be dug, but often they had to be several hundred feet deep to reach water. Even at that depth, a well was apt to produce only a small stream of four gallons per minute or so. Windmills provided the power to pump water out of the wells. The deeper the well, the larger the windmill required to fit the sucker rod and pump out the water.

H.C. and Alice took their son, Courtland, to England to visit Alice's relatives, and then to Germany, where they stayed for six months. While there, H.C. learned that Lane Fisher was putting his own brand on many of the calves. The Days returned to Wichita and H.C. traveled to Lordsburg, New Mexico, to see what could be done. He consulted a local lawyer, whose advice was, "Mr. Day, get a gun." H.C. was more inclined toward negotiation than a shoot-out. Lane Fisher left, but H.C. had to take over the Lazy B or lose his investment there. H.C. built a house near the Gila River, and a one-room school nearby for his children. He planted an orchard and a garden, brought a schoolteacher from Kansas, and moved in with his family. There Alice gave birth to three daughters, Eleanor, Nina, and Alice. Our father, Harry, their fifth and last child, was born at the family house along the Gila River in December 1898.

The Day family stayed at the Lazy B for ten or twelve years, until a new manager could be located, a pleasant man named Sam Foster. H.C. then moved his family to Pasadena, California, and to a more comfortable life. In the summers, H.C. visited the ranch, taking our father, Harry, along, and supervised improvements to the wells, the building of windmills and fences, and the management practices for the cattle and horses. Harry learned at his father's side how to minimize unnecessary expenses and how to accomplish improvements without major capital outlays. He learned well. As we were growing up, we saw that nothing would ever be thrown away if it had any conceivable practical use. Nothing would be wasted. Repairs would be made on any and all equipment right on the ranch with whatever means were available. A purchase of new equipment or objects was a rare event. No task was too small to be done as well as possible. No task was too large to be undertaken. And no day went by without hoping and praying for rain.

Harry had planned to attend Stanford upon his graduation from high school, but World War I intervened. He was drafted and began training, but when the war ended, he was discharged. At that time H.C. was ill and could not visit the ranch as was his custom. Sam Foster was producing no net income from the ranch and had paid nothing on the mortgage he owed H.C. for his part interest in the Lazy B. H.C. sent Harry to check on the ranch and report back. Harry did, but he had no happy news. In a letter to his sister Eleanor, written in November 1919, our father noted,

> *I have been way back up in the roughest mountains I ever saw for the last week or so range branding. We batched and lived on dry salt pork and fried sweet potatoes. We also slept on the ground and nearly froze. . . . This certainly is a terrible place to live and I hate it here, but I will have to stay here a few months until I get some money ahead. I expect to go east from here.*

Harry never made that trip east. H.C. died in 1921, and our grandmother Alice died five years later. The settlement of the family's estate and the mortgage-foreclosure proceedings stretched out over many years. A new ranch headquarters was built of adobe bricks some ten miles south of the Gila River and in the center of the ranch property, near Round Mountain.

In 1927 Harry went to El Paso, Texas, and bought some bulls from a rancher named W. W. Wilkey. Mr. Wilkey invited Harry to have dinner with his family. The Wilkeys' daughter Ada Mae was there, and an instant spark ignited between Harry and Ada Mae. Harry returned to the Lazy B Ranch the following day and began a correspondence with Ada Mae that spanned three months, after which they saw each other again in El Paso. The subsequent exchange of letters increased in frequency and intensity. In September they eloped, were married in Las Cruces, New Mexico, and returned to the Lazy B to begin their life together in the four-room adobe house at the new ranch headquarters.

Life was not easy. The ranch was producing very little income. The ranch house had no running water, no indoor plumbing, and no electricity. The cowboys bunked on the screen porch surrounding the house. The roads were poor, and automobiles were just beginning to be available.

Harry and Ada Mae lived the rest of their lives at the Lazy B. In time, they had three children: Sandra, Ann, and Alan. When Ann was small and learning to spell, she began calling Harry "DA," pronounced "Dee-ay," and Ada Mae "MO," pronounced "Em-oh" or "M.O." The nicknames stuck, and friends and family alike called them DA and MO henceforth. Harry and Ada Mae thought there was no better life anyone could live than on the Lazy B. Harry died at the ranch in his sleep on April 9, 1984, at the age of eighty-six. Ada Mae died at the ranch on March 3, 1989. In the pages that follow, we describe the life and some of the people and events at the Lazy B in the years that Harry and Ada Mae, and we three children, lived there.

Contents

Lazy B

Top: *H. C. Day on Eagle and Alice E. Day on Dunny.* Center: *Off to the one-room school: Harry, Alice, Nina.* Bottom: *H. C. Day and Alice Edith Hilton at the time of their marriage in 1879, with Donne and Helen Fisher.* Opposite: *H. C. Day, c. 1895*

1. *Early Memories*

When Time, who steals our years away,
Shall steal our pleasure, too,
The Memory of the past will stay,
And half our joys renew.

THOMAS MOORE, "SONG"

THE EARLIEST MEMORY IS OF SOUNDS. IN A PLACE OF ALL-encompassing silence, any sound is something to be noted and remembered. When the wind is not blowing, it is so quiet you can hear a beetle scurrying across the ground or a fly landing on a bush. Occasionally an airplane flies overhead—a high-tech intrusion penetrating the agrarian peace.

When the wind blows, as it often does, there are no trees to rustle and moan. But the wind whistles through any loose siding on the barn and causes any loose gate to bang into the fence post. It starts the windmills moving, turning, creaking.

At night the sounds are magnified. Coyotes wail on the hillside, calling to each other or to the moon—a sound that sends chills up the spine. We snuggle deeper in our beds. What prey have the coyotes spotted? Why are they howling? What are they doing? Just before dawn the doves begin to call, with a soft cooing sound, starting the day with their endless search for food. The cattle nearby walk along their trail near the house, their hooves crunching on the gravel. An occasional *moo* to a calf or to another cow can be heard, or the urgent bawl of a calf that has lost contact with its mother, or the low insistent grunt, almost a growl, of a bull as it walks steadily along to the watering trough or back out to the pasture. The two huge windmills turn in the wind, creaking as they revolve to face the breeze, and producing the clank of the sucker rods as they rise and fall with each turn of the huge fan of the mill.

The Lazy B Ranch straddles the border of Arizona and New Mexico along the Gila River. It is high desert country—dry, windswept, clear, often cloudless. Along the Gila the canyons are choked with cottonwoods and willows. The cliffs rise up sharply and are smooth beige sandstone. The water flowing down the riverbed from the Gila Wilderness to the northeast is usually only a trickle. But sometimes, after summer rains or a winter thaw in the mountains, the river becomes an angry, rushing, mud-colored flood, carrying trees, brush, rocks, and everything else in its path. Scraped into the sandstone bluffs are petroglyphs of the Anasazi of centuries past. Their lives and hardships left these visible traces for us to find, and we marvel at their ability to survive as long as they did in this harsh environment. High up on one of the canyon walls is a small opening to a cave. A few ancient steps are cut out of the bluff leading to it. To reach it now requires climbing apparatus—ropes and pitons. The cave's inner walls have been smoothed with mud plaster, and here and there is a hand-print, hardened when the mud dried, centuries ago.

Every living thing in the desert has some kind of protective mechanism or characteristic to survive—thorns, teeth, horns, poison, or perhaps just being too tough to kill and eat. A human living there quickly learns that anything in the desert can hurt you if you are not careful and respectful. Whatever it is can scratch you, bite you, or puncture you. When riding horseback, you have to watch where you are going. The branch of a hardy bush can knock you off; a hole in the ground covered with grass can cause your horse to stumble or fall. When you take a spill, it might be onto a rock or a cactus. When you get off your horse, it pays to look first to avoid stepping in an ant den, on a scorpion, or in the path of a snake. Over the years, Alan, Ann, and I each had our share of falls from a horse, insect bites, injuries, and other dangerous events, which we learned just came with the territory.

South of the Gila and to the east, the land is flat. For some ten miles it is covered with short burro grass and hummocks of tabosa grass. There are soapweeds—tall, hairy-looking yuccas, some with two or three trunks. In May they send up tall stalks with clusters of off-white blossoms that last about a month. These dramatic sentinels in the flat landscape are weirdly beautiful. The stalks, when dry, make good cattle prods, or fine lances for children's war games. The dry pods from the blossoms are good additions in dried-flower arrangements.

The mesa land is part of a large dry lake bed from an earlier time. It is hard to imagine this land covered with water. Places along the edge of it show signs of Indian camps. As children, we found many buff-colored pottery shards, an occasional metate, or grindstone, sometimes a projectile point or pieces of obsidian that had been flaked off in the process of making the projectiles. I would spend the hours waiting for DA to finish some work in that area looking around for some of these bits of Indian life and times. I would take them home to show MO, who greatly enjoyed finding such treasures. We would talk about the lives these early inhabitants led.

Water was scarce and hard to find. Every drop counted. We built catchment basins and dirt tanks to catch and store it. We pumped it from underground. We measured it and used it sparingly. Life depended on it.

There were thirty-five wells and windmills on the Lazy B, and it was a big job to keep them pumping. The windmills and pumps had to be oiled and serviced regularly. During periods of drought and dry weather—periods that seemed to predominate—the ranch crew spent most of their time keeping the wells working and hauling supplemental feed to the cattle. When a well went bad or a pump broke down, it was a serious matter. There might be only a day's supply of water in reserve in that area. The cattle could not survive more than a day of dehydration. There were times when we had to work through the night to try to get the well or pump repaired, to supply the livestock with water.

I recall some grim, difficult times when DA and the cowboys would have to stop all other work to repair a well that had ceased producing water for the cattle. Work would begin at daylight and continue into the night.

Sometimes the sucker rods had to be pulled out of the well and removed, one at a time, until the problem was located and solved. It could be a broken sucker rod deep in the well. It could be a corroded casing pipe that was allowing water to escape. It could be any number of things that took strength, time, skill, and energy to repair. There was little I could do to help. The work required more strength than I had. I could serve like an operating-room nurse—I would get a wrench, a hammer, or another tool that was needed and put it into my father's outstretched hand. More often, I read a book I had brought along or I watched the work and engaged in desultory conversation with the men.

If we failed to complete the repairs before the water tank was empty, we had to gather all the cattle and move them to another location where there was enough water and grass for them to survive.

The east part of the Lazy B is on the Lordsburg Flat—a large, flat, desolate area that is not the best grazing land on the ranch. The underground water is about three hundred feet deep and in places does not taste very good, but the older wells in that area all have splendid wooden windmill towers over them. In the 1920s a master craftsman constructed these towers on the site, with beautiful, long, straight timbers all cut by hand and mitered to fit, and they have weathered over the years to a soft gray color.

Some of the names of these watering places are colorful and descriptive. In the east part of the ranch is Z-Bar-L. It was named for the brand MO put on her cattle. The brand had no significance; it is just a brand DA had registered at an earlier time. A few miles away from there is Three Mills, named for the three windmills around the big water pond that served the cattle. When the first well was drilled, it was so weak and produced so little water that two more wells were drilled to supply enough water for the cattle. Wimp Well was named after the scrubby old fellow who drilled it. High Lonesome is the most descriptive name on the ranch. It stands alone as a sentinel over a a large, bare prairie that is roughly on the Continental Divide. When you are there, you can feel that High Lonesome is the proper name. Willow Springs is a shallow well located in a beautiful, narrow, rocky canyon. This is the prettiest location on the ranch.

The ranch headquarters is named Round Mountain, for the perfectly round volcanic cone that rises six hundred feet above the prairie about a mile south of headquarters. Round Mountain is visible from almost any-place on the ranch and appears on many air-travel maps. Cottonwood Spring is a flowing spring surrounded by large cottonwood trees located in the northeast part of the ranch, near the Gila River. We particularly enjoyed going to Cottonwood Spring; to see water seeping out of the ground was always a miraculous sight in that dry land. The cottonwood trees provided shade, and the canyon, with its steep, colorful walls, was cooler than the surrounding mesas. I could never resist digging in the sandy canyon floor until a pool of water would fill the hole. I also always scoured the canyon walls to try to find petroglyphs etched in the stone. The early Indians who made them left symbols of animal and bird life that have lasted thousands of years.

At eight hundred feet, Lost Lake is the deepest well on the ranch, located adjacent to a dry lake formed by drainage coming out of the mountains that surround it on all four sides. The dry lake bed would sometimes fill with floodwater in the monsoon season. The water flowing in would be brown, muddy, and full of leaves, sticks, debris, and foam from the flash flood. As the water receded over the succeeding weeks, it would leave wide areas of a coating of slippery mud. The cattle would walk through the mud to reach the remaining water, and their legs and even their bellies would have a coating of dried mud on them for months.

Sands Ranch, also a part of the Lazy B, is eight miles south of Lost Lake and was once the homestead of John Sands. He and his son Tom ran goats on this little ranch, but their main income was from the bootleg whiskey they made there. During Prohibition John and Tom took a wagonload of whiskey to Bowie to sell. They made the mistake of selling a gallon to a federal agent who was there to control bootlegging. When the agent attempted to arrest them, John pulled out his pistol and tried to shoot the gallon out of the agent's hand. John was killed in the shoot-out and Tom was shot in the arm. Tom's arm shriveled, and he could never use it again. His heart was no longer at the ranch, so he sold it to the Lazy B. The ranch hands dug a forty-foot-deep well on his land, and that area has always been known as Sands Ranch.

Robbs' Well is up the canyon about five miles east of Sands Ranch and was homesteaded by Fred Robbs. He was unable to make a living on this tough piece of land, but the well he drilled and the old wood shack next to it have always remained as Robbs' Well.

Antelope Well was drilled when Ann was about eight years old. When DA decided to drill a well in that area, he took Ann with him the day he went out to choose a site; the well got its name from a little herd of antelope they saw on the way. DA had brought a green willow limb with them, and he got Ann to "witch" the well with the willow limb. Some people are said to be able to locate underground water by holding a forked willow branch or a peach-tree branch over the area. When the branch pulls down, it indicates that water is below the surface. There was some question about whether they could hit water or not, since several wells had already been drilled in the area—all dry. At the place Ann selected, they ended up drilling through hard rock. During the drilling, the driller came to DA twice to ask for more money per foot for boring through such hard rock. With so much already invested, DA reluctantly agreed. At five hundred feet, they hit a good stream of water. Developing reliable sources of water and keeping all the wells, windmills, and pumps operative was a major part of the work at the Lazy B.

It is possible to survive and even make a living in that formidable terrain. The Day family did it for years; but it was never easy. It takes planning, patience, skill, and endurance. DA said he had to plan for the lean years and the low cattle prices, because there were so few years when there was plenty of rain and a good market for the cattle as well.

The CCC Camp in 1937. COURTESY OF REBECCA RICHINS

Opposite: *The Duncan train station.*

2. Local History

The Gadsden Purchase territory was
"so desolate, desert, and God-forsaken that
a wolf could not make a living on it."

ATTRIBUTED TO KIT CARSON
BY JAY J. WAGONER,
Early Arizona

*T*HE ORIGINAL INTERNATIONAL BORDER BETWEEN MEXICO AND the United States was established along the Gila River. After the Mexican-American War of 1846–48, President Franklin Pierce sent a diplomat named James Gadsden to Mexico to purchase some land. It was the era of transcontinental railroad building, and a southern route from New Orleans to Los Angeles required some additional land. Because of our victory over Mexico, Congress assumed that negotiations would be easy. Mr. Gadsden negotiated for the better part of a year and came back with his report. He had obtained an agreement from Mexico to purchase all of what is now the southern part of New Mexico and Arizona, as well as all of what is now the state of Sonora, Mexico, and all of Baja California. On the mainland side, the purchase was to extend south of the current city of Guaymas. This would have given the United States a deep-water port on the Gulf of California. The price was $15 million.

Unfortunately, while Gadsden was busy negotiating in Mexico, Congress had more pressing concerns. It was deeply embroiled in debate over issues of economics, tariffs, and slavery and secession. These pressing issues took precedence over desert land and rattlesnakes. Congress sent Mr. Gadsden back with a $10 million offer.

The compromise produced the present border with Mexico. On

December 30, 1853, the United States formally agreed with Mexico to purchase the area that became known as the Gadsden Purchase. The Mexican government accepted the $10 million, and the line of our present international border was drawn. This land was added to the territories of Arizona and New Mexico. All of the Lazy B Ranch lies within the area of the Gadsden Purchase.

New Mexico became a state on January 6, 1912; Arizona, on February 14, 1912. After the passage of the Taylor Grazing Act in 1934, the basic land-ownership pattern in Arizona and New Mexico was that approximately 70 percent of the land was owned by the United States, approximately 20 percent by the states, and the remaining 10 percent was privately owned. Most of the private land was situated around water sources. Access to water was the essential element in making a valid homestead or in obtaining grazing rights under the Taylor Grazing Act.

When H. C. Day founded the Lazy B Ranch in 1880, all the land was open range. There were no fences and no governing laws for the use of the public lands. Anyone could put cattle on the land to graze. The Lazy B and other ranches in the Southwest were essentially unregulated. H. C. Day was a shrewd businessman, and he knew it was in his long-term best interests not to overgraze the land, and he did not. The passage of the Taylor Grazing Act required land users to adjudicate their claims for the right to lease the grazing lands and to fence those lands for which grazing leases were approved. The federal government established district offices to administer the grazing-right claims and the eventual allotments of numbers of cattle permitted to graze. Government control at first was minimal. The entire Safford Grazing District of 1.5 million acres was staffed by one man and two secretaries.

The adjudication of grazing rights raised many serious and contentious issues. The principle that emerged was that the individuals who owned water—wells or ponds or stream rights—would be entitled to obtain grazing rights from the federal government on the surrounding grazing land for as far as it was practical for a cow to walk from the water to graze. There were many hotly contested disputes over grazing rights.

DA was appointed to the Grazing Adjudication Board. He spent much of his time for two or three years trying to resolve the disputes. How does one deal with two angry men who have each run cattle on the same range-land for the last twenty years or more?

Our neighbor Orville Rayburn was one such man. Orville was a scruffy-looking little man with small, cunning eyes. He seldom shaved or bathed. The only money he ever spent to develop water was to drill a well on his small homestead. He was eventually allotted four square miles of grazing rights around his homestead. He unhappily agreed to the allot-ment. But when the fencing crew arrived to fence his place along the agreed boundaries, Orville met them with his rifle loaded and in the ready position. "Get off my land!" he snarled at the crew through his tobacco-stained handlebar mustache. Not wanting to test Orville's resolve, the fencing crew left.

DA went to see Orville to determine what could be done. DA offered Orville 3,000 additional acres that had been allotted to the Lazy B. Orville accepted, and the fencing crew returned. He came out to his porch in his dirty long johns, holding his rifle cocked and ready. Once again, the fenc-ing crew left. DA could have forced the settlement. Orville had no right to any additional land. But DA felt in an awkward position. He was a neigh-boring rancher with his own much larger allotment awarded, and he was also a member of the adjudication board. DA finally yielded 6,000 addi-tional acres to Orville—acres that had been allotted to the Lazy B. Orville's attitude changed dramatically. The fence was built, and Orville would fre-quently visit the Lazy B headquarters uninvited. But Orville's self-anointed membership in the Day circle of friends was under careful scrutiny by MO. She was hardworking and fastidious in her household domain. Many times she watched Orville wolf down food she had pre-pared and then saunter down to the barn to help himself to horseshoes for his horses. He also took various items from the ranch house from time to time. Occasionally MO reprimanded Orville, but more often she just watched in silence.

One day our family was gathered in the living room, reading, playing checkers, and talking. Orville arrived unannounced and sat down. He propped his dirty boots up on a low coffee table and chewed his tobacco. "That boy of mine ain't worth a damn," he said. To emphasize his disgust, he spat tobacco juice across the room in the general direction of the fireplace. MO stood up immediately—all five foot, four inches of her—and asked Orville to leave. With her hands on her hips, she said, "Do not come back here again without an invitation, Mr. Rayburn." We saw much less of Orville Rayburn after that.

The final land allocation to the Lazy B Ranch was approximately 160,000 acres. Of that amount, 8,560 acres were owned by the ranch corporation, almost 30,000 acres were leased from Arizona, and almost 22,000 acres were leased from New Mexico. The balance was federal land administered by the Bureau of Land Management. The entire area consisted of roughly 250 square miles, an area about 16 miles across and 15 miles long. The size of the allotment was the result of the development of water in various locations through the years by H.C. and later DA. The Lazy B could sustain about two thousand cows, their calves, a few bulls, and some horses.

Top: *DA greets a visiting cowboy, c. 1926.*
Center: *DA (right) and his sister Alice.*
Bottom: *Branding a calf.*
Opposite: *DA riding Alvino.*

3. DA

Here are the facts. I am no more intelligent
than the law allows. My education is not what
it should be. My social position is nil. I am the
personification of poverty. Prospects for the
future bum. . . . Disposition terrible. . . . My
one redeeming feature is that I am healthy.

LETTER FROM HARRY TO
ADA MAE, JULY 15, 1927

$\mathcal{D}$A WAS THE BOSS, THE PATRIARCH. HE CONTROLLED LIFE AT the Lazy B for the people who lived and worked there, and for the animals that were raised and kept on the ranch. He was highly respected in that area of the Southwest. The Lazy B was the largest and most successful ranch in the region, and he had made it so. To his children and grandchildren he was smart and powerful. He was exceedingly kind to everyone, but everything had to be done his way. His children never heard him admit he was wrong about anything. He tended to be a perfectionist in his work and a careful business manager. He was not an expert cowboy or horseman, but he was an excellent rancher. He hired good cowboys and respected their work and abilities, and they respected his managerial ability.

DA went to high school in Pasadena, California, during the years Sam Foster ran the Lazy B. DA was handsome, a fine athlete, and a good student. He held several California state swimming championships. He always regretted that he did not attend Stanford and get a university education. He made up for it by reading widely the rest of his life and satisfying his curiosity about how things worked.

After his father's death, DA returned to the Lazy B at the request of the lawyers handling the estate to see whether anything could be salvaged from the ranch investment. The ranch had declined under Foster's management. There were many outstanding debts and no net profits. DA arrived in Duncan, Arizona, in 1922 with $300 in cash and no other assets. He was afraid to deposit his money in a checking account, because he thought the bank might close. He rented a safe-deposit box and put his money there. It was three years before he had enough confidence to put any of his cash in a checking account.

DA was lonely, frustrated, and worried those first years at the Lazy B. He never intended to stay, just to get things on a sound financial footing. On the instructions of the estate lawyers, he took over management from Sam Foster. There were only a few bulls on the ranch, which explained why the calf crop was so low. His first expenditure was to buy, on credit, a train-car load of bulls to increase the calf crop.

DA learned the basic lesson of every successful small business: the income must exceed the expenses. DA was a master at cutting expenses. He could fix almost anything that was broken. He saved and collected all kinds of things other people would discard: broken windmills, dysfunctional motors, gears, shafts, pump rods, fence posts—indeed, anything that might someday be useful. He had a forge and could shape metal. He learned to make and pour bearings from babbitt metal for the windmills and the engines. He might spend an entire day forming the casting—using metal, baling wire, and bread dough—in order to pour bearings for a broken windmill. Then he would spend another half day polishing the bearings to make them as good as any from a factory. He would not delegate these tasks because no one else would do them as well or carefully as he.

He kept books for the ranch every year he was there. Most of the book work was done at night because his days were full. The records in the early years show expenses in many months of less than $150, and for the whole year of $3,000. Even in the 1920s, that was quite an accomplishment for a ranch the size of the Lazy B. He never paid high wages, and he hired only a few cowboys. But the ones he hired were loyal and content to be at the Lazy B.

In the early years the only ranch motor vehicle was an old Model T truck. Most of the work was done on horseback. There was no electricity, no running water, and only outdoor toilets and kerosene lanterns.

Perhaps the toughest year for DA on the ranch was 1934. There was a severe drought—virtually no rainfall during the summer monsoon season—and the bottom dropped out of the market for cattle. The ranch could not afford to buy feed for the cattle. DA decided he had to reduce the herd. He gathered eight hundred thin cows to sell and then could not find a buyer. Only one man came to look at them. DA priced them at 1½ cents per pound. The buyer said, "My God, man, these are your old cows and thin cows." "That's right," said DA. "That's why I want to sell." The buyer said, "Well, I wish I'd known that. I wouldn't have wasted your time and mine, too. I wouldn't take that bunch of cows if you gave them to me. It wouldn't be worth the shipping charges."

DA was depressed. He had a wife, a child, and no market whatever for his cows.

The federal government adopted a program for cattle producers caught in the squeeze. The government agreed to kill the cows and to pay twelve dollars per cow for each one killed. There was considerable paperwork involved, and a veterinarian had to certify the cattle for destruction. The ranch was required to destroy or bury the carcasses. The sight of the cows and calves being shot that he and the cowboys worked so hard to produce, nourish, and save was almost unbearable for DA. A couple of months later the government agreed to buy some of the cattle in better condition for eighteen dollars each in order to provide meat for people who were going hungry. DA sold some additional cattle at that price. In September it started raining, the grass grew, and in time the ranch recovered.

Since adequate rainfall and decent prices for the cattle could not be controlled, DA focused largely on the expense side. Once he paid off the debts that existed when he took over the management, he determined never to borrow money for any reason. He passed over a number of opportunities to expand or to participate in other enterprises because each such opportunity would have required incurring a debt. During the Depression a good many fine ranches were lost when their debts could not be paid. DA survived the Depression debt-free and was in a position to earn good profits when beef prices skyrocketed during World War II.

Despite the federal programs to alleviate the Depression, President Franklin Roosevelt was heartily disliked by many of the ranchers. They were strongly opposed to an expanded role for the federal government. They believed in private initiative to solve all problems. DA thought William Howard Taft had been a good president and was not properly appreciated. Taft, in contrast to Roosevelt, had not sought an expanded role for the federal government. DA's conservative views held strong.

During the Depression, a Civilian Conservation Corps (CCC) camp was established near the ranch. Young men from urban areas around the country were sent to the camp to live and to work on the various projects to improve the public land. They built some roads, a dam in Horse Camp Canyon, and a few flood-control projects. DA would talk to the young men and their supervisors when they were doing work projects on the Lazy B. Most of the young men had never been out of their cities and had never lived outdoors or performed manual labor. They found they liked it. Years later some of those CCC campers would return to the Lazy B to visit the places where they had camped and worked. A number of them told DA that the experience there had helped them take hold of their lives and to accomplish things they would not otherwise have achieved. Even with that strong testimony, DA was reluctant to concede that any of the Roosevelt Depression programs were necessary, although he acknowledged that the CCC camp life was good for most of the young people who participated.

DA was a good listener and even a better talker. He took advantage of every visitor to talk for as long as the visitor would stay and listen. DA was also competitive and enjoyed playing various card games. He was a stickler for the rules and kept a volume of Hoyle handy to confirm the rules of whatever game we were playing. The intrafamily competition was keen at bridge, pinochle, gin rummy, and hearts.

It was not until the 1940s that, with the help of the Rural Electrification Administration, the Lazy B obtained electricity at its headquarters.

Before that there had only been an electric generator that DA would run for about three hours at night. There was an old AM radio in the house and one in the bunkhouse. The radio reception was poor and only worked when the weather was not too hot. The radio was a window to the outside world. During World War II, the Day family and the ranch hands listened to the news each day. We listened to some boxing matches when Joe Louis was the heavyweight champion. There were exciting times listening to events on the radio, thanks to some good radio announcers whom we knew well by voice but would never meet. The whole family also became regular fans of certain weekly radio programs—*Fibber McGee and Molly*, *The Great Gildersleeve*, *The Jack Benny Program*, and *The Shadow*.

DA could build or repair just about anything. He was good with his hands. His hands were those of an outdoor worker—the skin was thick, the nails were tough and damaged—but he could perform delicate tasks with those hands. He taught himself how to keep things going—how to build a gate, repair a windmill, build a house, construct a water tank, repair an ailing motor, keep financial records, survive a drought, make the most of a good rainy season, make do with what is at hand, help a friend, and encourage a child. He was a pretty good veterinarian and not a bad doctor on occasion. He could set a broken leg on a mother cow or doctor an infected eye. One time we found a cow whose uterus had come completely out of her vagina and was hanging, bloody and filthy, beneath her tail. DA brought her into the corral at the ranch and put her in a cattle chute where she could be tightly held. He then cleaned the tissue of the uterus, slowly and carefully, with fresh soapy water. He pushed it back inside the cow with his hand and arm and inserted—bottom first—a clean, empty wine bottle, to hold the uterus in place. He then sewed some stitches to largely close the opening around the neck of the bottle, and left it for a few weeks to see if the cow's condition would stabilize. It did, and a few weeks later he removed the stitches and the wine bottle and the cow went back into the pasture.

When a child or a cowboy got a serious cut or wound, DA would clean it with a disinfectant and try to close it with adhesive tape and bandages.

He made splints a few times for broken fingers or toes. He pulled out hundreds of cactus thorns and splinters. And a couple of times a suffering cowboy even persuaded DA to pull out a bad tooth. He thought some of the old remedies were best, such as the aloe vera plant for burns, Mormon tea for stomach ills, a cow-manure poultice for a sore muscle, hot tea and honey for a cough, and a dollop of Scotch or bourbon if all else failed.

DA had refined features—a straight nose, neither large nor small, and hazel eyes that were alert and twinkling. He went bald at an early age. Perhaps to compensate, he always wore a well-trimmed moustache. He was five foot eleven and well built. His most distinguishing characteristic was his genuine interest in everyone he met, whether poor or rich, educated or illiterate, well dressed or in rags. He never talked down to his children; he spoke to us as adults and wanted to know our thoughts and views. The value of hard work and honest, fair dealing were drilled into us constantly. Whenever any of us were at home, we could go with DA to help with his work. How many young people see their father leave for the office but don't really know what he does for a living? They might go to his office once in a while and see that he has a desk, but they probably don't really know or even care what he actually does on a day-to-day basis. On the other hand, Alan, Ann, and I knew exactly what DA did and could accompany him and help him most of the time. We could see how hard he worked, and we learned to appreciate the desert and how difficult it is to make a living on that arid land. All three of us, many times, saw DA spend an hour or more doing some little inconsequential job but having the patience to stay with it until he got it right.

"DA, can we take the twenty-two and go out behind the house to shoot some bottles?"

"I'll be just a few minutes here. I have to balance this ledger, and I'm ten cents off. As soon as I finish, I'll get the gun down from the shelf and we'll go shoot those bottles."

It might be an hour and a half before he found the error and corrected the ledger, but we children would wait patiently (or impatiently) for him to finish, knowing that he would surely complete the job before he went to do something less important than the ranch work. He was always willing to instruct us on the right way to do something, especially on how to handle money in a frugal manner.

As the first child, nine years older than the next, I received all the attention and love that DA had to give during those early years. The relationship we built was extremely strong and lasted through the years in a manner that both of us appreciated. I developed a love for the land and for the way of life on the ranch that has stayed with me. Spending hours each day at the dinner table discussing ranching, politics, or economics is a treat that many young people don't experience.

I usually accompanied my parents on their weekly trips to town. One time I was asleep in the back of the car, up on the ledge under the window, behind the rear seat. Our parents drove to Lordsburg and met MO's mother, Mamie Wilkey, who was coming for a visit. DA had purchased a case of dynamite to use for some blasting on the ranch and had it in the trunk of the car. When Grandmother Wilkey learned the dynamite was in the trunk, she was angry with DA and said, "You shouldn't treat my granddaughter like that! If that dynamite blew up, she would be hurt. And not only that—her head banging on that ledge will damage her brain." DA used to laugh later and said, "Well, for someone with a damaged brain, she's done pretty well for herself."

The good things we children learned from DA were many. One of the best was his awareness of the world and world events and his lasting interest in those events. He kept informed by reading periodicals such as *U.S. News & World Report, Time, Fortune,* and the *Los Angeles Times* newspaper. When television finally reached the Lazy B, almost everyone else in the country had been watching the tube for many years. The first reception the ranch received was very poor and sporadic, but it improved over the years. Watching television, however, never intruded into the dining room and always took a backseat to any other activity. All three children learned the art of discussion, but there was a negative side. DA always had to have the last word in any argument. All three of us picked up this trait, and we find ourselves as adults mirroring the same tendency. DA also had periods of moodiness and depression. He was very critical of MO and Alan during these periods. He wanted things done his way, which he was certain was the best way.

Saving money whenever possible was DA's watchword. He never minded any expenditure toward his children's education, but he objected strenuously to spending money for clothes, new furniture, or appliances. His one extravagance, beginning in the mid-1940s, was to buy a good new car about once a year. Living so far from town, he put many miles on his car each year, and he liked trading his old car in for a new one. He spent almost nothing on his own clothes. He wore long-sleeved, collared shirts and khaki pants each day. We never saw him in Levi's, which were favored by the cowboys. He wore boots to ride, but otherwise he liked soft-soled, comfortable shoes. DA had only one suit, a gray pinstripe worn at weddings and funerals. He had one or two sport coats and slacks and a handful of neckties. Even this was more than he needed, he said.

He always put on his old 7X Beaver Stetson cowboy hat whenever he went outside. Like all the men at the ranch, he had a line straight across his forehead where the hat brim sat. Above that line his skin was white. Below the hat line, his face was burned dark from years of too much sun. He had a newer hat, which he would wear to town or to special events. His regular hat was covered with a quarter century of dirt, sweat, grime, blood, and grease. It was totally disreputable. Once MO decided the hat was beyond enduring and, while DA was reading in the house, took the hat out to the trash barrel to discard it. When DA went outside, he looked for his hat and was very angry when he learned MO had thrown it out. He went immediately to the trash barrel, fished it out, and put it back on. He never did get rid of that old hat. "It is a perfectly good 7X Beaver," he would say.

His hat blew off one time in a big windstorm, landed in the water in a dirt pond at Tank 8, and sank. It was lost. A month later, when the tank dried up, DA went to the area and recovered his 7X water-soaked hat. "This hat is still good. It just needs to be cleaned and blocked—good-quality hats don't die from just a little water."

The muddy, soaked hat was sent off to the hat cleaners in Albuquerque, and when it came back, it looked like new. "Always buy a 7X quality hat or better, and it will last for many years," he said. When Alan came to the ranch, DA gave him a good hat with the admonition, "Take care of this, and it will last you a long time." It did.

DA treasured his old friends and his extended family. Every one of them was warmly welcomed at the ranch, and they were urged to stay as long as they could. Visits were never short. If someone drove as far as the Lazy B, he or she stayed with us for a while at the ranch. Most visits involved driving or riding around the ranch, shooting a few rabbits or birds, lots of eating, drinking, card games, and, most of all, talking. When company came it was exciting for all of us.

During World War II Lordsburg and Duncan prospered. Troops and goods moved by train and kept the railroad towns busy. Mining and ranching were also critical to the war effort and brought new people to both towns. A camp was built near Duncan to hold some German prisoners of war. Some Italian prisoners of war were later housed near Lordsburg. On various occasions the camps sent a few prisoners out as work crews to do a few projects on federal land. DA would stop and talk to them, as he did with everyone he saw on the ranch. He learned from the prisoners that they rather enjoyed getting out of the camps on work crews and seeing the countryside. They said they were treated well, and some expressed the hope of returning to the United States after the war.

Strangers occasionally simply drove off the highway and onto the ranch road out of curiosity. DA marveled at the complete lack of knowledge of visitors from the Northeast, who often had no concept whatever of animal husbandry and of what was involved in ranching. Other people came to the ranch looking for agates, especially the valuable fire agates that could be found on the surface of the ground near Robbs' Well and Antelope Well. The locals called these people "rock hounds." Some would come in campers and spend several days camped out and hunting for the agates. Some of the quartz and other rocks to be found were quite beautiful. DA kept a rock polisher at the ranch, and occasionally he would put a handful of small rocks in it and tumble them in the electric polisher for a couple of weeks. The results would be some lovely polished and smooth oval rocks with a great variety of color and grain.

Still other strangers would come to the ranch during hunting season looking for deer, antelope, and javelinas. These were the only visitors DA did not greet with warmth and pleasure. Some of the hunters felt free to drive their trucks, jeeps, and off-road vehicles anywhere on the ranch, trampling vegetation and leaving damaging tracks that could start erosion channels in the fragile soil. The irresponsible hunters sometimes shot the cattle when they failed to find game. And sometimes, for target practice, shots would be fired at the windmill blades, the gates, or anything else that provided a convenient target.

Multiple use of the public lands was a stated goal of the Bureau of Land Management, and DA agreed with the concept. He thought the ranchers were simply long-term stewards of the lands they used for grazing and that people should be free to visit those lands—to camp, hike, picnic, search for rocks, and even hunt, if they were careful with their weapons and targets. He deplored the sometimes careless visitors who left gates open so the livestock could move to different areas and who occasionally used their vehicles in ways that damaged the terrain. He also thought that on the occasions when he saw visitors and talked to them in a friendly way, mentioning the need to stay on the dirt roads and to close the gates they opened for passage, the visitors tended to respond in kind and tried to follow the suggestions.

DA knew that he expected and hoped to stay in the ranching business at the Lazy B for many years. To do that successfully, he depended on careful stewardship of the land, the grasses, and the water sources. He thought that grazing by livestock was the only likely and reasonable commercial use of the semiarid desert land. Overgrazing the land made it less productive in the long run and ran the risk of permanently reducing the grass and plant life. As a result, he was cautious about the numbers of cattle he maintained, as he was about everything else. "Keep the grass healthy, keep adequate water reserves, take care of the land, and it will take care of us," he said.

In some promising areas, DA would experiment with planting new, useful grasses to see how they would grow. One of the things he would do regularly was to drive out to check on his various experimental grass plots, as well as on projects designed to reduce erosion.

DA cared deeply about his older brother, Courtland, his sister Alice, and their families, as well as his sister Eleanor, who never married and lived until her death in the old Day house in Pasadena. His sister Nina died at approximately age twenty. When H. C. Day's estate was settled, the Lazy B went in equal shares to DA, Courtland, Alice, and Eleanor, and it was organized as a corporation. DA was the president and manager, and he felt responsible for producing some income from the ranch for his siblings. As the years went by, DA wanted to acquire additional shares of ranch stock so that he could eventually pass something along to his own children. In the late 1940s, Eleanor Day said she would sell her interest in the ranch to DA. That acquisition provided a welcome increment to DA's sense of accomplishment. After the death of his brother, Courtland, Courtland's shares of stock were purchased by the Lazy B corporation, which increased DA and Alice's ownership.

DA encouraged each of his children to accomplish whatever they undertook in a competent and professional manner. Slipshod work would be quickly uncovered, and he would redo it in a proper manner. He would not scold someone who performed a task inexpertly, but that person would know without being told that he or she had not met the desired standard. Each of his children would work hard to receive a nod of approval from DA.

I remember on one occasion noticing the poor condition of the screen door from the back porch to the outside. The door was exposed to the sun and the weather, and the paint was peeling off and it was unsightly. "DA, I'll be glad to paint the screen door," I said. "Do you think you can do it properly?" "Sure I can." "Well, give it a try."

I painted carefully to avoid covering the hinges and the screen, but the wood was badly weather-beaten and the surface was rough. After a half hour or so had passed, DA came to check on the job. "I think you'd better sand the wood first to get a better surface for the paint." "Oh. All right. Do we have some sandpaper?" "Yes, it is in the top cupboard on the back porch. You'd better get some paint remover first to get some of the fresh paint off. Then sand it. Then try again."

After scrubbing the freshly painted surface with paint remover and sanding all the wood surfaces to smooth them, I began painting the wood again. It looked all right, I thought. DA came out eventually to look it over. "You'd better cover the metal hinges with masking tape so you don't get paint on them," he said. "Okay. I'll do that." Finally, I finished and looked at the door. I thought it looked fine.

At dinner I asked DA if he had seen the screen door. "Yes. Did you clean the paintbrush and put the lid on the paint can and put it away?" "Of course, DA." "That's all right then." And that was all the thanks I received, but somehow I knew DA thought the job was done properly, and that was what counted.

DA also wanted his children to see some of the world beyond the ranch. He did not travel often, but when the rains came in the summer so that the financial prospects were brighter, he would consider taking the family on a trip somewhere. When I was small, those trips were usually to southern California to see the Day relatives, who all still lived there. One summer DA decided the whole family should drive the length of the Mississippi River from its source in Bemidji, Minnesota, to New Orleans. It was a long journey and no doubt tiresome for MO and DA to hear Ann and Alan fussing with each other and with me for thousands of miles. But we walked across the Mississippi where it bubbled out of the springs in Bemidji. And we followed the great river on its course through our country. We stopped at every state capital along the way and finally reached New Orleans, where DA ate his fill of raw oysters, and the family marveled at the old houses and quaint streets and names.

Another summer, when I was a student at Stanford, the family took the train from Lordsburg to New Orleans and then a banana boat to Honduras and to Cuba. In Cuba we visited a sugar plantation and a rum factory, enjoyed the Cuban music in some of the hotels and bars, and the lovely buildings and beaches in Havana.

Our favorite trip was when I graduated from Stanford. To celebrate, the family drove to Seattle to take a tourist cruise to Alaska. There was a labor strike in Seattle and the cruise was canceled. But MO was enterprising and began making telephone calls. She managed to charter a private yacht, and the family went by boat from Bellingham, Washington, to Juneau, Alaska. It was the most beautiful scenery any of us could imagine. To five dried-out desert dwellers, it was pure magic to be surrounded by water day after day. We anchored each night in a lovely cove and put out the crab pots. We nosed into icebergs to chip ice for cold drinks. We stopped at Indian villages and at a salmon cannery. We watched bear catch salmon in the streams. We caught and ate a few fish, feasted on king crab, and enjoyed every minute of that trip through the Inside Passage. DA corresponded with the boat captain for years afterward.

Top: *MO holding Sandra.*
Center: *W. W. Wilkey.*
Bottom: *MO (left) and
friend admire a
Hereford bull.*
Opposite: *MO, c. 1929.*

4. MO

Harry, I want to give you laughter
and courage, ambition and fulfillment,
and in that way, I shall find my own.

LETTER FROM ADA MAE
TO HARRY, JULY 1927

ADA MAE, OUR MOTHER, WAS BORN IN MEXICO IN 1904. MO'S father, W. W. Wilkey, and her mother, Mamie Scott Wilkey, were living then in Cananea, in the state of Sonora. MO was the first of their three children.

The Wilkeys were a handsome couple. W. W. Wilkey was one of seven brothers and grew up in Texas. As a young man he decided to go west and make his fortune. He took all the money he had—less than a hundred dollars—and bought a ticket on the Southern Pacific Railroad for as far west as his money would take him. His ticket ran out in San Simon, Arizona. San Simon was just a wide spot in the road, existing to serve the Southern Pacific with fuel and water on its transcontinental line. There was a little hotel there and he went in to inquire about jobs in the area. He was told that a local rancher could probably use a cowhand to stay out on one part of the ranch and tend the cattle there. W.W. met the rancher and got the job. There was a small one-room shack for shelter, a windmill and well for water, and a couple of hundred square miles to look after. It paid a small wage, but there was nothing to spend it on, so W.W. could set aside a nest egg.

He had been at his job a couple of months when two riders approached from the north early one evening. W.W. greeted them, and they asked if they could spend the night. "Sure. There's not much here, but you can roll out your bedrolls inside or out." "Thanks. Do you have anything we could eat? We've been riding since morning and could sure use some grub." "I haven't got much. Some frijole beans and salt pork. I can make some biscuits and coffee." "That will be just fine."

W.W. fixed enough food for the three of them and the two visitors wolfed it down. "We're bushed," they said. "We're headed down to Mexico and need to get an early start." After hobbling their horses and borrowing a little grain to feed them, they fell into their bedrolls and were soon asleep.

The next morning the two men were up before daylight. W.W. made a little breakfast—more biscuits, coffee, and fried salt pork. At daylight, the two travelers mounted their horses and headed south. "Thanks for the food," they said.

When W.W. picked up their tin plates from the table he found two twenty-dollar gold pieces under each plate. That was about a year's wages for W.W. He was very curious about his guests. A month or so later, W.W. rode into San Simon for some supplies and visited at the hotel and the bar. "Say," he asked, "did anyone see a couple of men on horseback about a month ago headed down to Mexico? One was riding a buckskin and the other was on a big sorrel." "Oh, hell. Them was probably them train robbers from up around Clifton. They robbed the train, took the mining-company payroll, and escaped down to Mexico. Did you see them two?" "Yes, I think I did," said W.W.

W.W. stayed in the cattle business. He would buy some feeder calves, put them in a feedlot, fatten them, and sell them to the packing houses after about six months. It was risky business because cattle prices were volatile. But he made more money than he lost and in time was prosperous. He met and married Mamie Scott when she was sixteen. She was a vivacious, precocious, brown-eyed beauty. They moved to Douglas, Arizona, after our mother, Ada Mae, was born. Then, after Evelyn and Scott were born, the family moved to Duncan. W.W. bought the Duncan Mercantile general store and the house next to it. Mamie ran the store, and W.W. ran cattle on a ranch he acquired north of the Gila River.

Ada Mae and her brother and sister attended school in Duncan. They met H. C. Day, Alice Day, and their four children when the Days visited Duncan from Pasadena. Harry was six years older than Ada Mae, and he took little notice of her then, but Ada Mae remembered DA as a handsome and attractive young man.

When Ada Mae was in high school, the Wilkeys sold the Duncan Mercantile and moved to El Paso, Texas. W.W. bought a second ranch east of El Paso near Fort Hancock. Mamie and her children enjoyed living in El Paso very much.

Ada Mae learned to play the piano, and she sang quite well. She participated in some high school musical productions. Upon graduation, she enrolled at the University of Arizona. Her father spent part of the winters in Tucson, where he had some cattle on feed. Ada Mae enjoyed her university days enormously. She was very attractive and had an outgoing personality. Her roommate and sorority sister was a pretty Texan named Agnes. Agnes graduated and married M. E. Maule of Houston. Ada Mae returned to El Paso on graduation and soon married a young dentist there. The marriage lasted only a few months. She never spoke of it, and I did not learn of it until I was about eleven years old. One of my school friends said she knew something about me and my mother. "Oh. What is that?" "I'm not supposed to tell," she said. "Come on. You have to tell me!" "Well, my mother says your mother was married to somebody else, not Harry Day." "I don't believe you," I said. "You are just making that up!"

I was shocked and frightened. Had I been adopted? Is that why MO and DA sent me off to school in El Paso? I asked Grandmother Wilkey. "Am I adopted? Was MO married to someone else?"

"Why are you asking that?" said Grandmother Wilkey. "Someone told me at school." "No, you are certainly not adopted. I was right with your beautiful mother at Hotel Dieu Hospital when you were born. And Harry Day is your father. You look just like him, too!"

"Was MO married before?"

"Yes. She was. For a few months. It didn't work out and that was soon over. We don't talk about that."

That summer I finally got the courage to ask MO the same questions. MO was surprised that I had heard about her previous marriage. "It was very brief," she said. "I never think about it. And DA is my husband and you are my daughter."

After Ada Mae's brief first marriage, she lived with her parents in El Paso. She taught school, played some bridge, and went to many parties and social events in El Paso. When Harry took over management of the Lazy B, one of his first acts was to buy some bulls to put out on the ranch with the cows. There had been too few bulls to produce a good calf crop. Harry purchased some of the bulls from W. W. Wilkey, and he always said he got Ada Mae as part of the bargain. When Harry went to El Paso to receive the bulls and pay for them, he went to W. W. Wilkey's house for supper and saw Ada Mae there. If there is such a thing as love at first sight, it happened that night. They stayed up and talked until very late, and found it hard to say good-bye. Harry said he would write, and so began a daily correspondence that lasted three months. The letters were passionate.

Harry wrote Ada Mae after their first weekend meeting in June 1927, saying that he started the letter as a short note

> *to tell you how extremely happy you have made me—how you have changed a dull, dreary life into something worthwhile—and to tell you again that I love you more than anything in the world and that I have never felt the same way toward anyone I have ever known before. It seems I have loved you always, dear, and you have always been mine.*

Ada Mae responded in kind. She wrote,

> *I would have died, I do believe, if your precious letter had not come this morning. And it surely made up for all my impatience for its arrival—it is the sweetest treasure I have ever had and I am going to*

*wear the pages out reading and re-reading every single word. Oh,
how I miss you, my beloved. I love you until it hurts and I am so lonesome for you!*

Mamie Scott Wilkey disapproved of Ada Mae's plan to marry and live
on the ranch in such harsh circumstances. Nevertheless, Harry and Ada
Mae eloped to Las Cruces, New Mexico, and were married there by a justice of the peace. They went on to the Lazy B Ranch, where they lived for
more than fifty years, until their deaths.

The house MO occupied with DA was anything but a honeymoon cottage. It was thirty-five miles from Lordsburg over rough roads, and, as
mentioned, it had no indoor plumbing, no running water, and no electricity. The two of them shared the house with several cowboys, who slept
on the screen porch. MO did a substantial amount of cooking for the crew,
and she was quite a good cook. She was an attractive-looking woman who
had never lived in an isolated environment like the Lazy B. The strong
physical attraction MO and DA had for each other overcame many of the
difficulties of ranch life. Those difficulties were many.

Washing clothes without running water or electricity in a tub, using a
corrugated washboard, was challenging and physically tiring. The wet
clothes would be hung on clotheslines behind the house to dry in the sun.
There was no bathtub. Instead, there was a large tin tub that would be
brought into the kitchen about once a week. Water would be carried from
the well in buckets and heated on the wood-burning stove. MO was allowed to take the first bath. Then DA. Then any cowboy who wanted to try
getting clean. That lifestyle is hard to imagine today, with our large bathrooms and ready supply of hot and cold running water.

MO never stopped trying to dress well and take care of herself. She
never wore Levi's or rough clothes. Before it was common knowledge that
people should avoid too much sun, she wore long sleeves and a hat whenever she was outside. She liked to read and began to accumulate books as
soon as she arrived. Another early acquisition—a gift from her father—

was an upright piano, which was placed in the office. MO played the piano occasionally and would sing a few songs in her clear soprano voice.

The living room was an oddly shaped square with a fireplace, a large sofa, and a few chairs. The office was as large as the living room but had only one window; the other walls had bookshelves. There were one bedroom and a kitchen. MO and DA occupied the bedroom next to the kitchen and the office.

In the early years of their marriage, MO rode horseback occasionally with DA. After I was born, MO seldom got on a horse. Her main challenge was to fix meals with the limited selection of food in the local markets and the lack of a refrigerator or freezer at the ranch. DA kept two or three milk cows at the ranch, so that one would always be producing milk. MO learned to make butter with an old churn that was turned by hand. She made cottage cheese from curdled milk. She kept a pot of frijole beans on the stove at all times. And beef was always available. Warm weather permitted her to grow a few tomatoes, cucumbers, and green beans. Local farmers grew melons, corn, and poultry. The ranch kept some chickens, and they produced enough eggs for daily use.

MO was blessed with an unusual amount of energy. She was always slender and was only five foot four, but she was indefatigable. She enjoyed entertaining company and never objected to cooking for guests. She was even-tempered and kind.

MO subscribed to various magazines and newspapers, including the *New Yorker, Vogue, House Beautiful,* the *Saturday Evening Post, Time, Life, National Geographic,* and the *Los Angeles Times.* She did most of her shopping for clothes from magazines. We learned as we grew older that the women in Lordsburg enjoyed seeing MO each week when she went to town to shop for groceries. They would always manage to gather around casually to see what she was wearing. It was the closest many of them came to seeing a stylish, well-dressed woman.

MO was a patient and loving mother. She read endlessly to all three of her children. She taught me to read by age four. She taught all three of us how to play various card games, including gin rummy, canasta, bridge, hearts, and booray. She was an avid walker. When we were small she would walk with us for hours and look for interesting things to see—a wildflower, a pretty rock, an unusual plant or insect. We would pick up these treasures and carry them home to put in a favorite place to keep forever. She made banana cupcakes for us every week, and various pies as well. In the summer, she would buy large blocks of ice to bring home to make ice cream in the old hand-cranked ice-cream freezer. We would each take turns turning the crank so that we would be allowed to eat the ice cream from the dasher when it was removed before being packed down for its final freezing.

MO was the only woman among a crew of men. In the early years the cowboys were invariably single men. They respected her, perhaps because she had an inherent dignity and a great deal of poise. Many ranch wives wore rough ranch clothes and had hands and skin resembling well-worn leather. MO managed somehow to do the work that other ranch wives did but still maintain her white skin, her good looks, and her well-dressed appearance. We took it for granted at the time, but in retrospect, it was a remarkable feat.

The most difficult decision came when it was time for me to go to school. Some ranch wives moved to town to live with their children during the school year. Others sent their children to boarding school. MO tried teaching me at home for a year, but she decided it was important for me to spend time with other children. MO's parents, Mamie Scott and W. W. Wilkey, offered to keep me in El Paso so I could attend school there. With some misgivings MO and DA decided I should spend the school year in El Paso from first grade through high school. Alan and Ann also lived there for a few years in grade school, but that was more than Grandmother Wilkey could handle, and they eventually returned to the ranch and attended school in Duncan. I was always homesick when away from the ranch. My grandmother was loving and caring, but the ranch was where I wanted to be.

MO liked to have visitors. She never complained about the extra work to take care of them; she wanted the companionship. Her brother,

Scott, and his family were regular visitors, as were DA's nieces and their families.

MO's niece and my cousin Flournoy was the most frequent visitor. Flournoy's father died of leukemia when she was very young. Her mother, my aunt Evelyn, had to get a job to earn some money. Flournoy stayed with our grandmother and me in El Paso. We attended the same school and shared many of the same friends. Flournoy was like a loving older sister to me and included me in all her activities. She was creative and fun loving, joyful and affectionate. MO and DA thought of her as their own, and I loved her as a sister. Flournoy spent most of her summers during grade school at the ranch.

Whenever visitors came both MO and DA would take them out on horseback or in jeeps and pickups, all around the ranch. They enjoyed showing people the cattle, the horses, and the different areas. Sometimes we would take picnics. Sometimes we would shoot a few quail or doves for dinner. And the conversations were nonstop. It was as though our parents had to make up for lost time when they had a chance to talk to people other than their children and the cowboys.

MO loved to travel. She would make the plans, and DA would complain and say he couldn't go. Often it would not be certain until the scheduled day of departure whether DA would decide he could go. Once they were on their way with friends, they had a wonderful time. They often traveled with the Lordsburg attorney Forrest Sanders and his intelligent and charming wife, Margaret, or with another ranch family, the Mahlon Everharts. Occasionally they traveled with MO's university friend Agnes Maule and her husband. The Maules were wealthy and lived in Houston in a beautiful home. Their life included many luxuries and lavish parties. MO looked forward to letters from Agnes. Several times a year Agnes would write long letters that gave detailed accounts of her social life, her travels, and her clothes. MO would read and reread every letter, and save them in a special drawer. They described a life she would have enjoyed but could not have, and yet she would not have traded her own for that of Agnes.

The weekly trip to Lordsburg was an important part of MO's life. She liked to go to a beauty parlor to have her hair washed and set and her nails polished. She liked to dial the numbers on the post office box and take out the mail. She liked to shop for groceries. Once a month some of the local women would take turns hosting a bridge luncheon. MO particularly enjoyed that day. When it was her turn to host it, the women would drive to the ranch for lunch and the bridge game.

She read all the magazines that arrived, cover to cover. Some of the magazines about houses and gardens had photos and articles about beautiful houses and handsome furniture. Although she would never live in a beautiful house, she would save the issues with articles and photos she particularly liked. There was very little storage space in the ranch house, and she filled up closets with the magazines, and when the closets were full she stored them under the beds. Ann and I would suggest from time to time that some of them could be thrown away. They never were.

Two special friends who lived in Duncan were an important part of MO's life—Hal and Louise Empie. MO and Hal knew each other from their days at the University of Arizona. Hal had graduated with a degree in pharmacology and obtained his license as a pharmacist. His real love and talent was painting, but Duncan had no pharmacist, so he had decided to open a drugstore there. He called it the Art Gallery Drug, and it was well known in the Southwest. No one could drive through Duncan without stopping at the Art Gallery Drug. Hal was a talented artist. He loved the Southwest, and he painted landscapes and portraits of the world about him. He filled the walls of his drugstore with his paintings, and sold many of them. Hal had red hair, blue eyes, and a twinkle and a smile for everyone. He also enjoyed tramping around looking for Indian artifacts. MO would join the Empies for many a day of looking for pottery and projectile points. The two couples also enjoyed playing bridge occasionally.

MO was always ready for an adventure. Several times when we were young she would arrange for the train that ran through the ranch to stop for us at Railroad Wash so we could ride in the caboose to Clifton for the day. The train would remain in Clifton for an hour and a half to take on a load of copper ingots from the Phelps Dodge mill. We would walk around Clifton, visit the old jail, or look in the mine tunnel and the general store, then get back on the caboose to ride back to the ranch.

On the Fourth of July, MO would make an enormous picnic lunch and we would drive nearly to the top of Mount Graham, outside of Safford, Arizona. We would enjoy our picnic in the cool pines at almost ten thousand feet! Then we would climb the fire lookout tower, and perhaps get caught in a thunderstorm before getting off the mountain and back to the hot desert.

MO was usually polite and not inclined to give offense when she spoke. But there was an inner core that at times could not be breached and that prompted her to speak out forcefully. One time was when Orville Rayburn took too many liberties in her house. Another occurred when the Valley National Bank decided to open a branch in Solomonville, Arizona, some fifty miles from the Lazy B. DA had since passed away, but MO was invited to a luncheon marking the occasion. She was seated next to the bank's chairman of the board. To make conversation, he said he understood she had a large ranch on the New Mexico–Arizona border. She said, "Yes, I have lived there many years." He then asked, "How many head of cattle do you own?" MO looked him right in the eye and replied, "If you will tell me how much money you have in your bank account, I will tell you how many cows we have on the ranch." We were proud of our mother for her reply. The bank chairman appeared duly chastened.

Of her three children MO felt closest to Alan. It is not unusual for little girls to adore their fathers and for little boys to be closer to their mothers. Although each of us felt loved by both our parents, MO was particularly close to Alan. It was nine years after my birth that MO became pregnant again. She had assumed she would have no more children. Both MO and DA were happy about the prospects of another child. I was away at school much of the time, and they looked forward to another child at home. Ann was a beautiful baby with blond hair and blue eyes. As she grew older she learned how to get DA to agree to most things she wanted. MO became pregnant the third time only eighteen months later. She was thrilled to have a son. Alan resembled the Wilkeys, with his square jaw, brown hair, and brown eyes. He grew up in a very permissive environment and had his own way in most things.

Both Ann and Alan learned how to make good cowhands and to do most of the things that needed to be done at the ranch. In turn they had almost total freedom in leading their own lives. Alan was quite wild as a teenager. The summer after his high school graduation, MO asked Alan what plans he had for the next year. Alan said, "I don't know. Maybe I'll work here on the ranch. Maybe I'll go to college." MO said, "Alan, I really liked the University of Arizona. What do you think about that?" Alan said it sounded okay to him. MO sent away for an admission application for the University of Arizona, and Alan filled out the forms and was accepted. Alan went to Duncan and bought some new Levi's and shirts in preparation. When the time came for classes to begin, Alan asked, "MO, where *is* the University of Arizona?" "In Tucson," she replied. "Where is Tucson?" Alan asked. "Get in your car, go to Lordsburg, and turn right." That is what Alan did, and he found it, just as MO had said.

MO was a tidy package of good looks, competence, and charm. She could fit in at a gathering of Arizona ranch wives or at an elegant party in Washington, D.C. She was the only female role model we had, other than Grandmother Wilkey. She made a hard life look easy. In a harsh environment where weather, the cowboys, and the animals were all unpredictable, she was unfailingly loving and kind. She created an appealing and delightful life for her family all her days. While some of the cowboys taught us that only the toughest survive, MO taught us that kindness and love can also produce survivors, and in a happy atmosphere.

Top: *Rafael Estrada, "Rastus."*
Bottom: *The saddle barn.*

PHOTOGRAPH © 1990

TOSHI KAZAMA

Opposite: *Rastus and DA tailing
up an old cow.*

5. Rastus

Honored and imitated among us were those
with special skills so long as the skills were
not too civilized.

WALLACE STEGNER,
Wolf Willow

OPERATING THE RANCH REQUIRED HAVING ABOUT FIVE EMPLOY-
ees year-round, and double that number for the spring and fall roundups.
Most of the full-time employees were single men who spent their entire
working lives at the Lazy B. There was no way to recruit cowboys; they just
appeared. DA would hire someone who asked for work if the fellow needed
help at the time. The regular ranch crew during our childhood included
Rafael Estrada (known as Rastus), Jim Brister, Claude Tippets, Ralph (Bug)
Quinn, Ira Johnson, LeRoy McCarty, and, later, Cole Webb.

The ranch work was very demanding in the spring, in the summer before the rain, and in the fall. Winter provided a somewhat easier time—
time to do needed repairs and special projects. But there was never a day
without things that needed doing.

One man was always at the Lazy B. He was an integral part of our life
there, and his constant presence helped make the ranch a secure and
dependable haven. His real name was Rafael Estrada, but no one could remember calling him anything but Rastus. He was born of Mexican-
American parents in Pinos Altos, New Mexico, in 1900. (Pinos Altos is a
wide spot in the road near Silver City.) When Rastus was about six or
seven, his father died. His mother remarried, and Rastus did not like his
new stepfather very much. He ran away from home and made his way to

Lordsburg, New Mexico, about fifty miles south of Pinos Altos. He asked around town for work. Somebody told him the Lazy B was having a roundup and that they could use a chore boy. Rastus took the job and went out to the Lazy B headquarters on a buckboard—a trip of thirty-five miles. He never left.

When he first arrived he worked as the roundup cook's helper. Before long everyone at the ranch just accepted him as part of the ranch family. He carried in wood for the cook's stove; he cleaned up the pots and pans; he helped hitch the horses to the chuck wagon. He learned to ride and in time became the horse wrangler. He would get up before dawn, saddle a horse he had kept in the corral overnight, and go out and find the horses and drive them in for the cowboys to ride that day. During the roundups he would move the extra horses along to the next roundup campsite.

In time, Rastus became one of the regular cowboys. He never attended school and did not learn to read or write. He was bright and interested in the cattle and the horses. He was friendly and warm; he had a kindly disposition and was totally honest. Whatever he said about something was true. You could count on it.

His features were well defined. He had a straight thin nose, rather thin lips, and dark brown eyes with a perpetual twinkle. His skin was a deep brown mahogany color. He had left home so young that he spoke English without an accent. His Spanish was limited to a few simple words remembered from his early years.

MO was his special friend. They often visited, and Rastus thought she could do no wrong. When we were babies he would take us up on the saddle in front of him and show us what it was like to sit on the back of a horse.

Rastus walked with a pronounced limp, which was the result of an accident at the ranch headquarters. He had climbed up one of the windmills to make a repair. The wind came up, and the windmill fan shifted direction, knocking Rastus off balance. He fell thirty-five feet and landed on his back. His right leg hit an anvil that was on the ground. The force of the fall knocked a piece of his tibia right through the skin of his leg. There was no doctor within several hours' distance. When his leg was finally set and healed, the right leg was several inches shorter than the left. He always had the foot of his right boot built up by a cobbler to make up some of the difference.

Rastus was fastidious about his appearance. He shaved every day and washed himself often. He had few clothes, but he washed them frequently. He would wear his shirt and his pants until the fabric was so thin you could almost see through it. Anytime there was a tear or rip in his clothes he would sew it up with tiny stitches that would have made the finest seamstress envious. He would not wear a new shirt or pants until the old ones were beyond repair.

When sitting around the bunkhouse, Rastus played cards—solitaire if no one wanted to play poker with him. He used the same deck of Bicycle playing cards until the spots were worn off and the cards were as limp as Kleenex.

One time in 1945 when MO and DA went to El Paso for a visit with us during the school year, Rastus went along. He bought a pair of Tony Lama boots and had a tailor make him a dress suit, a gray pinstripe. It cost $200, a tidy sum in those days. The suit was very nicely made. "Rastus," I said, "why did you get that suit? You never dress up. What are you going to do with it?" He laughed. "Oh, I got it to be buried in." "What do you mean? You're not going to die." "Well, maybe I will someday. You never know."

Rastus went to town about once a month. He would cash his paycheck and put the money in his wallet. There wasn't much he needed or wanted. A haircut. A barbershop shave. A couple of days sitting around the Bonnie Heather Bar playing poker. Maybe a visit to the town prostitute. When he was ready to go back to the ranch, he would find someone to give him a ride. He never drove a car, never owned one.

Rastus didn't spend all his money. Occasionally MO would invest some money for him. She would say, "Rastus, how much money do you have?" "Oh, Ada Mae, I don't know. Some." "Well, get out your wallet and let me see." He might have two or three thousand dollars in his wallet. "I will invest it for you—maybe get some El Paso Natural Gas stock." "Well, leave me enough to get to town," he would say.

MO would leave about $150, take the rest, and buy stock in Rastus's name. He really didn't understand what securities were. When he would receive dividend checks he would say, "I don't know why they're sending me this." He would endorse them on the back with an X, his mark, and the bank would cash them. Gradually, because of his stock holdings, he earned more in dividends than he did in wages from cowboying.

Rastus was patient and understanding. He had an inherent sense of distance and direction. He knew the best way to get from point A to point B. To watch him do his work was to see a master craftsman. During a drought or a dry spell, the cattle would have insufficient grass and forage to thrive. They would become thin and tired. Some would die. Some might be too weak or crippled to walk the necessary distances to find grass and water. Others might have teeth worn down so much that they would find it difficult to chew the tough dry grass. Rastus knew and recognized almost every cow. He knew when one was at the point where she needed to be brought into headquarters for extra feed and care. There wasn't room in the corrals to bring in all the thin cows, nor was there enough hay for all of them. Most had to survive out on the open range. To bring a thin, weak cow in eight to ten miles to ranch headquarters isn't easy. If the cow is out of energy and you try to prod her along, she might turn and fight. She might even charge the person on horseback, trying to knock down the horse and rider. If the cow is really weak and tries this, she may fall down herself and never get back up. Sometimes the cow will have an undernourished calf and will stop from time to time and bawl for the calf, waiting for it to catch up.

Rastus knew exactly how to handle a weakened cow. He knew how to avoid making her angry but still keep her moving along. He would come back to headquarters in the late afternoon, stirring up little swirls of dust in the dry trails, following an old cow that wobbled in her walk. But he would still have her goodwill. He would get her through the corral gate and get off his horse. We would start feeding the cow hay and grain and try to nurse her back to health. No one else on the ranch had the ability and patience Rastus had to handle cattle in a weakened and stressed condition. "She'll be all right," he would say, and she usually was.

We children thought it was a special treat to spend a day riding with Rastus. He never asked anyone to ride with him; he was content to be out alone. But we would sometimes ask, "Can I go along with you tomorrow, Rastus? Where are you going?" "Yes, you can go. But I'm going early—out to Old Camp. Think you can keep up?" "Ok, yes, sure."

We were not really sure at all. It was a challenge. Rastus always rode horses that traveled fast and were able to negotiate the rocky, rough terrain with ease. As children we rode smaller, gentler horses, but they were not as fast and not as good on the rocks. But Rastus never changed his pace. He would saddle up and set out in the morning after breakfast at a trot. He covered lots of miles. We would have to kick our horses constantly and push them to keep up. He might cover twenty-five miles or so in a day and look at more than three hundred cows and calves. If there were any problems, he would stop and take care of them. If a fence was down and cattle had strayed onto a neighbor's land, he would bring them back and repair the fence. If a well broke or a water hole dried up, he would move all the cattle in that area to another area where water was available.

When we rode with Rastus, we particularly liked to pick a day in late summer when he was going down to the Gila River area. He rode all day and never took a sandwich or water. If we came to a windmill and were thirsty, we would ask him if we could stop for a drink. "Go ahead. Get a drink." We would scoop up the water from the storage tank and drink until we could hold no more. He waited patiently. But we never saw him get off his horse to take a drink himself.

There were some farms along the Gila River wherever the valley flattened out and there was space for the fields. The farmers there knew Rastus and would always tell him to help himself to a watermelon from one of their fields. And he would. He would usually finish checking up on all the Lazy B cattle along the river by about 2:00 P.M. He would ask us if it wasn't about time for a watermelon. We were always so hot and thirsty by then that we felt we couldn't kick our horses another step. We would get off our horses, tie them up under a cottonwood tree, and walk out in the farm field to pick a watermelon. We would each take one back under the shade of the tree and cut it open with a pocketknife. The sweet, juicy melon would drip down our chins and onto our clothes. We would eat until we couldn't swallow another bite. Our hunger was over, our thirst gone. All too soon Rastus would get back on his horse to ride home. He would usually talk to us if we could catch up with him. If we didn't catch up, or if he didn't feel like talking, he was content to ride in silence, sometimes whistling a simple little tune.

Rastus would occasionally show a bit of temper. He expected other cowboys to perform their jobs adequately. If one got lazy or made a mistake, Rastus would know it and maybe say something. He also expected his horses to perform well. If one gave him trouble, he would yell at the horse and whip him with his quirt as hard as he could. When the punishment was over, he would get off the horse, rub him, talk baby talk to him, and feed him some grain. At the end of each day after his long ride, he would always feed the horse, rub it down, use the curry comb, and turn the horse out in the horse pasture. He thought horses should not be confined in a corral, even overnight. Because he didn't keep his horses corralled, he would have to go out before dawn on foot in the horse pasture to find the horse he wanted to ride for that day. Despite his limp, he never complained about wrangling his horse on foot.

He could look at hoofprints and tracks in the dirt and know how long ago a horse had walked there, whether it had carried a rider, and probably which horse it was. His memory was phenomenal. He could look at a cow and remember what the calf she had last year looked like, whether it was a steer or a heifer, big or small. He remembered each cow's history.

Life for Rastus was a little like playing poker. He was dealt what many would say was a poor hand in life—he was small, crippled, fatherless, a minority race in his birth land. He couldn't read, write, or drive a car. He had no wife. But he was skilled in the work he did. He enjoyed horses and

his outdoor life. He knew he was very good at what he did, and he demanded a high standard from those around him. He liked his extended
family at the ranch, and they liked and respected him. He had dignity and
pride. He was blessed with a cheerful and contented personality. He
played the hand he was dealt like a master—he succeeded in a way that
made him happy. From him we learned the contentment of doing the best
you can with what you have.

Top: *Jim Brister at a rodeo.*
PHOTOGRAPH BY DEVERE
HELFRICH, MARCH 16, 1956.
81.023.11140, "JIM BRISTER
ON A HORSE." DONALD AND
ELIZABETH M. DICKINSON
RESEARCH CENTER, NATIONAL
COWBOY AND WESTERN
HERITAGE MUSEUM,
OKLAHOMA CITY
Center left: *DA branding while
Jim Brister (right) looks on.*
Center right: *DA brands while
Jim Brister ropes.*
Bottom: *Branding.*
Opposite: *Jim Brister.*

6. *Jim Brister*

The answer to the challenge: . . .
to be invincibly strong, indefinitely enduring,
uncompromisingly self-reliant, to depend on
no one, to contain within himself every
strength and every skill.

WALLACE STEGNER,
Wolf Willow

*J*IM BRISTER ARRIVED AT THE LAZY B WITH HIS WIFE, MAE, IN 1924. Jim was born in Oklahoma in 1900. He ran away from home as a youngster. He did not want to talk about his abusive childhood, so we could only guess about his hardscrabble early life. He never spoke of having any relatives, and he'd never gone to school. His first job was as a swamper for a Wild West show based in Texas. He did the menial tasks—feeding and watering the animals, cleaning up after them, cleaning the equipment, and any other lowly job to be done. Jim applied himself to learning to ride and to rope and became one of the performers in the show. He grew fast and was over six feet tall; his shoulders and hands were huge. His red hair was covered by his cowboy hat.

About the time Jim became a performer in the show, the Wild West show heyday was passing. People could see Western movies on a screen in a theater. Attendance at the old-style outdoor shows dwindled, and local rodeos began to take their place. Jim and others who liked to ride broncos and rope calves would ride horseback hundreds of miles for weeks on end to attend and compete in some rodeo somewhere. Not many people had automobiles, and horse trailers were a thing of the future.

Jim was a top-notch rodeo performer. He could do all the events well. If he had a fault, it was that he made things look too easy. Audiences preferred seeing cowboys bucked off or chased by a wild cow. They loved the danger and excitement of the wild-cow milking. One cowboy would rope a wild cow and try to keep her still while his partner tried to milk her. The winner was the team that produced a bottle of milk within the shortest period of time.

Sometimes Jim would enter a rodeo and win every single event. He was legendary on the rodeo circuit. To earn some money to augment his rodeo winnings, Jim would go from ranch to ranch in the Southwest, riding the rough string of their horses. He would rodeo in between ranch jobs. A cowboy who rode the rough string made about twice the wages of an average cowboy—about sixty dollars per month. Jim would ride the unbroken horses and get them pretty well broken so the other cowboys could ride them, and then he would move on. Jim was incredibly strong and had a knack for sitting on a wild horse. It was a rare horse that could ever dislodge him from the saddle.

Jim married his wife, Mae, when she was eleven, according to Mae. He bought a motorcycle with a sidecar so he could take Mae with him from ranch to ranch. He would load Mae in the sidecar and tie his saddle on the back and go to the next ranch that needed a man to break horses.

The Bristers arrived at the Lazy B three years before MO. DA offered Jim a job riding the rough string and helping with the roundups, but there was no house available on the ranch for them. DA decided to build a little house for them at Willow Springs, which was a beautiful little remote canyon about ten miles from the ranch headquarters. DA and Jim took the wagon and a team of horses to Duncan to buy some lumber—some one-by-sixes, one-by-twelves, two-by-fours, and some corrugated tin for the roof. The two of them built the house. It had a kitchen, a living room, a bedroom, and a bathroom. The bathroom had a tub and sink but no toilet. They installed an outdoor privy near the house. For the next forty-nine years Jim and Mae lived at the Lazy B in that little house as part of the Lazy B "family."

Jim continued to enter rodeos on a regular basis. He would send word to DA that he would be gone a couple of days. He seldom missed a rodeo in

Prescott, Phoenix, Tucson, or El Paso. Sometimes he would enter the rodeos as far away as Cheyenne, Houston, Dallas, and Salinas. He helped organize the first rodeo cowboys' association in the early 1930s. It was called the Turtles, for reasons we never knew.

When Jim would return from a rodeo, if we saw him we would ask, "How did you do?" He would say, "Well, I won," or "I didn't win," and that was all. He never offered an excuse if he lost. He never blamed his partner, or a bad steer, or some failing of his horse. If he won, that was fine. If he didn't, that was all right too. You get the job done, or you don't. We learned from Jim that there were no excuses, only results.

Jim liked the Lazy B. In the 1960s he said that before long he might get a "steady" job at the Lazy B, with his forty-some years' experience.

Top: *Bug Quinn atop the last of the old horse-drawn and wooden-wheeled chuck wagons.* Bottom: *Bug Quinn with horse-drawn chuck wagon.* Opposite: *Ann, Bug Quinn, and Cole Webb.*

7. Bug Quinn

He was always up, his cooking done,
When the rest of us woke up.
It was laid out there for us to eat,
And he was sipping from his cup.

BOB E. LEWIS,
"THE CHUCKWAGON COOK"

$\mathcal{B}$UG QUINN WAS THE HAPPIEST OF ALL COWBOYS. HE WAS BARELY five feet tall and had a round face with a pug nose, a big grin, and twinkling eyes. The only things short about Bug were his legs. From the waist up he looked normally sized. We had to modify the stirrup leathers to make the saddle fit Bug. Once he was horseback, he could ride with the best of them. He saw the humor in every situation and could make light of any catastrophe. Everyone—except his wives—loved to be around him.

Bug's real name was Ralph Quinn. He acquired his nickname at the Lazy B. He was helping with the branding one day and was running back and forth carrying the hot branding irons to Jim Windham, who was branding the calves. Jim said, "Ralph looks just like a little lightning bug the way he turns back and forth to the branding fire." The name Bug stuck from that day forward.

Bug was married twice—neither time happily. He liked to drink and spent most of his paychecks in the bar. His wives found that unacceptable. In short, he was irresponsible, undependable, and thoroughly likable. He always said he could get even with both of his wives by outliving them.

When Alan was about five, he wandered down to the bunkhouse one day. Just as he reached the door, Bug came running out, followed by his wife, who had a hammer in her hand and was trying to hit Bug over the head with it. Bug was trying to run fast enough to avoid being hit. Alan was shocked and watched in fascination. Bug escaped injury, and Alan returned to the house to evaluate what he had seen. In later years, when Alan asked about the incident, Bug laughed and said it was just one of many battles, most of which he lost. He told us another story about the same wife. They were in San Francisco when she became angry with Bug and chased him down the street, hitting him with her purse. Bug was on the waterfront running toward a dock. He could see Alcatraz across the water. He said he wanted to turn around and hit his wife, but the image of Alcatraz was strong. Finally, his anger overcame his qualms and he turned around and hit her. Down she went, and Bug went straight to a ship at the dock and signed on as a cook. While he was at sea, he received a letter from his wife asking for a divorce and offering to pay for it. He wrote back saying, "For that price, let's get a dozen." That was the end of that marriage.

Bug's first job at the Lazy B was in 1916, building a fence at High Lonesome. He cut the posts in the Peloncillo Mountains, on the west side of the ranch. The fence he built is still standing today, although the barbed wire is badly rusted. Bug continued to work at the Lazy B off and on until 1993. For a time he worked as a regular cowboy. Later he took the job of roundup cook. He said, "Frosty mornings and bucking horses made a cook out of a pretty good cowboy." When he stayed on the job, he worked hard. When he went to town and started drinking, it was a different story.

In the 1920s Bug and our foreman, Jim Windham, went to Duncan and got a little drunk. They were driving a Lazy B truck and ran into the train, which was stopped at the crossing. The truck was destroyed, and both men were thrown through the windshield. Neither man was seriously injured, but DA fired them both the next day when he discovered that the truck was totaled. Bug thought the whole thing was funny because Jim Windham had been thrown through the windshield and somehow Bug had gone out the same hole. Jim Windham was annoyed that Bug hadn't made his own hole in the windshield. The railroad company was angry about the damage to its property. DA was angry with both Bug and Jim, but he got over it and rehired them. Bug laughed about the whole thing and told the story many times in subsequent years.

Bug joined the Coast Guard in World War II, but he did not like the service, and after a while he went AWOL. He returned to Duncan, but for some reason he was never court martialed. Through the years, Bug often ended up in jail for a few days when he got drunk. He told us he had his own private cell. After the war Bug decided to run for justice of the peace in Duncan. His campaign platform was that if he was elected, he would stay out of jail. He thought that as justice of the peace he could just sign himself in or out of jail. He was elected for one term and managed to stay out of jail throughout his term. He refused to perform any weddings during his term as justice of the peace, saying, "The Constitution prohibits cruel and unusual punishment." As soon as his term was up, he landed back in jail, where he felt more at ease than on the bench.

Bug was independent to the point of irresponsibility. One time when we were rounding up cattle near the highway from Duncan to Lordsburg, Bug was riding near the highway. Some of his friends came driving along the highway, saw Bug, and stopped to visit. He asked them where they were going, and they said to the Mardi Gras in New Orleans. His friends said, "Why don't you come along with us?" Bug said, "Well, I believe I will." He got off his horse, unsaddled, loaded his tack in the trunk of the car, and turned his horse loose with a swat on the hindquarter. When Bug's horse came in without a saddle or a bridle, DA said that he knew Bug had just taken off. He was angry, of course, but it didn't do any good since the man was hundreds of miles away by then.

Another time, when Bug was much older, he had done all the work for the day by noon one Saturday. He asked if he could take the one old ranch pickup we had and go to town to get a haircut. DA said okay. Monday morning arrived, and neither Bug nor the pickup was at the ranch. DA received a telegram from Berkeley, California, from Bug asking for enough money to return to Duncan. He had gotten to Duncan on Saturday, gotten drunk, caught the bus to Phoenix and then a plane to San Francisco. When he'd sobered up, he had no money or job, but, then, this was nothing new for Bug. It was merely one more Bug story for the cowboys to pass around and laugh about.

Bug was generous, and if he had anything that a friend needed he would give it or lend it willingly, and he was always loyal to his friends. He would sometimes borrow money from Rastus and pay it back a few days later, just so Rastus would feel needed. In 1996 Alan visited Bug in Duncan. He was ninety years old, almost blind, and couldn't hear well but was cheerful. He said the only thing he was sad about was that his old friends and my parents had all passed on and he was the last of his generation to be alive. He passed away a year later, and Alan gave one of the eulogies at his funeral.

Top: *The Lazy B.* PHOTOGRAPH © 1990 TOSHI KAZAMA
Bottom: *Lunchtime.* Opposite: *Claude Tippets (right), who worked for over half a century at the Lazy B.*

8. *Claude Tippets*

Blessed is he who has found his work.

THOMAS CARLYLE,
Past and Present

$\mathcal{C}$LAUDE TIPPETS WAS UNIQUE AMONG THE COWBOYS. ALL THE other cowboys measured themselves by self-imposed standards of how they could handle horses, a rope, and work with cattle. They valued the traditional cowboy crafts. Claude measured himself by how well he could build a fence, construct a corral, or lay a water pipe. He was never satisfied unless each fence-post hole was exactly square, and precisely the proper depth, and unless each corner of the brace fitted together properly, with no crack or separation showing. He would work for an hour or a day, if necessary, to make each piece fit correctly. No job would be left until it was perfect by his own high standards.

On completing a gate in a corral he would look at it and say, "I want this gate to be here and still working when I am dead and gone." Many of his projects are there and still working today, many years after his death.

For a young man to learn patience and precision from Claude was not an easy job. Young people tend to be in a hurry all the time, and "Get the job done quickly" is their watchword. Alan was no exception. One time Claude said, "We need to put this fence corner in, up west of Big Tank. Would you like to help me?" Alan agreed, thinking it would be a three- or four-hour job. Now, the pickup ride just to get to the spot with the posts and the equipment needed was an hour and a half and hot and dusty, so according to Alan's calculations, the job should be half over by the time they arrived.

The soil where the postholes had to be dug was very rocky and difficult to dig. The holes each had to be two and a half feet deep in order for all the braces to be even. When one hole had a big rock at a depth of two feet, three inches, Alan said, "This rock is too big to get out, so let's just say that two feet, three inches is enough." Claude, of course, answered, "Well, the brace won't fit right if one post is higher than the other two." Then he laughed and recalled the time when a laborer who didn't like to dig holes deep enough had started cutting the bottom of a post off so that it wouldn't stick up too far and it would look like the hole was deep enough. "We wouldn't want anyone to come up here and pull this post out and find out that we had cut it off, would we?"

"We are four miles from the nearest road, and no more than five people will see this brace in the next ten years," replied Alan.

"Well, if you're getting tired and don't want to finish this hole, then why don't you go rest in the pickup, and I will finish the job," said Claude.

An angry Alan continued digging the hole and probably didn't learn that lesson for ten more years. When a seed like this is planted in the desert, it sometimes takes a long time to grow, but it will always be there.

One summer when Alan was sixteen, Claude said the corral fence at Z-Bar-L was falling down and needed to be rebuilt. "Would you help me fix it, Alan?" "Sure, Claude. I'll help."

They had to dig, with a digging bar and shovel, postholes for about forty posts. Unfortunately, just below the surface of the ground was a layer of caliche. Caliche is always hard and tough to dig through, but at Z-Bar-L it was extra hard, like concrete. Alan and Claude were able to dig only two holes each day, working nine hours straight. They would take turns pounding the caliche with the crowbar for about ten minutes, then cleaning out only about a quarter of an inch of the stony soil.

After a few days of this, Alan asked Claude if they couldn't find some easier way to do the job. Claude said, "Well, if we could finish this quicker, there is another hard job waiting. It's all work in one place or another.

What does it matter?" It took them most of the summer to finish the corral fence at Z-Bar-L.

As the years went by Alan grew to appreciate Claude more and more. Claude never changed and never looked for approval, nor did he ever complain about tough conditions but always tried to do his best in any situation.

Claude worked at the Lazy B from 1918 until he retired, in 1984. He was away for a brief period during World War II; he was drafted at age thirty-nine. The army gave him basic training, pulled out all of his teeth, and gave him a set of false teeth and a uniform, including a necktie. He was proud of the fact that he was strong and could keep up with the young men. He was released at age forty and returned to the ranch. Claude said he'd smoked and drunk a lot as a young man, but we never saw him smoke or drink all the years he was at the ranch.

When Claude got out of the army, he was happy to be able to throw away the false teeth that the army had made him wear. And he never got false teeth again. It took him a little longer to eat than most people, but he would eat steak or hard candy any time it was served. In between roundups he did some of the cooking at the bunkhouse, and he would cook typical cowboy food. Cowboys all like their steaks cut fairly thin and cooked until they are past well-done. "Tough" is one way to describe these steaks. But the sight of Claude easily eating a fresh biscuit with stewed apricots on it was pure pleasure in action.

Claude was as strong at sixty as he had been at forty. He taught all of us a thing or two about stamina and strength. His horse fell with him when he was in his thirties and he never saw a doctor about his injuries, but from then on he could not raise his right hand above his head. Claude's honesty and high work standards were a good example for all of us.

He drove his old pickup so slowly that the motor was always in danger of stalling. The old truck lasted many years with Claude's care and attention. On roundups Claude rode every day and never complained. He was kind to his horses and would volunteer for the hard or boring jobs.

DA did not have to tell Claude what to do on a daily basis; Claude would go out around the ranch in one of the pickup trucks and check the windmills, and the salt and water for the cattle. He had an excellent memory. When he saw something amiss, he would decide what was required to fix it, and on his next trip to that spot he would bring the necessary supplies to repair the problem and make it right. He had the patience to take all the time he needed to do the job.

One time DA sent Claude to Horse Camp to get the pump running on the water well there because the tank was low and the cattle were short of water. The pump engine was an old one-cylinder Stover that ran a flat belt to the pump jack on the well. The Stover engines were all manufactured before 1920. They were very temperamental and hard to start. DA was a wizard with them and had the magic touch, but Claude could not make the old engine run. He stayed at Horse Camp three days working on it. He would crank it and crank it with no effect. The cattle were almost out of water when DA drove up. He found Claude sweating and swearing at the balky engine. DA asked, "Does it have fuel? Does it have a spark?" Claude replied, "I've been working on it for three days. Of course it has fuel and a spark to the magneto. That isn't the problem." DA went over to the engine, cranked it one time, and it started right up and ran without a problem. Claude was so angry at this turn of events that he said, "I quit. There's no use working at this outfit anymore." After a few days in Duncan, he cooled off and returned to the Lazy B.

One time when the cowboys were rounding up in the east pasture, Claude's horse stepped in a hole and fell with him. The fall broke two of his ribs and knocked the wind out of him. The cowboys sent for help to haul Claude home in the pickup, and Alan volunteered to ride Claude's horse home. Claude was not a young man by this time, and he had let his stirrup down at least six inches on the left side so that he would not have to raise his foot so high to get on the horse. His pride was such that it would not allow him to ask for help. As Alan rode Claude's horse home, he discovered that one stirrup being a lot longer than the other causes you to sit tilted sideways on the saddle. When Alan dismounted, he said, "Claude must be a lot tougher than I thought he was to be able to ride sideways all day in this saddle."

When Claude finally retired, in 1984, he moved to a small house owned by Bug Quinn about a mile from the border of the Lazy B. He continued to check the water and the windmill for us at New Well about twice a week and would report any problems. When he retired he took his saddle, an old one with a silver horn, and he took his tack and his spurs. He said he might need them sometime. Alan was visiting Claude and Bug at the little house one day in 1986. Claude got up and handed his old spurs to Alan. "I won't need these anymore," he said. It was an emotional moment for Claude and for Alan. When a cowboy gives up his spurs it is usually the beginning of the end. Claude knew it and Alan knew it. It brought tears to the eyes of both men.

Not long after that Claude was taken to the hospital in Safford, Arizona. Alan went by to visit him. Claude, like many of the cowboys, had never married and had no children. But he had various relatives in the area, and they were hanging around the hospital. Claude told Alan his relatives were like the vultures out at the ranch, waiting for him to die so they could get his money. He asked Alan to write a will for him. Alan explained that he couldn't do that, but he offered to ask a local lawyer he knew to write one for Claude. Claude told Alan what he wanted, and Alan had a simple will prepared for Claude that same day. Claude was very relieved. A few days later the telephone rang at the ranch at 2:30 A.M.; it was Claude's doctor saying he was dying. Alan got up and drove the sixty miles to the hospital as fast as he could. He walked into Claude's room and held his hand a few minutes before he passed away. Alan was grateful he could be with Claude because Claude wanted it that way. We were proud to know him.

Top: *Our peg-leg cowboy in the 1920s.* Bottom: *Trailing a herd of cattle.* Opposite: *Driving a herd of cattle.*

9. Trail Ride to Mexico

The trail work is something by itself.
The herds may be on the trail several months,
averaging fifteen miles or less a day.
The cowboys accompanying each have to
undergo much hard toil, of a peculiarly same
and wearisome kind.

THEODORE ROOSEVELT,
Ranch Life and the Hunting-Trail

*I*N 1928 THE RANCH WAS VERY DRY. THERE WERE TOO MANY CATTLE, and no rain fell in the summer. The grass was short, dry, and of poor quality. The Depression was around the corner, and cattle prices were low. The range was still open and unfenced, and anyone who wanted to keep some cattle could just put them out and let them roam. The mother cows were so thin they couldn't produce milk to feed their calves. Some cows began to die of starvation, and most were too thin to breed for the following year. DA decided to lease a ranch in Sonora, Mexico, and put his breeding herd there over the winter until conditions improved. He gathered about two thousand cows and calves and a crew of cowboys to drive the cattle some 120 miles south to the Mexican ranch. They were on the trail at Thanksgiving near Animas, New Mexico, when a storm had moved in, and the cowboys were cold and wet all day. That night a rancher in Animas let them rest their cattle overnight in his pasture, and told the crew they could sleep in an old chicken house on the property. Bug Quinn said that chicken house was a very welcome sight for all of them. He called it the Animas Hilton.

Another night, while they were camped, something spooked the cattle, and they stampeded. Anything can set them off: a sudden noise, a cowboy striking a match, an unexpected cough. Once they run, all hell breaks loose. The men struggled out of their bedrolls, into their boots, and onto their horses. They had to try to head off the cattle in the lead and turn them back into the herd. It required riding as fast as the horses could go, a full gallop over unfamiliar terrain in the dark. The next day they had to ride all the surrounding areas to locate the stray cattle lost in the night's stampede.

Bug had started the journey as one of the cowboys, but the man who was hired as the cook had been to town before the trip started, and he developed a bad case of venereal disease. DA let the cook go and Bug volunteered to be the new cook. It turned out to be a fine choice. Bug cooked all the traditional cowboy food—biscuits, beans, and beef—but they tasted better when he cooked them. He planned ahead and never ran out of food, no matter how many unexpected guests showed up. He slept very little and was up starting breakfast by 2:00 A.M. He would do some lunch preparation at the same time. The food was always ready and served with a smile and a story. The coffee was strong enough to walk on its own. There was always a pot of stewed apricots to spread on the biscuits.

The cattle reached their destination before Christmas and remained there a year before returning to the Lazy B. The ranch was leased from the Gavilando family, whom DA said were honorable people. During the year in Mexico, rain fell on the Lazy B, and conditions were good when the herd returned. DA never spoke about the financial picture of the year in Mexico. Bug said it had been a financial disaster and that it was hard on the cattle to travel so far. Bug must have been right, because DA never again moved his cattle during a drought on the Lazy B.

The housing on the Gavilando ranch was simple: a few adobe huts with dirt floors. Pigs ran loose around the houses, and they would eat anything that wasn't tied up in a tree. One time the cowboys butchered a couple of beeves and spent several days cutting the meat in thin strips to season and dry in the sun as jerky. They hung it all up on some clotheslines to cure, but the pigs pushed the clotheslines down and ate all the jerky.

Bug loved the time in Mexico. Whiskey was cheap, and life was easy. Most of the cowboys traded for new horses while they were there. Coming back across the border the next year, there were a few problems about proper papers and bills of sale for the horses. After a few days of delay and negotiation, the cattle and horses were allowed to cross the border and return to the Lazy B. On the return trip, Jim Brister was running after a stray cow when his horse stepped in a badger hole and fell. Jim just stepped off his horse as the horse went down. Fortunately, the horse did not break a leg, and Jim got right back on and kept going.

A few days after they got back to the Lazy B, our great-uncle, Brooks Scott, was at the ranch for a couple of days to ride with us. He was racing to turn back a cow when his horse stepped in a hole and fell. Brooks stayed on the horse, and it rolled over on him. Brooks was badly bruised and the wind was knocked out of him. Jim rode up and laughed at him. Brooks was just lying in the dirt—too injured to get up—but he said, "Damn, Jim. Why are you laughing at me? Haven't you ever seen a cowboy hurt before?" Jim said, "Well, you didn't have to stay there and let him roll on you. You could have gotten loose and stepped off." Jim lived in a different world. Problems for most people on horseback were not problems for Jim.

The cattle drive to Mexico became the subject of many a story in the years to follow.

Top: *Playing cards at the ranch house:*
Scott Wilkey (MO's brother, far left),
MO (center), DA (far right).

Center: *The ranch house.*

Bottom: *MO working in the kitchen.*

Opposite: *DA at the dining room table.*

10. *Ranch Family Life*

---

*There is another question I want to ask you.
Have you ever stopped to think about just what
living with me will be like?*

LETTER FROM HARRY TO
ADA MAE, AUGUST 1927

*T*HE RANCH HOUSE WAS BUILT IN THE EARLY 1900S AS A PLACE
for some of the cowboys to live. DA's parents, H.C. and Alice Day, had
their house along the Gila River on farmland. But the bulk of the range-
land was south of the Gila, and a more central location was needed for the
men who rode the range and looked after the cattle. Two wells had been
drilled at the location of the house. Water was found at about six hundred
feet, although each well produced only about five gallons per minute when
pumped. The main source of power was the wind, which blew much of the
time. Two Stover ten-horsepower single-cylinder pump engines were
used when the wind did not blow. Two giant windmill towers were con
structed over the wells.

The two huge windmills at the headquarters were the dominant feature
for miles around. The windmills were Sampson twenty-foot mills. This
means that the fan is twenty feet across. These were the largest ever made
in the United States, as far as I know. The towers were constructed on-site
out of eight-by-eight-inch square timbers, with all the joints mitered to a
perfect fit. The whole appearance of them was graceful. Later windmills
built on steel towers appear spindly in comparison to these two giants.
When they were pumping they made their own distinctive sounds—the
creak of the wood as it responded to the pressure of the wind, the sounds of

the rods going up and down to pump the water, the sound of the gears in the head of the windmill as they turned from the upstroke to the downstroke in the pumping cycle.

Over time these big inanimate objects almost came to life. By producing water, the very lifeblood of the desert, they made us very dependent on them. Because they seldom broke, they were like helpful friends more than just pieces of machinery. They stood as silent guardians of the landscape when it was still, and when the wind started to blow, the tail of the mill always turned to face away from the wind. The wheel would only face the wind directly when the wind was less than ten miles per hour; in higher winds, the wheel would turn progressively more out of the wind the harder it blew. We could look at the tails of the windmills and see what direction the wind was coming from and how hard the wind was blowing by how much the fan was faced into the wind. In a really hard wind the windmills would almost turn themselves off and remind us of a peasant in a shawl with his back turned to the wind.

All visitors to the ranch were always captivated by the windmills—the beauty, grace, and size of them. They were as close as any mechanical object can be to having personalities—the kind, benevolent friends who stood so stately, predicting the weather, and always ready to produce water when nature decided to cooperate.

The house was built of adobe bricks made from a clay pit just north of the building site. Felipe Zuniga from Duncan, who had built other adobe houses, came out to the ranch to make the adobes and line them up in rows, slanted to expose both sides of the bricks to the air and the sun until they dried. The design of the house was square, with four rooms—a kitchen, a living room, an office, and one bedroom. A screen porch wrapped around three sides. There was no bathroom and no running water. A wooden privy was installed about seventy-five yards from the back door and to the west. The exterior and interior of the adobe walls were plastered. The floor was poured concrete. The kitchen had a sink, some cupboards, a wood-burning stove, a kitchen table, and some chairs. The living room had a fireplace that was needed only a few days and nights in the dead of winter.

When DA was sent to the Lazy B, after his father's death, to run the ranch until the estate was settled, he lived in the adobe house with the ranch crew. The old Day house on the farm had burned down, so DA was still living in the adobe house when he courted Ada Mae. Despite his passion for her, he thought it would be impossible to bring a wife to live at an isolated house with no indoor plumbing and no electricity that had to be shared with the cowboys. Ada Mae's mother, Mamie Scott Wilkey, agreed with him and did not want to see her lovely eldest daughter move to such a remote and primitive place.

Harry wrote to Ada Mae in early August 1927 about what he thought their lives would be like if she married him and moved to the ranch.

> *I have been thinking and imagining what we would be doing if you were here. In the morning we would probably ride some place on our horses and see how our cattle are getting along. We might find a calf that needed doctoring or one that needed attention of some kind. When we got back to the ranch we would prepare and eat lunch together. After that we would read, write letters or rest until it cooled off a little. Then we would get in the car and go up to the tank for a swim. In the evening if conditions permitted we might listen in on the radio or you might sing for me or we might do any one of the thousand and one little things that have to be done in any home. One or two days a week we would have to go to Duncan for provisions and our mail. Occasionally we would have to go to Clifton or Lordsburg on business. Dearest, are you sure you wouldn't soon tire of a life like that? Oh, I am afraid.*

Harry's fears grew stronger and, in a letter to Ada Mae dated August 12, 1927, he wrote:

> *I just counted my money and I have five dollars and sixty-one cents in my pocket. I have eighty-nine dollars in the bank. I owe ninety-eight dollars taxes on our farm. . . . [Just] as soon as I can establish*

*a living source of income I am going to you wherever you may be and
ask you to come back with me.*

In response, Ada Mae wrote:

*Harry, I might better be dead than away from you like this indefi-
nitely.*

Neither MO or DA ever discussed with their children what changed
DA's mind about getting married. Their daily correspondence ceased on
September 12, 1927, and they eloped on September 16, 1927, to be married
by a justice of the peace in Las Cruces, New Mexico. Mamie Wilkey's parting
advice to her daughter was, "Ada Mae, don't ever learn to milk the cow."

All things are possible to two people as deeply in love as DA and Ada
Mae. Hardships became just challenges to be met and shared. Ada Mae
was by nature ready for adventure and full of energy. She was a willing
cook and not afraid of hard work. But she heeded her mother's advice and
confined her work to her household and did not work in the barn or corrals. She enjoyed riding horseback with DA in the early years of their
marriage, at least on rides that were not too long or tedious. She didn't
mind heating water on the old woodstove, or bathing in a big round wash-
tub. She did not miss her life and friends in El Paso, because she wanted
nothing more than to share DA's life. DA, in turn, was happier than he
had ever been.

The ranch was producing very little net income in the years that DA
first managed it. It had lost money steadily during Sam Foster's management, and DA was careful with every penny he spent. He was determined
to stop the deficit. The stock-market crash in 1929 produced a drop in
price for many goods and for salaries. It also meant a drop in cattle prices.
There was no money for new clothes or for travel. Ada Mae and DA stayed
home and tried to cope with the Great Depression. They had plenty of
beef to eat, and frijole beans were cheap. At the end of the year in 1929
they had a small profit. But Ada Mae was pregnant.

Somehow DA had not counted on having a child, at least not until they had better housing and a little money. The prospect filled him with foreboding. Ada Mae, however, was confident that they could cope with parenthood despite their limited facilities and resources.

The lawyers for the H. C. Day estate decided that mortgage-foreclosure proceedings should be brought against Sam Foster. Nothing had been paid on his interest in the Lazy B, and the attorneys thought the legal proceedings would be brief and conclusive. Suit was filed in the federal district court in Arizona. The Fosters decided to contest the foreclosure, and DA was required to spend a great deal of time going over all the records of income and expenditures during the years Sam Foster had managed the ranch. When the time approached for Ada Mae to give birth to her baby in March 1930, she decided to go to El Paso, Texas, and stay with her parents. There she could have the assistance of a doctor and go to a hospital for the birth. DA, however, spent most of the month of March in Tucson, attending and testifying at the mortgage-foreclosure hearing in federal district court. Ada Mae delivered her little daughter on March 26. DA went from Tucson to El Paso to see Ada Mae and her baby in the hospital. He stayed one day and returned to the ranch. He wrote Ada Mae before going to bed that night.

> *We will work everything out some way. . . . I carry in my heart a picture of your beautiful face, with your wonderful love shining through your eyes, framed with a white pillow. I also have a vivid picture of Sandra (is that spelled correctly?). Although I cannot say that I feel any great parental love for Sandra yet, I would like to see her and touch her again.*

DA did not see us again until mid-April, when Ada Mae returned to the ranch with me. Mamie Wilkey was reluctant to let us return to the ranch, and she wrote DA to urge him to leave the ranch.

There were no disposable diapers in 1930, and there was no doctor within two hundred miles of the Lazy B. But Ada Mae cheerfully assumed the duties of motherhood without complaint. The cowboys carried buckets of water to the house from the wells. They helped keep the woodstove supplied with wood kindling. Ada Mae washed and boiled diapers and nursed her baby. DA slowly and reluctantly grew accustomed to his new role as a father. In time he grew to love his daughter dearly and to think that perhaps they could manage after all.

As the first child, I was always the darling of my daddy's eye. I was an easygoing baby and ready to learn. I loved the ranch and adored my father. I loved MO, too, but the bond between a little girl and her father is often something special. How lucky I felt to be able to share as much of his life as I did!

The cowboys were more enthusiastic than DA about having a baby at the Lazy B. As soon as I could sit up, Rastus took me up on his saddle and rode around the yard with me on horseback. Rastus called me "Tanny," an approximation of how I pronounced me own name at age three. All the cowboys would try to hold me and entertain me. Ada Mae never lacked for baby-sitters, but they were not at all what one would expect in a city. My baby-sitters were tobacco-chewing, unshaven, unbathed, Levi-clad, and tough as nails, but they would talk baby talk and try for hours to keep baby Sandra happy.

My skill with a horse was not great, but I was not afraid of horses, and I loved to get out around the ranch. I cannot remember a time when I did not ride. The cowboys seemed to enjoy my presence and later said that, since I was the first child, they took special care of me. Before I rode occasionally on the roundup, it had been an all-male domain. Changing it to accommodate a female was probably my first initiation into joining an all-men's club, something I did more than once in my life. After the cowboys understood that a girl could hold up her end, it was much easier for my sister, my niece, and the other girls and young women who followed to be accepted in that rough-and-tumble world. Ann was a big help on roundups, as was Alan's daughter, Marina, in later years.

I had a soft spot when it came to stray kittens, crippled birds, and even baby mice. MO and Ann were afraid of mice and hated them, but I was not afraid of them and even had some as pets at one time. I was very afraid of most insects, however. Ann and Alan delighted in chasing me all over the house with a June bug on a string or a cricket in hand.

I was about seven years old when DA and MO decided to build a separate bunkhouse for the cowboys and to add on to the original house for themselves. The ranch had produced some net income each year, the price of cattle had increased, and several years of decent rainfall persuaded them that it could be done financially.

DA drew the plans and hired Felipe Zuniga to come to the ranch to make some adobe bricks. He designed the bunkhouse with two bedrooms, a large kitchen, and a bathroom. Next to the bunkhouse he built a two-car garage and a storage room. A covered porch was built along the front of the bunkhouse.

The main house was extended by a new wing, adding two new bedrooms and a bathroom, plus a wide hallway connecting the new wing to the old house. DA then designed a large glass-enclosed case about five feet by ten feet, which was outside near the bathroom. It faced south and was tilted up about forty-five degrees. He painted the interior black and ran water pipes up and down the interior of the shallow case. The pipes were also painted black. He then sealed the case with a double layer of glass. He connected the pipes to the water supply and to the shower and washbasin in his new bathroom. It was a perfect solar-energy water heater at a time before any such device had been built. Having indoor plumbing and hot water was better than the Biltmore Hotel for the Day family.

DA and his employees did all the work that went into building the bunkhouse and the new addition. The kitchens were equipped with running water, and he installed a water tower to serve both the house and the bunkhouse. He installed a propane gas tank outside each building and replaced the woodstoves with gas stoves. Eventually he installed an electric generator, which could provide electric power for a few hours each day. By 1937 the ranch had made a giant leap into the twentieth century.

Through the years the ranch house was the center of the Day family life. DA awoke early and would light a cigarette before getting out of bed.

Then he would put on his khaki pants and a well-worn shirt with a collar and long sleeves. He would go in the kitchen and heat water in the teakettle to make a cup of tea. In the living room, in the armchair closest to the kitchen, he would smoke another cigarette or two, drink his tea, and read some of the magazines and newspapers that had arrived in the week's mail.

MO was the next one up. She would dress, come to the kitchen, and make a pot of coffee. Before long she would prepare something for breakfast. It might be eggs and bacon, french toast, or pancakes. Occasionally she would make a pan of biscuits. DA would watch the proceedings in the kitchen and offer advice on what to cook and how to cook it. He never tired of criticizing MO's methods of cooking, but he never tired of eating her meals, either.

We children would do our best to sleep late, but usually DA would come in and say, "You'd better get up if you're going with us today."

"Ummm. Where are you going?"

"Several places. Probably Z-Bar-L and maybe Cottonwood."

"Oh, wait for me. I want to go, too."

"Well, we can't wait around. You'd better get ready—*pronto.*"

That would send us scurrying around to get dressed, have a little breakfast, and get outside to the bunkhouse so we wouldn't be left behind. More often than not, we would find DA squatting down on his haunches on the bunkhouse porch, talking to the cowboys. They would all be smoking and talking about some of the things that might need doing at various locations on the ranch.

"Ira, how much water is left in Tank 5? How long will it last?"

"Oh, probably another couple of weeks. A couple of old cows were stuck in the mud there yesterday, and I had to pull to them out. I probably ought to get up there with the tractor and try to blade away some of the silt and mud."

"Rastus, where are you going today?"

"I thought I'd go up to New Well. There's a cow there with a swollen udder. I want to see if she lost her calf. And I want to check the fence over at the Rayburn side. I think maybe a few of his cows got through and are in the New Well pasture."

"Well, I expect you'd better check it out."

"Claude, we ought to check on the salt blocks over at High Lonesome. There wasn't much left a week or so ago. And it wouldn't hurt to oil that windmill."

"Okay. I reckon I'll take the Chevy pickup and head over there."

"It doesn't look like any rain clouds are going to come up today. The wind is from the west. The barometer is steady."

"We could sure use some rain. Them cows are lookin' thin. Startin' to eat the prickly pear. You know they're hard up then."

"Well, I expect I'd better get on my way to Z-Bar-L," DA would say. "Sandra, you ready to go? I'll just go get the .22 Hornet in case we see some rabbits or a coyote."

After puttering around, getting a burlap water bag, the .22 rifle, another pack of cigarettes, and a handful of wooden kitchen matches to put in the jeep, DA and his children were finally on their way. In the jeep we drove with the windows down. The dust kicked up by the tires rolled into the jeep, and before long we were covered with a fine layer of dirt. As we drove along the unpaved road, DA kept up a steady stream of conversation. When he spotted some cattle, he would leave the road and drive across the terrain to check on them. He wanted to see which ones they were, how they looked, whether there were any special problems. He never tired of looking at the cattle, checking the grass, tinkering with the water supplies, and watching everything around him.

"Do you see what I see?" he would say.

"No. What? Where?"

"Right over there below the hill."

"I don't see anything. What do you see, DA?"

"Look right over there. Do you see the three little light-colored animals?"

"Oh, you mean near the mesquite bushes on the flat area?"

"Yes. They are looking at us. They see us."

"What are they?"

"They're antelope. We'll stop here so we don't scare them off. See? Their heads are up and they are nervous. Yup. There they go." And we watched them bound across the ground as though they had wings—over the hill and out of sight.

"Oh, DA, aren't they fun to see? They won't let us get close. Where do they stay most of the time?"

"They like to stay on flat, grassy areas like those near Summit. They want to be able to see in all directions to protect themselves. We used to see many more of them. The hunters have pretty nearly killed them off."

"Why are they allowed to hunt so many? Why doesn't the state limit the hunting?"

"I'm not sure. The state probably wants the income from the sale of hunting licenses. And they never come out and check on the conditions here."

"Let's drive over here and look at something," said DA later. We jounced along over some rocks and gullies and over a hill until we reached an area about the size of a football field. It was completely bare of grass and vegetation and had a number of low mounds of dirt scattered around. We stopped the motor and watched. Each mound had several small holes in it, and soon the little tan head of a prairie dog peeked out of one. It was standing on its hind legs, holding its front paws up and looking all around, making little chirping sounds. Then another prairie dog popped out of another mound with an answering chirp. In time several scampered out and ran to another mound or to an area beyond the mounds.

"Aren't they cute, DA? Can we catch one?"

"No. You'll never catch one. And they are real pests. They eat all the grass and plants in the area. Look how they have picked it clean! And they multiply like mice. I am not too happy about having so many prairie dogs around."

"Does anything eat the prairie dogs?"

"Oh, I suppose coyotes catch a few occasionally. And maybe a fox can catch them. Or even a hawk, if it is fast. They say the ferrets live on prairie dogs. I've seen an occasional ferret but never in the prairie-dog town."

DA started the motor, and we went on past Summit and the Lazy B shipping pens, past the road to the Fuller ranch, and on to Z-Bar-L. In the remains of a little one-room wooden house there, a cowboy could camp for a while. There was a well, a big windmill, a steel-rimmed water tank, and some troughs with float valves to keep them full for the livestock to drink. DA checked the float valves, the level of water in the troughs, the storage tank, and the size remaining of the salt blocks.

We children walked over past the corrals to a sandy area where we could find a few shards of ancient Indian pots or, if we were really lucky, part of a projectile point or some pieces of the special flint stone the Indians used to make their arrowheads. The area used to be a shallow lake and, when water stood there, Indians would camp nearby to hunt the birds and animals that used the lake.

It was hot; we got the water bag, unscrewed the cap, and had a drink. The water was cool from the evaporation of the bag, but it tasted like the wet burlap.

"DA, when are we going? It's hot."

"Pretty soon. I want to oil the windmill." So he climbed up the windmill tower, hoisted himself onto the narrow platform, and tied down the mill so it could not turn and knock him off. Then he oiled the gears and moving parts, released the mill, and climbed back down. "We need to wait a while until the wind blows so I can see if the well is pumping all right."

We got a stick and drew squares in the dirt and played hopscotch while we waited. A buzzard circled overhead looking for anything dead or dying that it could eat. A hawk swooped by on the prowl. Finally a breath of air stirred, and a little later a light breeze came and the windmill began to turn. It creaked as the tail turned to follow the wind and to head the mill into the wind. As the wheel turned, the sucker rods began to move up and down, and we could hear them as they rose and fell in the well casing. In a few minutes, water began to pour out of the pipe into the storage tank. DA held his ear on the pipe that housed the sucker rods to hear whether they were functioning properly. If not, he knew he would have to return with a crew to help him pull all the sucker rods out, one at a time, uncouple them, and find the problem. That was a job he didn't enjoy. It took several days and was hard work for at least three or four men.

"Ready to go, DA?"

"Yep. I'm ready."

"Can I drive?"

"You know you *can*. You mean '*May* I drive?' "

"Okay. *May* I drive on the way home?"

"Yes. After we leave the highway, you *may* drive on the ranch road."

One of the things the Day children liked to do was drive the various vehicles at the ranch. DA let us do that from a very early age. As soon as we were big enough to see over the dashboard, DA would let us sit on his lap and steer the car or truck. And as soon as we were tall enough to reach the pedals on the floor and still see over the dashboard, he would let us drive on the ranch roads. He would sit next to us so he could grab the wheel if necessary, but he seldom did despite our wanderings. And we loved the excitement of driving.

Ann and Alan paired up when they were small. Alan would sit down on the floor of the car and push the pedals—the gas pedal, the brake, and the clutch. Ann would steer the car and work the gearshift. She would say, "Speed up," and Alan would push down the gas pedal, or she would say, "Stop!" and Alan would push the brake pedal, or "Shift," and he would push in the clutch. Sometimes that arrangement produced some wild rides when the steering and the gear shifting failed to coincide.

Another constant part of ranch life was beef jerky. It was made by taking very thinly sliced raw beef, sprinkling salt and pepper on it, and drying it in the sun. In the early days before refrigeration, when a beef was butchered during warm weather, it was very difficult to use the entire beef before it spoiled. As a consequence, we would use a quarter or even half of the beef to make jerky in order to preserve it.

Jerky is usually eaten in its dry form but can be incorporated into a number of dishes that are cooked on the stove. Shredded jerky heated in gravy and served over a biscuit is a quite nutritious and tasty breakfast. The most standard use of jerky, however, is to put a few pieces in the jacket pocket or chaps when going outdoors. A piece every hour or two keeps hunger away and also serves to satisfy the need to chew. Almost nothing is more difficult to chew than a piece of sun-dried jerky from the front shoulder of a ten-year-old cow that ended up on the butcher block. It might take half an hour to render a piece of tough jerky into a form tender enough to swallow.

Alan enjoyed eating jerky so much that at a relatively young age he got involved in the cutting and drying of it. As time went on, he became the primary jerky producer on the ranch. It is pretty much a thankless job, so everyone was happy when Alan took it over. Over the years he experimented with various other seasonings for the jerky. He felt the traditional salt-and-pepper coating could be improved upon. He tried teriyaki, jalapeño, and even prickly-pear-cactus juice. There are many varieties. What one person thinks is delicious, another cannot tolerate.

In the early days, jerky was made from any part of the beef, and the most time-consuming part was the slicing of the meat. You need a very sharp knife and a lot of patience. When the jerky strips were hung outside to dry, it would usually take a week or so for them to dehydrate. There was no way to keep the flies from swarming around the meat. The standard cowboy joke involved deciding how much of the coating was pepper and how much was fly specks on the meat. The quality improved when the beef could be dried on a screened porch. A few years later, Alan designed some drying trays to dry the meat near the fireplace in the winter, when the fireplace was used to heat the house.

Eventually the ranch acquired an old walk-in cooler from a restaurant that had gone broke. We could keep meat much longer in warm weather. The ranch also had a large freezer so we could age the beef properly, then cut it up, package it, and keep it in the Deepfreeze until we needed it. The addition of an electric meat saw and a slicer to slice the meat thin made the jerky production much easier. We sent sacks of the jerky as Christmas gifts to friends and family. Guests who came to the ranch would often ask about jerky when they first arrived and would say how they remembered the jerky from their previous visit. All in all, jerky was a better snack than cookies, candy, or doughnuts, and everyone in the family still enjoys it to this day. Alan still makes jerky, and it is always much better than any that is sold in the supermarkets.

As with most families, we had certain traditions. Thanksgiving always meant having as many family members as possible at the ranch. MO arranged to get a large turkey from one of the local farmers. She cooked for several days. The immediate family and usually a few relatives or other friends would gather in midafternoon in the small dining room and share the abundant meal. DA carved the turkey after sharpening the knife on his whetstone. I was usually asked to say the blessing. The conversations continued long after the meal ended. We would eventually get out of the house and try to walk off some of all those calories.

Christmas meant more planning for both gifts and holiday meals. We always drove to the mountains outside Silver City, New Mexico, to select and cut down a piñon pine for our Christmas tree. We would take a picnic and drive north of Lordsburg to the national forest. We drove first to Tyrone, an old copper-mining town since closed down. Then we would drive to the old house in the woods once used by President Theodore Roosevelt for a hunting trip. Finally, we would eat our picnic lunch. Afterward, we would find a tree we thought would be the right size for the living room. As with all families, we often argued among ourselves about which tree was the best. The piñon pine is the most fragrant of all the conifers. The fragrance permeated the house when we put it up.

DA would not allow us to put up the Christmas tree or decorate it until Christmas Eve. We spent much of that day installing it and covering it with lights, ornaments, and tinsel. We always went outside to check the stars before settling in for the night. Milk and cookies were always left by the fireplace for Santa.

After Christmas, DA told us the tree had to be down by New Year's Eve. Then we would turn on the radio and try to stay up until it was at least New Year's Eve in New York City before going to bed.

On the Fourth of July we took a picnic to Mount Graham, outside Safford, Arizona. The trip took several hours, and it often rained once we were on the mountain. The cool, wet air was welcome to all of us. When we returned to the ranch that evening, DA would light some firecrackers to make sure we observed that important date in the proper manner.

Birthdays called for angel-food cake baked by MO and homemade ice cream. Making the ice cream was a major production. We had to buy block ice in town and coarse salt. MO made a basic custard with milk, eggs, sugar, and vanilla. Then she added the heavy cream we had accumulated from the milk each day. We put it all in the metal ice-cream container and fitted it into the larger bucket with the paddles inside and a handle outside to turn them. We broke up the block ice with an ice pick and fitted it around the metal container in the larger bucket and spread the salt over the ice. Ann, Alan, and I took turns cranking the handle. It took about three-quarters of an hour to freeze. When one of us tired, another would take over. As the ice cream hardened, it was much harder to turn the crank. When we could turn it no more, we called to MO to open it up. She removed the salty ice at the top and then the crank handle. Finally, off came the top, and she lifted out the paddles, or the "dasher," as it was called. The child who had cranked the hardest got to lick the dasher first. Then we all piled ice cream in our bowls and ate until we felt a pain in our foreheads from the cold ice cream. The hard work somehow made it taste better.

The most important times of the year for us were the roundups in the spring and fall and the resulting sales of cattle. Everything else we did led up those special events. All else paled by comparison, although one event came close. It seldom snows at the Lazy B, and when it does, not much falls and it soon melts. In the winter of 1949 we had the biggest snow of our history. One January night it snowed two feet. Alan was ten and Ann eleven. They were ecstatic the next morning to see their world in white. They had never seen anything like it.

The storm was large and covered all of New Mexico and into the Midwest and part of Nebraska. South Dakota got five and six feet of the white stuff. Many cattle froze to death or were smothered by the snow.

At Lazy B we had some old cows that DA had gathered in the fall to sell. Some were thin and weak and should have been sold much sooner, but DA had a common failing that many cowmen have. It was hard for him to sell an old cull cow—his thought was always, "She has been a good mother and has raised so many calves. Maybe next year she will produce one more. Besides we are in the *cow* business, so why get rid of our main product?"

In any event, we were ill equipped for a snow—we had no chains and only one jeep with four-wheel drive. DA decided to feed hay to the old thin cows at High Lonesome. He sent Claude and LeRoy McCarty to feed them. They took the pickup to haul the hay and the jeep to pull the pickup out when it got stuck. "DA, DA can we go along?" Alan and Ann did not want to miss all of this adventure. Their school was closed for at least a week because of the snow. Life could not get much better for a youngster. So off they went to feed the old cows, slipping and sliding and occasionally stuck, but never for too long. Finally, within sight of Summit and the railroad work station, both the pickup and the jeep got totally stuck and could not be moved. Claude, LeRoy, Ann, and Alan were wet and cold, and had no proper shoes or clothing. Claude walked about half a mile to Summit and borrowed a large jack that weighed close to one hundred pounds. He carried it back, which was no small feat, to help jack up the vehicles. The vehicles were finally moved and the men were able to find some of the old cows needing the hay and to feed them. The next day they tried again, and reached a few more cows. The excitement was getting more like a muddy routine.

A few cattle died, but the net outcome of the big snow was a great amount of moisture available to seep into the ground to cause the grass and weeds to grow as the weather warmed. The big snow gave us the greenest, prettiest, and lushest spring any of us could remember. The cattle all got fat and happy, and the life cycle on the ranch got a big boost. We all wished we could get a snow like that every year, but that we might be better prepared next time with overshoes and waterproof clothing!

The clothes worn for ranch life have always been distinctive. Tourists from abroad come to the West to see cowboys, and they look for long lanky men wearing blue jeans with cowboy boots on their feet and big Western hats on their heads. This garb has grown so popular that it is hard to tell the cowboys from the dudes. Levi's first appeared in California during the 1849 gold rush. The miners found them to be the toughest pants they could buy. Word of mouth after that made them the pants favored in the West by anyone who had to work outdoors. As mining became more specialized, the clothing changed to fit the needs of the miners. But Levi's served the needs of the cowboys. They are long lasting and resist the punctures of most small objects other than cactus. They have wide belt loops that accommodate the type of belt favored by cowboys, and they come in all waist sizes and lengths.

Alan always dressed just like the cowboys, but MO managed to have clothes for Ann and me that were more feminine and made of better materials. DA and Rastus never wore Levi's but instead chose khaki pants for their work. All of the other cowboys wore Levi's. No one ever made fun of those two for not wearing Levi's, but if a dude or visitor didn't have standard Levi's, the others would always make fun of them.

Footwear for cowboys is always some form of boot. A boot with a high heel is not likely to slide all the way through a stirrup by accident and then leave the rider hung on the horse in case of a fall. The high tops of the boots keep leaves and trash from getting inside the boot when you are riding through trees or under brush. Many cowboys tell of rattlesnakes striking at them but not being able to penetrate the high top of the boot with their fangs. Boots are expensive if they are custom-made or made from special leather. They can be the most comfortable footwear you can wear or the most uncomfortable. If boots are bought too tight they can be excruciatingly painful. Rastus had small feet but bought his boots too tight. One time he was crossing the Gila River and his horse stepped into a quicksand bog. Rastus had to get off and struggle to get out of the bog himself. After the rest of the cowboys had thrown their saddle ropes over his horse and pulled him from the bog, we had to cut one of Rastus's boots off because it had filled with quicksand and it was so tight to his foot that we could not pull his foot out of the boot.

Most cowboys have two pairs of boots—a pair for work and a pair for going to town. A decent pair of boots might cost a month's wages, but cowboys always seem willing to spend that much for their footwear. DA had a good pair of boots and a pair for town. We children grew so rapidly that we had only one pair at a time. MO had one pair, but she seldom wore them because she rode horseback so rarely.

Shirts are almost always long-sleeved. The sleeves give some measure of protection from scratching by thorns when riding through brush, and also give protection from the sun. The best way to tell a real cowboy from a dude is to look for very suntanned hands and face and very pale skin on all other parts of the body. No self-respecting cowboy will take his shirt off to get a tan.

The cowboy's hat is as much a part of him as his boots, and he probably wears it about as many hours a day as he does his boots. It is usually broad-brimmed, and creased in the crown. Some prefer black and others tan, but all the hats show dust and dirt almost from the first day they are worn. Hats sometimes last many years and show the marks of many days working in the hot sun and dust, and the rain. The sweat stain that eventually appears around the band is a testimony to many hard days. A hawk feather or silver concho might be stuck in the band to show the owner's individuality, and many a fight, either good-natured or serious, ensues from someone messing with another cowboy's hat. If the boss really wants to get 100 percent effort from his crew for a roundup, all he has to say is that if they all work hard for the entire roundup he will buy them each a new Stetson hat when the roundup is over. We did this more than once at the Lazy B. Ann and Alan had cowboy hats by the time they were five. I never wanted a hat and never wore one.

Cowboys always own their own saddle, bridle, and spurs. Each cowboy has his own preference for each of these items. Rastus and Claude each had a pair of spurs that had been custom-made by a good spur maker when they were quite young. They each wore their spurs every time they rode, until they died. Jim Brister owned many sets of spurs but usually wore just one favorite pair. Spurs are the tool the cowboys use to help give signals to their horses, and they are not harmful when used correctly. A little touch with the spur on one side will help the horse prepare to turn the other way ahead of a cow who might otherwise have run past him. Losing a spur is about like losing a wallet. After wearing spurs for many years, you feel almost undressed getting on a horse without them. The spurs that DA wore didn't match each other, and it always looked odd to see him walking around with unmatched spurs. Alan offered to buy him a nice new pair of spurs, but he never accepted the offer and always wore that odd pair. In their spare time at the Lazy B, the men would sometimes make spurs. Some were functional and would sit on the boot at the correct angle, but none were ever as pretty or shiny as the spurs that could be bought in a store. Each of us as children had small spurs, although I usually did not wear them.

Almost all cowboys have chaps. They help ward off the thorns and cactus spines the cowboys ride through, and when they fit properly, they form a barrier to keep the inside of the legs from rubbing as much on the saddle. They also shed water when it rains or snows, and give some measure of protection from the cold. Chaps are merely heavy leather pants with the seat part missing. They can be of several different designs, but all serve the same purpose. They usually last for many years, so cowboys don't change chaps as often as they do their boots or hat. Some chaps have pockets in them so that the owner can carry his gloves or a pair of pliers or spare leather for spot repairs. Cowboys usually wear chaps only when they are actually riding horseback. Since chaps are so heavy, when the rider dismounts he usually takes off his chaps. Some of our cowboys enjoyed working with leather and made chaps in their spare time. If made correctly, the fit on these handmade chaps is better than the fit from chaps purchased in a store.

In the 1960s, a new breed of cowboy began to appear. They called themselves buckaroos. These cowboys dressed differently from our old-line cowboys. They wanted to draw attention to themselves and did so in part by their manner of dress. They wore boots with heels so high that some of these men wobbled when they walked. They tucked their pants inside their boots, and the chaps they wore only came down to their knees. Their hats were usually even larger than a traditional cowboy's hat, and might have no crease at all. The buckaroos were all quite proud of their ability as riders, and they resisted any mechanized form of work on a ranch. Most men who work on a ranch know that part of their work will be manual work and part will involve driving a tractor or a pickup. The work might include loading or unloading hay, fence building, or mechanical work on equipment. Buckaroos usually disdained this kind of work. They went from ranch to ranch looking for jobs that only required them to ride horseback. Fifty years ago such a job was easy to find, but now there are very few ranches that have jobs where the work is all horseback. These men all wished they could go back in time fifty or a hundred years, and most of them would have fit into those years better.

Saddles come in all shapes and sizes and prices. Jim Brister had several championship rodeo saddles that probably cost three or four thousand dollars each. Claude and Rastus each rode saddles that they had bought in the 1940s and that cost no more than $150. All horses are shaped differently, and saddles sit on the backs of horses differently, depending on the shape of the saddle and of the horse. Some perfectly good saddles that are made to sit on the back of a big horse will hurt a small horse, and the reverse is true for a saddle made for a small horse but used on a large horse. Some saddles make the rider feel like he is sitting on top of a board, while other saddles make him feel like he is sitting down in the saddle. When a new cowboy brought out his saddle, we always checked it when he put it on one of our horses to make sure it didn't hurt the horse's back.

My saddle was given to me by DA when I was about seven. It was a nice small saddle with attractive leather work on it. Alan and Ann each used my saddle at times until they got their own.

Life at the ranch involved all of these components—association with our old-time, long-suffering, good-natured cowboys; living in isolation with just one another and with few luxuries; eating mostly beef and beans, dried fruit, and biscuits; riding horseback for long hours in the heat and dust; seeing the plant, animal, insect, and bird life of the Southwest close at hand; and enjoying the love and companionship of MO and DA, not just on evenings and weekends but all the time. It was not until I grew up and moved away from the Lazy B that I learned just how unusual my early life was.

Top left: *MO holding Alan with Ann and Sandra, age eleven.* Top right: *Sandra, age ten, holding Alan, at three months.* Center: *Sandra (left) and Flournoy as flower girls at a wedding.* Bottom: *Friends from the Radford School for Girls in El Paso visiting the ranch during spring vacation. Left to right: Pat Murchison, Sandra, Cita Fletcher, Beverly Timberlake holding Ann, Paquita Zork, and Chana Harvey.* Opposite: *Sandra at age twelve.*

11. *School Days*

Do they miss me at home?
Do they miss me?
'Twould be an assurance most dear,
To know that this moment some loved one,
Were saying, "I wish [s]he were here."

S. M. GRANNIS,
"DO THEY MISS ME AT HOME"

$\mathcal{E}$XCEPT FOR ONE YEAR, MY SCHOOL DAYS WERE IN EL PASO. When MO and DA decided I was old enough to travel alone on the train, they would drive to Lordsburg to meet the eastbound Southern Pacific train to El Paso. The train whistle could be heard several minutes before we could see the train. In those days the engines were powered by coal, and a column of smoke was visible from the engine's smokestack. The brakes squealed as the train slowed, then stopped at the station. Steam puffed out of various parts of the engine. The conductor came out of one of the passenger cars and put a step stool down on the ground for those leaving or boarding the train. Not many passengers used the Lordsburg station. My mother always spoke to the conductor and made him promise to keep an eye on me until El Paso. DA gave him a tip to help jog his memory.

I climbed on board and sat at a window waving at MO and DA as the train slowly moved along the track and out of sight of my parents and the town. I then looked around to see who else was in the passenger car. I felt rather grown up and important to be riding on the train by myself, but I was also somewhat afraid of talking to strangers. During the war years the train was full of soldiers and sailors going from one post to another. They would often try to talk to me, but I was still shy.

The conductor, true to his word, walked through the train cars and checked on me every so often. After about four hours and brief stops in Deming and Las Cruces, New Mexico, he went through the train calling "El Paso. Next stop."

The railroad track from Las Cruces to El Paso follows the Rio Grande River through a green valley. There were some orchards, mostly of pecan trees, and some fields of cotton and hay. They were followed by a number of metal buildings, a copper smelter, and a power-generating plant as the train approached El Paso. Finally, the train stopped and I got off and walked to the station, where Grandmother Wilkey waited.

In the early grades my cousin Flournoy also lived with our Wilkey grandparents in their bungalow in El Paso. Flournoy and I attended the local public grade school until the fourth grade. Then Flournoy's mother remarried and the new family moved to Corpus Christi, Texas. I missed Flournoy very much.

My parents decided to send me to Radford School for Girls in El Paso. They thought I would receive a better education there. Grandmother drove me to Radford School every day. Radford had a few boarding-school students, several of whom were daughters of ranchers or mining-company officials who, like me, lived many miles from any town. I was glad I could live at my grandmother's house instead of at the school.

The classes were small and the teachers were kind and caring. My dramatic-arts teacher was a red-haired woman named Miss Fireovid. She insisted that I memorize various short essays and deliver them in public. These were frightening and painful experiences, but her insistence on proper and clear enunciation of the words and looking at the audience have stayed with me ever since. Arturo Gonzales taught the art classes. Those classes required no homework or preparation, and I looked forward to them. Mrs. Feuille taught history and social studies; I thought she knew everything, and I tried hard to please her. Because we were in Texas, we studied Texas history first and foremost.

The friends I made at Radford are my friends to this day. Most of them had never lived outside a city and knew nothing of ranch life. And I knew nothing of city life. My friends Cita, Pacquita, and Beverly invited me many times to spend the night at their houses. Their houses seemed very grand compared to our house at the Lazy B. They had several bedrooms and bathrooms and large dining rooms. The furniture was elegant, and there were maids and gardeners, lawns and flowers. It made me feel awkward and a bit uneasy to be in such surroundings.

When I was in the sixth grade, our spring break at school coincided with my birthday in March. MO and DA said I could invite some of my friends to come to the ranch for four days. It was arranged, and four of my El Paso friends made the trip to the Lazy B. We slept on couches and on the floor in sleeping bags. DA gathered several gentle horses in addition to Chico, Flaxy, and Swastika (named for an old brand shaped like a swastika), and all of us rode on a few short rides. Most of my visitors had never been on a horse. We drove up to the Black Hills and picked poppies. We went to the corrals to try to milk the milk cow, and to find eggs in the henhouse. We looked at some of DA's best bulls, and saw some newborn calves. We played card games in the house. Everyone had a wonderful time. After that, I felt a little more at ease with my city-born friends, and they had good memories of their visit to the Lazy B.

In 1942 I was ready to enter the eighth grade. All the years that I had attended school in El Paso I'd felt homesick for the ranch. "Why can't I stay home and go to school? I'll ride the school bus in. It will be all right. You'll see," I told my parents. With some misgivings MO and DA finally agreed. I enrolled in the Lordsburg public school. Each school day MO or DA drove me over the eight miles of ranch road to its intersection with the highway from Duncan to Lordsburg.

At that intersection the State of New Mexico had built a three-room pueblo-style stucco building on the south side of the highway to serve as a port-of-entry station. Earl Kinney and his wife, Manny, lived there and served as the "staff." It was Earl's job to stop all motor vehicles traveling east to Lordsburg and to ask whether any fresh fruits or vegetables were in the vehicle. If so, Earl would inspect them for evidence of certain insects or disease that might be transmitted to New Mexico crops. He also checked all commercial trucks to be certain the required New Mexico fees and licenses were paid. The Kinneys were a friendly, pleasant couple from Tennessee. They had accepted the lonely assignment because the warm dry climate was beneficial to Earl's weak respiratory system.

Each school day I would wait for the school bus in the port-of-entry office, visiting with the Kinneys. The drive from there to school in Lordsburg took over an hour, with all the stops along the way. I spent the day at school, and as soon as it let out I got on the bus to return to the port-of-entry station to meet one of my parents. Usually Manny Kinney would offer me a homemade cookie before my parents came. It was dark when I left the ranch in the mornings and dark when I returned. Because I did not stay overnight in Lordsburg, I had no chance to become acquainted with my new classmates outside of class. The teachers probably did their best, but I have no memory of any academic challenges that year. The only friendship that developed was with the daughter of a neighboring rancher, Helen Gruell, who also rode the bus part of the way with me.

Across the road from the port of entry was a 160-acre homestead owned by a man named Jim Black. Jim had a shabby two-room wooden house facing the highway and a windmill for water. He installed a gasoline tank above ground and a hand-cranked gas pump, and he put up a big sign advertising gas, oil, cigarettes, and soda pop for sale. Jim kept about ten head of cattle, and more often than not he left his gate open to allow his cattle to graze on Lazy B land. Once in a while we would see a car stop at Jim's station to buy gas, but he clearly had very little business.

Occasionally, DA would stop in to let Jim know we had found one of his cows and put it back in his pasture. Jim was usually unshaven and wore baggy khaki pants and a soiled shirt. He also usually wore a black fedora hat and smelled strongly of alcohol. A ragged-looking woman lived at the house with Jim, as well as a frightened little daughter a few years younger than I. I was always curious about the little girl. She would not answer when I said hello and instead would hang on to her mother's dress and try to stay partially hidden. On several occasions when we stopped at Jim's place we saw the woman's face black and blue. "DA, what happened to Jim's wife?" "I don't know." "Yes, you do. Did she have an accident?" "I suspect Jim was drinking and probably hit her too hard," said DA. "Can't you do something about it, DA?" "No, Sandra. I don't think I can." "Well, I think we ought to tell the sheriff." "I think we'd better leave well enough alone, Sandra."

I asked the Kinneys what they had seen of their neighbors across the road. They said Jim went to town about once a week and usually left the woman and child at home. The child did not attend school. They thought Jim drank most days and that the woman and her child were afraid of him.

After the school year ended in Lordsburg I decided that I should return to El Paso for high school. The long commute to school was not something I wanted to repeat, even for the privilege of staying at the ranch. My parents were relieved because they thought I would learn more at the El Paso school. I returned to Grandmother Wilkey in the fall and enrolled in Austin High School.

The Kinneys had become friends of MO and DA, and they would drive to the ranch now and then to have dinner and a visit. Earl also went to the ranch every month or so to go bird hunting, which he enjoyed. After a few years, the State of New Mexico closed its ports of entry and the Kinneys moved away. The Day family missed their closest neighbors, the Kinneys, very much.

Jim Black decided he would do better to sell his homestead to the Lazy B, which he did. We never knew where that pitiful family went, but the sight of them stayed with me always as a poignant picture of human failure.

With the departure of the Kinneys and Jim Black, the buildings were removed and the ranch road led only to the highway and to memories of our former neighbors and my long commute to school in 1942.

Top: *Alan and Ann, at ages nine and ten, respectively.*
Center: *A cattle drive.*
Bottom: *Mae Brister and Alan (age two) watch as the men eat lunch during a roundup. Opposite: Alan at age ten.*

12. *Making a Hand*

It was probably a step in the making of a cowhand when he learned that what would pass for heroics in a softer world was only chores around here.

WALLACE STEGNER,
Wolf Willow

$\mathcal{A}$ MILESTONE FOR A RANCH CHILD IS THE FIRST TIME THE child can get a foot in the stirrup without help. Another is being old enough to ride alone beyond the familiar places around the headquarters and then find your way home again. And still another is driving a motor vehicle. The biggest milestone is being able to provide useful help on a cattle drive or a roundup—solving problems rather than causing them.

As soon as we were old enough to ride, we would ask to go out with the cowboys to the different areas of the ranch, through the cactus and mesquite and over the rocky hills, to gather the cattle in a particular area for sorting, branding, cutting out those to be sold, and then herding them to a holding pasture to await shipment. In time each of us learned enough to become useful. Alan and Ann were better ranch hands than I was because I was away in El Paso for school from the time I was six. On days when we rode on the roundups we were happy if we could stop for three drinks of water during the long day, and ecstatic if we could also have lunch somewhere along the way. Sometimes there was no time for either a drink of water or lunch. The job had to be done while there was daylight to see what we were doing.

The cowboys did whatever job was required. They met the unexpected as though they'd known about it all along. They never complained, and they made the best of everything along the way. If a fence had broken and some cattle had gotten through, the cowboy finding the condition fixed the fence and gathered the cattle and drove them back to where they belonged. If a windmill wasn't pumping, the man finding it tried to repair it. If a newborn calf was still too weak to walk but the mother cow and calf needed to be moved, the calf would be carried on the saddle in front of the cowboy.

Each of us had some brushes with cactus thorns. One day Alan was riding and his horse was moving fast and brushed Alan against a cholla. Cholla is sometimes called the jumping cactus because it seems as though the thorns actually jump out at you if you even go near it. Alan's leg was covered with cholla thorns from above the knee to his calf. He had to endure the pain and discomfort for half a day because he was out on the cattle drive too far from any other rider to get help and he was too small to be able to get down off his horse and to remount. MO was nowhere near to pat him on the back to say, "You're all right. Don't worry."

If our horse stumbled or jumped a ditch unexpectedly and caused us to fall off, there usually was no one around to dry our tears and lift us back on the saddle. We had to move quickly to catch the horse's reins and find a big rock to stand on to give us the height to get back in the saddle unaided.

Alan's first roundup was in 1945, when he was five, and before he had started school. He begged to be allowed to ride on the spring roundup, in May. MO and DA talked it over and decided he could ride on some of the days when the distance traveled was not too great. Each roundup lasted about thirty days, and each day the crew fanned out over a different area of the ranch to gather all the cattle in that area and bring them together just before noon at a preselected place where they could be held or corralled and sorted, and the calves could be branded.

Alan's first day was in Old Camp Canyon, a place about eight miles long and with extremely rocky terrain. The mountains rise steeply from five hundred to one thousand feet above the canyon bed. Two side canyons feed into Old Camp Canyon, Lightning Canyon from the east and Rock Tank Canyon from the southwest.

The crew got up that day at the ranch headquarters about 3:30 A.M. DA awakened Alan and told him to get dressed. Alan pulled on his Levi's and boots and got his jacket and a hat. The night was dark; no moon shone. The stars were so bright they seemed almost close enough in the sky to touch. The Milky Way cut a broad bright swath through the heavens.

The cowboys and Alan and DA gathered in the bunkhouse for breakfast at about 4:00. Most were quiet and still sleep starved from the short time they had been in bed. Bug Quinn had a breakfast ready on the stove. Hot coffee brewed in an old tin pot. The grounds floated up in the murky cup. Pans of hot, thick biscuits were on top of the stove. Tubs of butter and pots of honey and jam were on the old square table in the corner. The table was covered with a piece of oilcloth so old the original design could scarcely be seen. Pans of bacon and sausage were also on the stove, and there was sausage gravy to spoon over the biscuits. Bowls of cooked dried prunes and apricots were on the table.

The crew finished breakfast and gathered around the pickup truck and the jeep to drive to Robbs' Well, where the horses had been corralled the night before. It was still dark when the vehicles arrived at Robbs' Well, some five miles or so from the ranch headquarters. The men went into the corral, each with a lasso in hand, to catch their horses. The horses ran around the corral in a circle, not wanting to be caught. But when the rope settled around the horse's neck, the horse surrendered and followed his captor and stood while the bridle went on, then the saddle blanket, and, finally, the saddle.

DA helped catch Alan's horse and saddled it. Every rider gave one last tug on the cinch below the horse's chest to be sure it was tight enough. Then everyone mounted. Alan needed a boost from DA to get on. His legs were still too short to reach the stirrups without help. As the crew left the corral at Robb's Well, a little daylight began to show in the east, to their backs. They rode to the west in silence. There was an undercurrent of excitement. Each day brought different problems and challenges: some days the cattle drive and the branding went smoothly and efficiently; some days there were multiple problems. The uncertainty contributed to the excitement.

After riding west about half an hour, DA signaled a stop. The sun was coming up and the sky was clear. DA told each man which area to cover. "Claude, how about going along the ridge above Lightning Canyon? Jim, take the south side of Lightning. Rastus, take the bottom of Lightning. Ira, head on over to Rock Tank Canyon and keep them headed to Old Camp. I will head over the ridge toward Rock Tank Canyon and Alan can stay in Old Camp Canyon and make sure the cattle don't go back up the canyon to Robbs' Well."

Everyone started off in the general direction that he had been assigned. Each man had to find and gather all the cattle along his assigned "beat" and move them on toward the center so that before noon all the cattle would have arrived in Old Camp in time for the branding. Alan proceeded to the intersection of Rock Tank Canyon and Old Camp Canyon, where he was to meet the men from either side, along with the cattle they had gathered.

Alan stopped where he thought the others would join him. The sun climbed high in the sky, and the heat began to settle in the canyon. The longer he stayed, the hotter it got. His horse nibbled at the sparse dry grass underfoot. Cicadas made their incessant buzzing among the mesquites, and Alan needed to pee. It had been several hours since breakfast. The problem was that if he got off his horse, he couldn't get on again by himself. He didn't see any big rocks around to stand on. He sat on his horse for what seemed an eternity. The buzz of the cicadas grew louder and louder. The sun grew hotter. Sweat formed under his hatband and rolled down his neck and back. Time for a five-year-old moves slowly. Alan knew where he was. He knew the cowboys were supposed to come along with the cattle they had found. But it had been such a long time. Probably the men had ridden on ahead and forgotten him. The buzzing was incessant. The heat was intense. The pressure on his bladder was uncomfortable. He was thirsty. It went on so long that tears flowed down Alan's cheeks, making little wet trails through the dirt on his face. His thoughts kept coming. "They told me to stay here and meet them. But maybe I should turn around and go back up the canyon to find them. Or maybe I should just stay here longer, and sooner or later they will come and get me. Maybe I am going crazy. Is this what it's like?" After what surely was an eternity to a five-year-old, there was the sound of one of the cowboys yelling at some cattle, urging them along. And then another one off in the distance. "Hey, Alan, get that old cow over there and bring her along. Come on, now." Thank God they were here. "You okay, Al?" "Oh, yeah. Sure."

Gradually all the men appeared with the cattle they had found. Everyone kept the cows moving along to Old Camp, where Bug Quinn was waiting with a fire going, the coffee made, and lunch ready. Alan was able to get off his horse and pee behind a bush. He got a drink and ate some lunch. There was no more buzzing in his ears. He decided he wasn't crazy after all.

After lunch, the calves were branded, earmarked, and vaccinated. Alan got back on his horse and helped keep the cattle from wandering off. The yearlings were separated from the herd and driven to a separate pasture. The mother cows and young calves were driven partway back toward Robb's Well. The sun was going down in the west when they got back to ranch headquarters. Alan had made a hand.

*Round Mountain, near Jim Brister's house in
Willow Springs, and Lazy B horses.*

PHOTOGRAPH © 1990 TOSHI KAZAMA

Opposite: *Water mills at the Lazy B.*

13. Rain

Shook from the tangled boughs
of Heaven and Ocean,
Angels of rain and lightning.

PERCY BYSSHE SHELLEY,
"ODE TO THE WEST WIND"

*A*S CHILDREN WE REMEMBER DRIVING AROUND THE RANCH with our father hour after hour, bumping slowly along over rocky terrain to check on a windmill or a water pipe or tank, to see if there was a salt block at a certain place, or if a cow with sore eyes was doing all right. We would watch the skies constantly, hoping for rain. Rain was our life's blood.

It produced the grass and vegetation the cattle had to have to survive. In all the arid Southwest, rain was the essential element—the most treasured event—prayed for, hoped for, anticipated, savored, treasured, celebrated, and enjoyed—every drop. In summer when the big cumulus clouds would begin to form around noon on the days there was moisture moving in from the Gulf of Mexico, we would watch those clouds. When they produced rain it was often in the late afternoon. The clouds would grow dark, almost black. There would then be a strong wind—blowing dust, leaves, small bits of everything lying around. Then a sudden stillness—the earth silent and waiting for the momentous event. Then the crack of lightning touching something on earth with all the electric fury of the universe. Seconds later the incredible sound of the thunder, the sound produced by the lightning bolt rolling through the clouds above. And then—wonder of wonders—the first few big wet drops of rain forming muddy places on the dusty windshield. Then more and more until we would just stop the pickup truck and sit inside it, unable to see even the closest objects outside because the rain would come in waves, sheets, torrents. Joy. Wonder. Incredible gift from above. Our salvation. *Rain.*

After a few minutes, it would slow. Again we could distinguish our surroundings. More lightning, more thunder. Now just a shower, a sprinkle. And we could watch the eye of the storm move off a few miles in another direction, the dark clouds meeting earth in a different spot. The thunder, the lightning now more distant.

Then we would watch with wonder the changed world about us. The dry, dusty soil was wet, muddy, brown rivulets of water running down every slope and gully. The grass and plants sparkling with drops of water clinging to them. The greasewood bushes—normally so gray green and dull—releasing their incredible perfume, produced by the rain on their dense oily leaves. The birds chirping frantically, the rabbits peeking out from their burrows. Everything stirring and excited from the rain, and no one more excited than my father. We were saved again—saved from the ever present threat of drought, of starving cattle, of anxious creditors. We would survive a while longer.

And as proof we would look in wonder at the rainbow that had formed in the sky with the end of the rain. There it would be with the sun shining through—all the colors so vivid—the arch going high up in the sky and the ends touching down where we could see them—right over the next hill, down by the soapweed near the gully.

"You know what the old-timers say?" DA would ask. "No, what?" "They say there is a pot of gold at the end of the rainbow." "No, really?" "That's what they say." "Do you believe them?" "Of course, why not?" "Have you ever seen it yourself?" "No, not really." "Well, let's go, Daddy. Let's go find it. It is right over there. Don't you see? The end of the rainbow is right there by the hill. Come on. We'll find that pot of gold." "All right. We'll go."

And off we would go, sliding along the wet slippery mud, jouncing across country—rocks, cactus, and all. Tough going. Hanging on tight as we slid along, up and down scary places. But a strange thing would happen. As we approached the hill where the rainbow ended, the rainbow would have moved—off to the right, more distant still. "Oh, let's keep going—let's get there and find the gold."

After a while, DA would say, "You know, I think we'd better turn back and go home. Your mother will be worried about us. And that rain may mean the canyon will run with water so we couldn't cross it and get home." "Oh, darn it. We were so close. We could have found it. Oh, well, next time. Promise we'll find it next time."

When we'd get back near the headquarters, the canyon we had to cross would be filled with rushing, muddy water if there had been a hard rain upstream. No car or truck could be driven across. If the water was not too high, DA would just wade across and carry us over, one at a time. Then we could walk the rest of the way home.

Rain put our parents in a very happy mood. They would go from one room in the house to the next to see from every window whether the rain was still falling somewhere on the ranch. DA would go out and check his rain gauge several times to see how much rain had fallen. He would enter the precise measurement in his old, dusty record book, along with the date. He kept the rain records throughout his years at the Lazy B.

"Well, Ada Mae, how about a Cuba Libre to celebrate?" "Yes, that's a good idea. I'll get the ice." DA would go into the kitchen and open the doors under the kitchen sink. At the rear he kept some liquor. Jim Beam bourbon, Johnnie Walker Scotch, and Ron Rico rum. He would get the rum and carefully measure out an ounce into each glass and fill it with Coca-Cola. He and MO would sit in their chairs, next to the kitchen, looking out toward the northeast at the windmills, the corrals, and the road leading to the ranch. "Where do you think the rain started?" "Up by Big Tank. Then it moved on towards Robbs' Well. It hit us when we were out in East Pasture. It was a pretty good rain. It only measured a third of an inch here. But it was more in East Pasture. God knows, we needed it." "Do you think it put water in Big Tank?" "I think so. The canyon is already running a little down here. It probably put water in Big Tank, Tank 4, and Tank 5. We'll go see tomorrow, if we can get out in the jeep."

The happy atmosphere would continue all through dinner. Later we would walk outside to see if it was still cloudy. The dirt tank behind the house had filled with water from the flow in the canyon. After we went to bed we could hear the first sounds of the spadefoot toads, which had emerged from their holes under the bed of the dirt tank. By morning there would be thousands of toads making their calls. The sounds of the toads making their love calls at night would last through the night, each night for a week or ten days, until apparently the sexual urge was satiated and we could all get some sleep.

The desert spadefoot toad is among the most amazing of the desert animals. It lives in desert areas where ponds of water form. As the pond dries up, the toad buries itself in the soil beneath the pond, digging burrows from three to seven feet deep. They can remain in hibernation for several years if necessary. When the pond fills again with water, the toads emerge, and the males begin their incessant coarse croak to attract a mate. After mating, the female deposits one to two thousand fertilized eggs in the pond. The tadpoles emerge within five days or so. The tadpoles transform into toads within a few days, and the life cycle begins again.

Our most contented nights in the summer were the nights after we had enough rain to fill the tank behind the house and we could hear the toads all night long.

Top: *Lazy B headquarters*

Bottom: *The first motor vehicle at the Lazy B.*

Opposite: *Three Mills.*

14. Making the Rounds

------------- --

*When the big rain came that lasted
forty days and forty nights, Southern Arizona
got half an inch.*

R. LEWIS BOWMAN,
Bumfuzzled Too

*T*HE DAY FOLLOWING A HEAVY RAIN IN AUGUST, DA WENT DOWN
to the bunkhouse to talk to the cowboys about where each one should go
that day. DA was eager to have someone go to each area of the ranch to see
how much rain had fallen, whether the various dirt storage tanks had received some water, whether any of the cattle or horses had been struck by
lightning, and whether the floodwaters had done any damage. The men
were squatting at the edge of the bunkhouse porch. Rastus had taken a
packet of cigarette papers out of his shirt pocket, along with a little cloth
bag of Bull Durham tobacco. He held the cigarette paper in the fingers of
his left hand, making a little trough in the middle of the thin paper. He
tugged on the string of the tobacco pouch with his teeth and opened it
slightly. With his right hand he poured a little tobacco into the cigarette
paper, then tugged on the string again with his teeth to close the pouch.
He tucked the pouch back in his shirt pocket and, using both hands,
spread a line of tobacco all along the trough of the cigarette paper. He then
carefully rolled the long side of the paper over the tobacco and into a neat
little cigarette, which he licked along its edge to seal it. After folding one
end a little to close it, he struck a kitchen match on his jeans to light the
cigarette.

The other cowboys also made and lighted cigarettes, and all of them talked about the rain—where it had started and what areas it might have covered. DA pulled a pack of Lucky Strikes out of his shirt pocket, took out a cigarette, and carefully placed it in a well-worn silver-and-black cigarette holder. He reached in his pants pocket for a kitchen match. He held the match upright in his right hand and struck the head with his thumbnail to light it. "Rastus, do you want to head over to New Well and check things out there and over by Franklin? Claude, how about going on over to High Lonesome and the shipping pasture to see whether Railroad Wash held up? Ira, you might as well check out Cottonwood and the Burch place. I'll take the jeep and head up to Robbs' Well and over to Big Tank and Tanks 4 and 5." After fifteen minutes of talking about the rain, DA got up and walked back up to the house and sat down in his usual chair by the kitchen door with his cup of tea. "What are you making, Ada Mae? Bacon? I don't know why you don't fry up some salt pork. That's a lot better. And how about some biscuits this morning? I have to get going pretty soon." "DA, can I go with you?" "Yes, sure. Get ready. We will take the jeep. I need to take along some salt blocks. We'll leave pronto."

There was no telling how long we would be gone. Maybe three hours, maybe seven. DA wouldn't be rushed, and he liked to check on everything. The amount of rainfall and the amount of water captured in the tanks would determine the condition of the cattle in the fall and the weight of the calves. These were matters to be carefully observed.

After breakfast we settled in the jeep and drove down the ranch road to the Round Mountain Wash, near the ranch headquarters. Water still ran in the bottom of it, but it looked like it was not more than a foot high. DA put the jeep in four-wheel drive and we entered the wash. The wheels sank in the mud. The engine strained. He put it in a lower gear and stepped on the gas. Reluctantly, the mud gave way, and we rolled out the other side of the wash and up the hill. White, puffy clouds were beginning to gather on the horizon. The air was still and very humid. Water stood in puddles here and there in the ruts of the dirt road. When there was a particularly wet, muddy area in the road, DA left the road and drove around it to avoid making deeper ruts in the roadbed. The cattle were spread out.

With water standing in so many places, they could fan out in every direction to forage for grass and still have some drinking water nearby. In a few days some of the old dry tabosa grass would begin to turn green. The short burro grass would begin to grow.

We drove some five miles to Robbs' Well and found areas that had received only a sprinkle the day before. At Robbs' Well DA parked the jeep and walked over to the water trough to see if it was properly filled. He checked the float valve, then checked the windmill. A very light breeze had come up, and the wind mill turned lazily in the breeze. The pump was working, and a little stream of water was flowing into the steel-rimmed storage tank. He put out a block of salt for the cattle near the trough. Cattle, like people, crave salt in their diet. They will get a drink and then stand and lick the salt block until they have their fill.

We returned to the jeep and drove west toward Big Tank. Big Tank got its name because it was the largest of the dirt water storage basins DA had dug to collect water from a couple of canyons feeding into the largest canyon, Railroad Wash. It had taken months for Ira, using the Caterpillar tractor, to move the dirt out and build a dam to hold the occasional flood-water that flowed after a rain. When full, the tank covered several acres, and it could hold water almost year-round. It was well located at the foot of the Black Hills, the volcanic mountains on the east side. There was no well and no water up in the mountains, so Big Tank was a vitally important asset.

As we neared Big Tank the road became very rough, filled with the ever present volcanic rocks. It was no more than a pale track over the rocks. The jeep slowed to barely five miles an hour. There were fewer muddy places in the road because there were so many rocks that the water could not gather in pools. The rain had been heavier near Big Tank.

Big Tank had gained several feet of water, and more of the brown, muddy water was still running into it from the two feeder canyons. DA looked satisfied and stopped to light a cigarette, again striking the match head with his thumbnail. "Let's go over and check the spillway," he said. We got out of the jeep and made our way along the top of the dirt dam to the side where the spillway allowed any overflow to drain off into the canyon below. It looked all right.

We retraced our steps, our shoes by now covered with mud. Back in the jeep we bumped along the road to Tank 4 and Tank 5. It was about 2:00 P.M. "DA, I think I'll eat my apple. Do you want one?" "No. Go ahead. Let's drive on back the other way near Round Mountain." By now, the clouds were building up into tall columns in the sky with dark blue edges.

"DA, do you think it is going to rain again today?" "I don't know. It looks pretty good, but there is not much wind and the wind is not coming from the east. It's hard to say."

"DA, why don't we ever go to church on Sunday?" "It's too far to go to town. Besides, most of the local preachers aren't very good." "Do you believe in God?" "Yes, I do. I know some people question whether God exists and whether all those Bible stories are true. I don't know about the stories, but when you watch the world around us and see how the earth orbits the sun, and how the moon orbits the earth, and see the laws of nature work, you have to believe that some power beyond us has created the universe and has established the way nature works. It is remarkable to see how the clouds form and produce rain, which produces the grass and plants, which sustains animal, bird, and insect life, and which in turn sustains human life from generation to generation. It is an amazing, complex, but orderly universe. And we are only specks in it. There is surely something—a God if you will—who created all of this. And we don't have to go to church to appreciate it. It is all around us. This is our church."

"Well, if there is a God, I wish he would make it rain again. We really need it. The cows are thin and there is no grass for them. Do you think it will rain again soon, DA?"

"I don't know. There are a few clouds there in the east. Maybe they will gather up pretty soon and produce some more rain. You'd better do a better rain dance, Sandra."

Cattle in pasture. PHOTOGRAPH © 1990 TOSHI KAZAMA

Opposite: *Alan, age fourteen, with Smokey.*

15. Turning Thirteen

Years he numbered scarce thirteen
When Fates turned cruel.

BEN JONSON,
Epigrams

*T*HE SUMMER ALAN TURNED THIRTEEN HE LEARNED ABOUT HIM-
self and the ranch. The ranch was a place where a growing boy could test
himself. Alan wanted to find out what he could do and how he could do it.
Or maybe he just wanted to find out how much testosterone he was producing. Probably most young people feel the need to test themselves, perhaps in sports or against some obstacle that they think is very difficult and
that they will have to work very hard to achieve. In a city, that testing could
be trying to make the varsity team as a freshman, trying a deepwater dive
with scuba gear, making a parachute jump, or having a fight with the
school bully. In Alan's case, the challenges he found were right on the
ranch.

DA's style of management was to provide general directions and goals
but to avoid, when possible, assigning specific jobs to anyone. Our cowboys had been there for many years, and DA expected them to know what
to do and when to do it. When a well needed work, he might pull one or
two of the cowboys away from what they were doing to work on the well,
but mostly the cowboys decided on their own what needed to be done and
would simply do it. Rastus and Jim rode horseback most of the time.
Claude worked on fences and corrals. Ira was our mechanic and machinery and equipment operator. If any one of them had too much to do alone,

he would ask one of the others for help and it would be given. When we were available during the summertime, we would visit with each of them to see who needed help.

At the start of Alan's thirteenth summer, he was told that the thing that needed doing was breaking some young horses to ride for the ranch. We had no one else that summer to do the job.

We kept a stallion and a band of about ten brood mares. Usually we had some young cowboy who was willing to break horses, and he would get the young horses gentle enough for the other cowboys to ride. During the first part of the breaking process with a young horse, the horse doesn't know what the rider wants from him. Most of the rider's time and attention at first is spent teaching the horse what the rider wants the horse to do. The cowboys, of course, want a horse that they can ride and is trained to work with cattle. The horse breaker would teach the young horses those basic things, and then our older cowboys would select the young horse that they liked for their string of horses. The cowboy would then teach the horse how to work the cattle. This final training could take years, and no one else would ride that horse once it was selected for the cowboy's string. If it turned out the cowboy couldn't get along with the young horse he had selected, he would put the horse back in the common pool of horses. The common pool of horses would be assigned to our temporary cowboys during the roundup time.

Getting the young horses started could be quite an adventure. Some are easy to break and cause no problems, but others are stubborn or mean, or will run off or try to buck. You never really know what to expect when you get on a young horse. This is the adventurous part of horse breaking, and the part that tests the rider repeatedly. Each young horse has his own personality, and trying to figure out what makes him tick is the challenge. Alan had no mentor that summer for this challenge. Jim Brister would have helped Alan, but he didn't live at the headquarters, and during the summer he might only come to the headquarters two or three times. The other cowboys would just smile and say that these horses really needed breaking and that they were glad Alan was doing it. They might ask how their favorite colt was progressing, but they never gave him advice on how to do it. Every day, Alan learned from the horses more than they were learning from him.

Our stallion had Hancock breeding. This is a bloodline in the quarter-horse breed with a reputation of producing good, tough cow horses, but they are also hard to break. Most of them were not pretty looking and had rather large heads with Roman noses. After Alan worked with them for a while that summer, he was prepared to agree about how tough and hardheaded they were. Alan and the horses were probably a pretty good mix in the hardheaded department. The ranch had eight young horses that summer, and Alan decided to try to break all eight. That was a tall order. DA always said, "If you want something done, do it yourself." And Alan wanted a big challenge. Or as Alan said later, maybe he was so cocky that he didn't know when he was overmatched. Maybe it was some of all of these things.

A year before Alan started to break them, the horses had been weaned from their mothers and kept in the corral for a couple of weeks. During that time they were taught to lead with a halter, to eat grain, and to load into a horse trailer. We had also spent a few hours with each of them, petting them and picking up their feet and just making friends with them. They were too small to ride at that age. The colts are taught to carry a rider when they are large enough to carry someone and old enough to learn.

The colts were all between two and three years old that summer, and the largest of them Alan named Dave. He was a buckskin, which means he was tan colored with a black mane and tail. He was quite gentle and very strong. Jim Brister later claimed him and rode him for many years. Dave was very heavy-headed and hard to handle. He required a very strong hand to rein him to stop or turn. He never bucked with Alan, but Alan had to constantly pull on him to turn him to the right or left or to stop, and he never felt quite strong enough to do the job. When Jim took him, he didn't mind that heavy neck because Jim was so strong that it was easy for him to turn or stop Dave. Dave had a good gait and could travel long distances with ease. Jim liked big, well-gaited horses, so it was a good match when he took Dave.

The prettiest of the colts was Tango, a sorrel with a shiny red coat. He was not a big horse, but he had the smallest, prettiest head of the group. Tango was smart and lazy. From the start Alan had to push him hard to get anything out of him. Some colts will run off if they get into a gallop and are not held back tightly, but Tango would only go as fast as Alan made him go, and when Alan stopped kicking him, Tango would slow down and stop. Tango bucked once or twice while Alan was breaking him, but his heart was never in it, and Alan found him pretty easy to break. On the trail, Alan was always kicking and spurring to keep the horse going. Tango was light reined and easy to handle, and he liked to work cattle. Ann liked Tango because he was so pretty and gentle. Ann claimed him for her string of horses.

Smokey was the toughest of the young horses. He was a medium-size blue roan and rough looking. He was stubborn, very headstrong, and liked to buck. He could buck Alan off with ease and did so many times. Alan would get on and might go around the corral three or four times with no problem. Then with no warning Smokey would put his head down and start bucking. Alan could never ride him successfully when he was bucking and would have probably never gotten him broken if Smokey hadn't just stopped bucking all on his own. His record bucking Alan off was six times in one day. Once in a while Alan would land on his feet, but more often he would land on his head or his back or some other place that would hurt. LeRoy McCarty, an occasional cowboy, was watching the day Smokey bucked Alan off six times. LeRoy said that every time Alan and Smokey would go out of sight behind the barn, the horse would come back a minute later without Alan. Alan would come walking around the barn and catch him and get on again. The sixth time Alan came walking up, still smiling, he had landed on his face in a pile of cow manure. Some manure had stuck to his front teeth, and when Alan smiled, LeRoy thought he had knocked out his two front teeth. LeRoy suggested that six times was enough for one day and that maybe tomorrow would be a better time to try Smokey again. Alan was ready to agree.

When Alan finally got Smokey around some cattle, he was a completely different horse. He was attentive to the cattle and wanted to work them and herd them. He had a natural ability to work with cattle and a strong desire to do so. Later, when he was fully broken, he was the best cutting horse Alan ever rode. The first time Alan was driving cattle while riding Smokey, a cow ran off. Smokey, without being directed by Alan to chase her, took off running to get around the cow and bring her back. Alan didn't know what Smokey had in mind, so he tried to pull him back and stop him, but he couldn't. Smokey had made up his mind to bring this cow back in spite of everything Alan could do, and he did. Alan was amazed and learned to give Smokey his head around cattle because he was going to do the right thing even without being urged. When Smokey got older and was unable to make the long trips out to gather cattle, Alan would occasionally keep him close by, and when the cattle were gathered in the corral, Alan would saddle Smokey just to work the cattle.

Alan took Smokey into his own string of horses and rode him until the horse was too old to ride. Even though he was the toughest of the colts to break, he had the biggest heart and by far the most ability to work cattle of any of them. Out in the pasture just riding along, he was pretty lazy, and the rider had to keep spurring him to get him to travel at a reasonable pace. But when there were cattle to be moved, he was totally alert and had a great amount of energy. No spurs were needed then to get him to go. It was like having two different horses, a lazy one for trail riding and a high-powered one for working cattle.

One of the colts, Shoreleave, had muscles on his front legs that didn't work properly. His legs appeared not to be properly developed, and when ridden, he would stumble frequently with his front legs. He never fell with Alan, but Alan became concerned that Shoreleave would never be able to take the kind of riding that we had to do on the ranch. After some soul searching, we sold Shoreleave.

Junior was a big blue roan horse that turned out to be a good solid all-around horse. None of the cowboys claimed him, so he was usually just an extra horse during roundup time. He didn't give Alan a lot of problems when he was breaking him, but he did buck a few times. Once in a while Alan even stayed on Junior when he bucked. Junior gave Alan an early sense of success because the horse was not difficult to break, and he turned out well. Junior had a good disposition and was easy to handle, with a nice gait for riding long distances. Most ranches would be glad to have a horse as good as Junior.

The other big blue horse that closely resembled Junior was Little Joe. He was the nicest of all the colts Alan broke that summer. He was very gentle right from the start and always wanted to do what Alan wanted him to do. He was really strong and could pull almost anything. He had a fairly short gait and didn't walk very fast, but he had an easy trot and could cover a lot of country. His biggest fault was that when he was running and stopped rapidly, he would always stop on his front legs and would jolt his rider. Good quarter horses halt mostly with their hind legs and are much smoother when they stop and turn. Despite the problem, Little Joe always had a happy disposition and wanted to do anything that his rider commanded. Because he was so rough when he stopped, he wasn't as good at working cattle as Smokey. But he was strong and very, very gentle. After he was broken, whenever a small child or a guest wanted a ride, we would put the person on Little Joe because he wouldn't spook or jump suddenly. Alan loved this big blue horse and rode him often for the rest of Little Joe's life.

After Little Joe had been broken for several years, Alan and the Lazy B cowboys were rounding up the East Pasture one day when a bobcat jumped up close to Little Joe and ran off. Alan, being young and full of testosterone, gave chase, and after a pretty good run, ended up roping the bobcat around the neck and one front leg with his saddle rope. He was very proud of having been able to rope the bobcat, but in the heat of the chase had never stopped to think how he might get his rope off. This question arose only after he had the bobcat on the other end of his twenty-five-foot rope.

They were near a cattle-water pond called Horseshoe Tank, so Alan decided to drag the cat as far as the water tank, thinking that when the other cowboys came to Horseshoe Tank, they might help him free the bobcat. But the cat did not want to cooperate. At one point Alan dragged him too close to Little Joe, who was not very happy about this whole episode anyway. The bobcat jumped at Little Joe's rump, and even though Little Joe jumped away to avoid him, the cat scratched his hip. This made the horse even more wary of the angry animal at the end of the rope.

When they finally arrived at Horseshoe Tank, the horse and the bobcat were both panting and stressed. Alan decided to give them both a drink of water and rode out in the tank so that he could pull the wildcat into the water. The horse was too frightened to drink, and the cat ducked his head under the water and inhaled water into his lungs. Alan saw this happen and pulled the cat out of the water as quickly as he could. It was too late. Rather than face captivity, the cat had drowned. Alan was shocked and grief stricken. It had started out as an exciting chase, and Alan had never anticipated this turn of events, nor had he intended to kill the bobcat. Another lesson learned.

Alan's goal was to ride each of the young horses once a day. If he only rode for an hour on each, it was an eight-hour day even if he had no problems. But just to catch and saddle a bronc can take an hour when they are first being trained. Alan was not always able to ride each one each day. The first few times he would ride a young horse he would ride him in the corral. The horse cannot run off in the corral, and if he bucked Alan off, the horse could be caught more easily than if he were out in the pasture. After Alan had ridden each of them a few times in the corral, he rode each one out in the pasture. On a longer ride he would set a gait and teach the horse to hold that gait and travel cross-country. Sometimes, however, after a ride in the pasture, when he would turn toward home, the horse would want to run all the way in, and it would become a contest as to whether he could hold the horse back or whether he would go at a dead run.

A typical day on Alan's thirteenth summer began at 6:00 A.M. with breakfast. He went down to the corral while the air was still fresh and cool, although the dust never settled as long as livestock were there. When Alan would walk into the corral, the colts would all snort and roll their eyes and bunch up in one corner of the ring. He would open the barn door and drag his saddle out and lay it in the dirt. He would get a halter and a hobble rope and go out to see if he could catch the colt that he wanted to ride. This could be rather difficult, especially during the first part of the summer, when he had not caught each of them very often. They would all bunch up in one corner, crowded as tightly as they could, to stay away from Alan. When Alan finally separated the one he wanted to catch, he would trap him in one corner and start walking up to him slowly while talking in a soothing voice. Sometimes the colt would stand there long enough for him to get his hand on his neck and start rubbing him. But sometimes the colt would be so frightened that he would bolt past Alan to rejoin the group again. When Alan would finally get his hand on the colt's neck and speak soothing words and stroke his neck, the colt would calm down a little.

After rubbing and stroking and talking to him for a while, Alan would be able to slip the halter over the colt's head and lead him near the barn. The next step was to get the hobbles on him. The hobbles are simply pieces of rope looped around the front legs so the horse is restricted in its movement. Sometimes young horses are very skittish about things wrapped around their legs, but after two or three tries they would stand still to let Alan firmly tie the hobbles around their front legs. This helped control them while Alan was saddling them. The first step in that process was to put the saddle blanket on the colt's back. The first few times the blanket settled on a colt's back, he would spook and jump, and the blanket would fall off. The colt would finally get used to the feel of the blanket. Next would come the saddle. The weight of the saddle and the stirrups banging on his sides would almost always make the colt throw it off the first few times before finally, grudgingly, allowing it to stay on his back.

Every move was done with kind words being spoken and much petting and rubbing. The girth or cinch would now be ready for tightening. No young horse likes to feel the cinch tightening up under his belly. Some would kick at it, or jump, or run backward, but as with all the other processes, they would soon learn to stand still until it was cinched up tight to hold the saddle in place. This whole process might take a half an hour. Later on, when the horse became accustomed to it, it would take only five minutes. Next Alan would substitute a hackamore for the halter. A hackamore is like a bridle except there is no metal bit to go in the horse's mouth. The hackamore has a hard piece of rawhide that goes over the nose and a pair of soft cotton reins for the rider to hold.

Alan would then remove the hobbles and lead the colt around the corral to allow him to become accustomed to the feel of the saddle on his back with the stirrups swinging free at his sides. Some horses pay no attention to this, and others are quite frightened by the stirrups. Many times the colt will jerk loose and buck all around the corral with the saddle. After leading the colt around for a while, Alan would get up close to his side and use the reins to turn the colt right and left. When the colt got the idea of turning, then Alan would pull the rein on the left side and put his foot in the stirrup on the left side. While turning the horse to the left, Alan would swing up into the saddle. Alan learned that if a horse was moving when he got on, it was better than if he was standing still. The reason is that if a young horse is standing still and you try to make him go, his first move is often a jump forward, followed by a second jump, and he would then be bucking. If the horse is turning while the rider gets in the saddle, it is possible to keep him turning and, in time, turn him in the other direction, and the horse is less likely to start jumping forward and bucking. Of course, this didn't always work, and most of the wrecks Alan had were in the first couple of minutes after he mounted the horse.

Some of the bad things that can happen when getting on an unbroken horse are that the horse might start bucking, or he might run off, or, worst of all, he might rear over backward with the rider. This last possibility worried Alan the most because it is very hard to get out and away from the saddle when a horse is going over backward with the rider. Staying in the saddle and having the horse land on the rider, crushing him with the saddle horn, is not pleasant. Having a horse run off is not a pleasant experience either. The horse is usually so concerned with what is on his back and how to get rid of it that he doesn't watch where he is going. He can step in a hole and fall. He can run blindly into a gully and fall. Usually when the horse runs off with a rider, the horse will bow his neck and not respond to any pressure of the reins. The best thing to do is to try to get the horse running in a big circle and eventually slow him down. When the rider loses a stirrup or gets out of position on the saddle and starts to go off, it is time to begin thinking about finding a soft place to land, but the choice is usually not the rider's. There is usually time for only a fleeting thought that this is going to hurt when you land, and it usually does.

Alan put all his energy to work that summer. Every time he mounted one of the colts he wondered what would happen. He learned to stay focused on being in control and teaching the colts with kindness the things he wanted them to know. But in his mind, all of the bad things that could happen to him were never far from the surface. A horse seems to know when the rider is afraid, yet it is hard not to be fearful with an unbroken horse. And just when Alan thought he had done something well with a young horse, the next one would respond totally differently and make him feel foolish again. The adrenaline was pretty high each time he got on a new horse, but things calmed down if the ride went well.

There was excitement for Alan every day that summer, but by September he found the horses were responding and learning, and he was not always waiting for the next jump or run. The days went by. Alan would ride one of the colts, then unsaddle. He would be hot, dusty, and thirsty. Alan would walk into the barn, get a drink of water, and then splash water on his face and head to wash off some of the dust and cool off. Then out the door to catch another horse and repeat the cycle. If Alan had any notions that this was glamorous work, they were certainly dispelled forever by the end of the summer. There was, however, much satisfaction in seeing a young horse progress and learn in a willing manner the things Alan tried to teach him. This satisfaction was even greater with the tougher horses because they usually would go days or even weeks with little progress, but then suddenly something would click in and they would make great strides in a short time. Alan was too young to have much initial patience with the young horses, and perhaps the most important lesson Alan learned was to govern his own impatience.

Alan's confidence grew as the colts became easier to handle. Alan was taking the broncs out for long rides in the pastures and was using them to gather and handle cattle whenever possible. The summer monsoon rains had started and green grass was growing on most parts of the ranch. The air had a fresh feel to it. This is always a particularly good time on a ranch. The green grass makes the cattle feel good and the horses too. It even rubs off on the cowboys.

With about a week left before school started, Rastus came riding back from New Well one day with the news that he had put a sick bull in the small holding pasture near the corral there. This was a remote location on the ranch about twenty miles northwest of the headquarters. It was far too long a distance to drive the sick bull home by horseback. To get to New Well one took the main ranch road to the highway that ran east and west through the ranch, then headed west along this highway toward Duncan, then followed a dirt road south for about five miles to New Well. It was five miles of the road from hell, over some of the worst soil on the whole ranch. The soil was a very fine-textured clay. In dry times it was almost as soft as blowing sand, and was very difficult to travel over because it was so soft. With a two-wheel-drive vehicle you were never sure that you could avoid getting stuck. If the wheels ever started to spin, the vehicle would dig in almost instantly and be stopped dead. If one could keep traveling without spinning the wheels, although a large cloud of dust would be raised, one could still traverse the road. But pulling a horse trailer, as needed to be done to haul the bull home, was going to be a big problem.

When it rained and the clay soil got wet, it was even worse to traverse. The clay would get so slick that there was no traction. A motor vehicle could go nowhere. If it rained for a long period and the moisture penetrated deep into the soil, the vehicle would simply sink all the way to the axle and be stuck for a long time. On the morning it was decided to haul the bull home, three cowboys and Alan took the pickup, the old horse trailer, and the old jeep that was kept around the ranch for its four-wheel-drive capability. Alan put one of the broncs he was riding into the trailer so that he could bring the bull into the corral at New Well and then load him for the ride home. It hadn't been raining much in the New Well area, so they weren't worried about getting stuck in the mud. But in late August thunderstorms can pop up with very little notice. When they left that morning the skies were blue, with only a few clouds building up. As they got to New Well, the clouds became more threatening, but they went on, and Alan was able to get the bull into the corral without incident. Getting the bull into the trailer was an altogether different proposition. After much struggling, the men ended up just grabbing the bull, and all four of them simply manhandled the bull into the trailer. This hot, dusty struggle took about an hour. They were all happy when they finally got him in the trailer. The bull was in the front of the trailer and the horse in the back. They started home.

It began to rain about the time they left New Well. There was a chain in the jeep that could be used to tie the jeep to the pickup to pull the pickup if it got stuck. As they bounced along, they had to stop several times in order to attach the chain to the jeep and pull the pickup out of the mud. Alan was riding in the jeep, which had no top, and he was the one elected to jump out and tie the chain to the pickup whenever it was stuck. They were rushing to try to reach the highway before the rain got too heavy, but they didn't make it. About halfway from New Well to the highway, the bottom just dropped out of the clouds. The rain fell so hard they couldn't see fifty feet. Along with this heavy rain came the lightning. There have been many lightning storms on the ranch, but the cowboys said there was never one as intense as that lightning storm. The lightning was striking so furiously that there was almost a continuous sound of thunder. A Lazy B cowboy had been killed by lightning, along with his horse, in the early years. His old saddle with the small holes all through it from the lightning was still hanging in the barn, and Alan had looked at it many times while growing up. The lightning wasn't in the distance; it was all around them. It hit so close several times they could see dust fly up where it hit the ground and penetrated deep enough to throw the dust up. The men were all deeply concerned, but they didn't know what to do except to plunge on and try to reach the highway. The rain was so sudden that it hadn't had time to sink more than a couple of inches into the clay. If they stayed much longer, the moisture would penetrate much deeper and the road would be totally impassable.

It was like going through the chamber of horrors, except that the danger was real and not make-believe. Each time Alan jumped out to attach the chain to the pickup, he was very afraid that he would be hit by lightning before he could get back in the jeep. And even the jeep was not a safe place.

The final hurdle they had to cross before they reached the highway was Railroad Wash. This is a deep, wide, usually dry watercourse. It only has water in the bottom two or three times a year, when big storms hit. Railroad Wash drains about 150 square miles of land, and when there is a major rain on this drainage the wash turns into a raging river one hundred feet wide and six feet deep. They all knew that Railroad Wash would be running a great deal of water very quickly that afternoon. Their hope was to get across before the water got too deep. They hoped to be going fast enough when they drove down into the wash to be able to use their momentum to help climb out the other side. But the clay and mud were too slick. The pickup got stuck in the bottom of the wash with the jeep halfway out on the incline. The jeep was struggling to climb up the side and pull the pickup with it. There was not enough traction to do it, and there they were. The rain was pouring the water in, and lightning was popping everywhere. Railroad Wash was rising fast. As Alan jumped out of the jeep to look the situation over, he stepped on a large mesquite thorn, which penetrated the thin sole of his worn-out boot. The first step he took broke the thorn off in his foot. At that moment thirteen-year-old Alan was having about as much of a crisis as he could cope with, or maybe more.

DA demanded total loyalty from his employees and his children. He also expected them to use good judgment in their work. It didn't take much time for Alan to figure out that they had used really poor judgment. There they were, stuck in the bottom of a normally dry wash that was about to be a very wet wash—with a horse and a bull in the trailer. The pickup, the trailer, the bull, and the horse were about to be swept away in the rising flood. To make matters worse, the bull had lain down in the trailer and refused to get up. They could have unloaded the horse and saved him, but all the rest looked very much in jeopardy. Alan was hopping around, trying not to put weight on the foot with the thorn in it. Alan knew DA would be very angry with all of them for using poor judgment, but he would be particularly angry with Alan. Family members were always judged by a higher standard than everyone else. It didn't matter that Alan was only thirteen. He knew that he was accountable for everything that went on, and would be judged accordingly. Alan didn't know whether he was more afraid of the lightning or of DA.

Alan happened to spot an old nylon saddle rope under the seat of the jeep. Because one of its three strands was broken, it had been discarded by the cowboys. Nylon ropes had become available only a couple of years before, and most cowboys still used the hemp ropes that were standard before nylon. None of them had used nylon enough to know how strong it was, or how versatile; a hemp rope used in the same circumstance would have surely broken. When Alan spotted the rope, he suggested that they tie the rope onto the chain and then onto the jeep, so that with a longer line the jeep could be up out of the wash, on flat ground, and would perhaps have more pulling power. They all thought that the rope would probably break, but they were desperate. If that failed, they planned to unload the horse and save him, but the pickup, the trailer, and the bull would be lost.

The water was running deeper under the pickup as they unhooked the chain from the jeep, and within five minutes would have swept it away. Hemp ropes do not stretch when they tighten; they either hold or break, with no stretch. The men were able to move the jeep to flatter land and attach the nylon rope to the chain, which was still hooked to the pickup. The old nylon rope started to stretch as they drove forward with the Jeep. It appeared to stretch at least ten feet, and looked like it was about to break. Finally, the pickup started to move. The jeep was churning up mud with all four wheels and the pickup was slowly moving up the hill. The rain was pelting and the lightning crashing. The pickup came out of the wash, and it was only a short distance to the highway, where travel was safe. Alan had never felt more relieved in his short life.

When they got back to the ranch, they told DA they had been stuck in the wash, but they did not mention how bad their judgment had been to get them in that predicament. Alan used a pair of pliers to pull the thorn out of his foot, and he limped for a few days, probably as a badge of honor. He started school the next week. His life at school seemed rather quiet compared to his thirteenth summer. Alan was more confident in school that year, as well as at the ranch. And the old bull recovered and lived to a ripe old age, happily siring hundreds of calves along the way.

Top: *Branding.*
Bottom: *Lazy B roundup,*
1940s. Opposite: *Alan*
branding a calf.

16. The Roundup

But though there is much work and hardship, rough fare, monotony, and exposure connected with the round-up, yet there are few men who do not look forward to it and back to it with pleasure.

THEODORE ROOSEVELT,
Ranch Life and the Hunting-Trail

*T*HE RANCH YEAR IS CYCLICAL. INCOME IS PRODUCED TWICE A year, in spring and fall, when the cattle are sold. Gathering all the cattle scattered over almost three hundred square miles is an enormous job. Each spring, in May, and each fall, in November, we would round up the cattle. We covered about ten square miles each day on horseback and worked in that area to gather the cattle, brand the calves born since the last roundup, and separate out the yearlings and any old cows or bulls to be sold. We hired extra help for the roundups—a cook and another five or six cowboys for the time it took to complete the job.

Every state in the West has laws providing that no cattle can be sold unless each animal sold has been branded with the registered brand of the seller. Each rancher tries to put his brand on each of his calves as soon as possible, both to discourage theft of the calves and to be prepared for the eventual sale. Calves are ready for sale when they are six to twelve months old. In a normal year a calf weighs between four and five hundred pounds. We normally produced about one thousand calves each year. We would keep approximately two hundred heifer calves to use as breeder cows at maturity and sell the remaining calves.

The process of selling the calves could take several rounds of negotiations with a cattle buyer; or, in a year when feeder calves were in short supply, a single brief conversation might suffice. In late winter or early spring, or in late summer, we would see the dust cloud forming on the ranch road that signaled the arrival of a car. It would eventually arrive in the gravel area in front of the house or the bunkhouse, and the driver would get out and walk around a bit. DA would go out and greet the visitor and invite him inside for a cup of coffee or a glass of iced tea. They would sit in the living room. MO and any of us who were there would join them. The conversation would last an hour or more, concerning where it had rained last and when, how range conditions were at the Lazy B and elsewhere in the Southwest, how the cattle looked there and elsewhere, and what the prices had been on any known cattle sales in recent months. There would be talk of mutual friends and acquaintances. But no mention would be made of the purpose of the visitor's trip to the Lazy B. If lunchtime or dinnertime rolled around, MO would invite the visitor to join us for a meal. During the meal, the conversation might extend to President Franklin Roosevelt and some of his programs, which the ranchers particularly disliked, or to the economy generally, or to the price of cattle feed.

Finally, the visitor would say he'd better be getting along. DA would walk out to the car with him, and often the visitor would turn the key and start the motor. Then he might say, "Harry, I think I could use some calves this spring. What would you take for the steers?" "Well, I don't know. What are you paying?" They would talk a bit about the price, and if it sounded all right, they would shake hands. DA would say, "I think I can have them at the shipping pen on May twenty-ninth. Is that all right?" "I think that will be okay. I'll see you the twenty-ninth over at Summit."

It was many years before a written contract of sale became commonplace. And for many years sales would be made without a down payment. Gradually, the practice changed, until not only a written contract but a down payment were required.

Once DA had a buyer for the calves, he would start planning for the weeks ahead. Thirty or so of the horses must be gathered and new horseshoes put on. The fences in the various pastures used to hold the cattle to be sold must be checked and any repairs completed. The extra roundup help must be hired. The roundup schedule must be fixed. All told, about forty-five consecutive days of work were required for each roundup and sale.

Shoeing the horses takes several days. Each hoof of each horse must be examined and trimmed with a rasp, and a properly sized horseshoe must be selected. The iron horseshoe must be fitted and then nailed to each hoof. Some of the horses put up quite a fuss as they are worked on. More than one man usually gets kicked in the process. The horseshoes are needed because much of the ranch is rocky, and without horseshoes the horses can injure their hooves and become lame.

The saddles need to be oiled. Grocery supplies must be purchased. The chuck wagon must be cleaned out and resupplied. In the meantime, the usual maintenance of wells, windmills, and troughs must be carried out.

The start of a roundup is always a time of excitement and anticipation for everyone involved. Although the basic routine is always the same, there is also something new to experience each time. It might be a new horse or two to ride, a new saddle to use, or a new cowboy hired for the crew. Someone would inevitably be bucked off a horse, which in turn would provide fodder for the ensuing jokes and the teasing. Sometimes a cowboy would be seriously injured from a fall, a kick, or some other accident. Most of the crew would feel pretty sore the first few days of the roundup. The days are long, with ten hours or so in the saddle and chores to do before and after the roundup work. After a few days in the saddle, it begins to feel more comfortable and the days are not quite as difficult. But after twenty consecutive days, the crew gets tired and cranky, and everyone starts looking forward to the end. One sure signal that the end is in sight is when the cook gets crabby. At the beginning, our cook, Bug Quinn, would be cheery and full of jokes. But toward the end the cowboys learned to stay clear of Bug or risk a tongue-lashing. DA always said roundups were hard on old men and little boys. That remark made Alan mad, and he tried his best to prove DA wrong.

Those who completed an entire roundup had a real sense of accomplishment. Most who did it realized they had experienced something few people have a chance to do and something that few people are capable of doing.

Each day of the roundup the crew tries to gather all the cattle in the area to be covered and bring them to a designated place for branding and sorting. Some of the places used have corrals, which makes the work easier. Some are in open country, which means several people on horseback have to keep all the cattle herded together while one or two men work inside the herd to rope each calf to be branded and drag it to the branding fire. A couple of other cowboys have to be on foot to wrestle the calf to the ground and tie its legs together with a pigging string. The roper keeps roping all the time, and sometimes as many as eight or ten calves are tied down at one time. If the roper misses a few calves as he tries to catch them and the ground crew has no calves tied up to brand for a few minutes, they tease the roper unmercifully for being slow.

DA usually applied the branding iron to stamp a Lazy B on the left hip and a straight line, or "britchen," under the tail. Someone else would use a knife to cut the tip off each ear, which was the registered earmark for the Lazy B. It is the custom for ranches to have not only a brand but also an earmark. As the calves age and the hair grows out, it can be hard to see the brand from afar. But the earmark is distinctive and can be spotted at quite a distance from the animal.

After the branding, another cowboy checks each calf for the sign of horns, and if there are horns starting to grow he takes a special sharp tool and a hammer to gouge them out. Of all the things done to a calf, the dehorning is the most painful. Because of that, in the 1940s DA began buying only polled Hereford bulls to try to breed cattle that did not have horns. He succeeded to a great extent, and most of the Lazy B calves thereafter never produced horns. Each calf was also vaccinated for blackleg, a preventable bovine disease. All the male calves were castrated, which took only a couple of skillful cuts with a sharp knife. The entire process of branding, dehorning, vaccinating, and castrating a calf by a skilled crew takes only a couple of minutes, after which the pigging string is untied and the dazed calf stands up, a bit wobbly, and bawls for its mother. The mother cow, meanwhile, is anxiously looking for her calf and bawling to it as well. Cattle do not see very clearly, and cows identify their calves mainly by smell. When the mother cow finds her newly branded calf, she licks it and nudges it, and stands while the calf nurses, finding solace in the warm milk and its mother's udder.

After each unbranded calf in the herd had been branded, DA, Rastus, and Jim would ride among the herd and single out the yearlings to be sold. Each one and its mother would be cut out of the herd, driven out of the herd to form a second, smaller herd of cattle to be kept together for transfer to a holding pasture until a few days before the shipping date. Any cows that were too old to breed or were infertile or sick would also be culled out, along with any bulls DA decided were no longer able to breed. They, too, would be sold.

The last task of the day is to move all of the selected cattle to the holding pasture, which might be several miles away. Some of the cowboys must drive them by horseback to the pasture. Other cowboys have to make sure there are enough horses in a corral for the next day's work and that they are fed. Then and only then can the crew return to headquarters to do the chores there—milk the milk cow, feed the horses at the headquarters, check the chicken coop for eggs, and fall into bed until before dawn the next day.

The hours were long. Sometimes the chores would not be finished until 10:00 P.M. The next day, at the start of the day's ride, the cowboys might say, "Well, by golly, maybe this time the boss will buy us a new Stetson hat! Or at least take us in to the Bonnie Heather for a night off." Claude might ask Alan, "How much do you pay us per day?" Alan would smile and say, "You know how much we are paying a day." Claude would say, "Okay. That's fine, but how much are you paying us for the nights?" His point was well taken after five days in a row of eighteen-hour days.

After the various holding pastures are full of cattle from different parts of the ranch, and the delivery date is near, all the cattle in the holding pastures are moved to a central larger holding pasture. The two hundred or so heifer calves to be kept for the breeding herd are then separated from their mothers and taken back to the corrals at the headquarters to be fed hay and cottonseed meal to teach them to survive without their mother's milk.

The day before the scheduled delivery date, the calves to be sold and their mother cows are driven by the crew on horseback to the location on the ranch called High Lonesome, where there is a windmill and troughs with plenty of water for the cattle to drink. The cattle are kept near the water to give them ample time to drink their fill. The standard agreement for the sale of the calves always provides that the animals to be sold will not be given access to water on the day they are weighed for the delivery. The sale price is based on an agreed upon price per pound, and the buyers do not want to pay for a belly full of water.

The cows and calves are then driven to a smaller holding pasture for overnight. Before dawn the next day the roundup crew saddles up and drives the cattle slowly to Summit and the shipping-pen corrals. Summit is on the spur line of the Southern Pacific Railroad. The track runs from Lordsburg, New Mexico, to Clifton, Arizona, where the daily train picks up a load of copper from the Phelps Dodge smelter in Clifton. A couple of families live in little railroad-owned wooden houses at Summit. The men living there work as repairmen for the railroad.

An effort is made to keep the cattle calm and free of stress. The crew, however, is tense and watchful. Above all, we want to avoid having any cattle run off or get excited, because any stress causes the calves to lose weight. Getting all the cattle into the corrals at Summit is the most difficult part. As we get the cattle close to the corrals, one rider goes ahead and opens the main gate. Then the crew tries to get the herd of cattle—numbering more than a thousand—circling around near the corral gate. One of the men rides in and tries to drive a few cows into the open gateway. They don't want to enter, but if one or more will do so, the rest will usually follow on inside the corral. Every rider's heart is pumping fast until the entire herd is corralled.

Next is the task of separating each calf and driving it into an adjacent corral without its mother. This is when a good cutting horse is worth its weight in gold. It takes great agility and quick reactions for a horse to get between a calf and its mother and get the calf into the next corral. One man stands at the gate and must immediately close it as the calf enters the next corral.

Once the calves have been separated, they must be weighed. The weighing doesn't start until the cow buyer shows up to verify the weights and numbers. The scales, which are made to hold thousands of pounds, are kept locked until the weight-and-measures inspector has certified that they are properly tested and in working order. The buyer of the cattle always reserves the right to reject a certain small percent of the cattle to be sold. The buyer usually rejects the largest of the calves, in order to save money, and any that have an unusual set of markings or any evidence of injury or illness. Again, the ones that are rejected are separated from the rest and put in a separate corral. Then ten or twelve calves at a time are driven into the small area of the scale and are weighed as a group. The heifers and the steers are weighed separately. A careful tally is kept by both the seller and the buyer of the numbers and the weights. When all have been weighed, a total is made of the number of heifers sold and their total weight and the number of steers sold and their weight. Those weights are then multiplied by the agreed price per pound. Normally, the price for the steers is several cents higher than for the heifer calves because experience has shown that the steer calves gain weight faster than the heifers. The buyer will pasture the calves on green grass to promote rapid weight gain over the next six months or so. When the weighing is completed, the calves are loaded into railroad cars or truck trailers for shipment to their next home.

The day of the shipping is the culmination of at least six months of work on the ranch. There is no income until the cattle are shipped, and the amount of income depends on the weight of the calves and the price DA was able to obtain for them. That price in turn is determined largely by world-market factors, over which neither the producer nor the buyer has any control. The weight of the calves is determined largely by weather and grass conditions, over which the producer has no control.

MO and Bug, the roundup cook, always prepared a particularly hearty and good meal for shipping day. There were extra people to feed—the buyer and perhaps his family, the brand inspector, perhaps the truck driver and a neighbor or two.

DA was always on edge until the last calf was loaded and he had the bank draft in hand to take into the First National Bank of Lordsburg to collect and then deposit in the Lazy B account. He never ate much on shipping day; his stomach was queasy. DA and the entire crew were covered with dust and grime from being in the corrals all day with the cattle. The mother cows, which had been separated from their calves for most of the day, would bawl for their calves and walk anxiously around their corral. The sound is constant and deafening. They are thirsty. Their udders are full of milk and taut. Everyone is tired yet relieved to have the calves loaded and on their way. But the real end of the roundup is not yet at hand.

Alan remembers a particular day in November, the day after the shipping. We were up again before dawn. Rastus had wrangled the horses by 4:30 A.M., and they were in the corral at the headquarters. We had breakfast at the bunkhouse and went to the corral to select our fastest horses for this day. We loaded them in the horse trailer, along with the saddles, saddle blankets, and bridles, and rode in the pickup and the jeep to Summit. We got there just after sunup. The cows were still bawling and showing signs of agitation. They had been without water for some thirty-six hours. We had to move the cows back onto the range in the areas where they would graze; soon their udders would stop producing milk, and they would again come into heat and breed for another calf the following spring. We knew that when we opened the gates, the cows would come out running. There would be no way to stop them. We had to try to keep them generally together and to gradually turn them in the direction we wanted them to go, toward the central part of the ranch. The trip would take about three hours. The cows would run fast the first mile or so and then continue at a steady trot. The horses we rode had to be fast enough to outrun any strays and keep the cows headed in the right direction.

Alan was still getting ready to cinch his saddle tight and to mount his horse when one of the cowboys opened the corral gate. The cows stampeded out of the corral and into the adjacent pasture. Alan jumped on his horse to stay with the herd. One of the cows suddenly headed back and to the side, and Alan's horse made a quick pivot to stay with the cow and turn her back. The cinch had not been tightened, and Alan's saddle slipped to the side. That started his horse bucking wildly, and Alan went flying off and to the ground right next to the corral. No one stopped to help, and he managed to get to his horse and grab the reins and calm the horse long enough to put the saddle back on, tighten the cinch, and gallop after the stampeding herd. He would hear from the cowboys for weeks afterward about his mistake.

Top: *Main Street in Lordsburg.* Bottom: *The livestock train.*

Opposite: *Sandra and her horse, Swastika (left); Flournoy with Chico.*

17. Going to Lordsburg

*If you're just treading water
you're not making much progress.*

R. LEWIS BOWMAN,
Bumfuzzled Too

$\mathcal{I}$T WAS JULY AND OUR COUSIN FLOURNOY WAS AT THE RANCH FOR most of the summer. Flournoy and I were inseparable, and I was never happier than when she was at the ranch. It was hot—over 100 degrees in the heat of the day. We slouched on the couches in the house, reading. After lunch we put on bathing suits to go for a swim in the steel-rimmed tank. We wore thong sandals to walk the two hundred yards from the house to the windmill and tank. The tank was fenced, and we had to open a wooden gate and climb an old wooden ladder up to the top of the steel rim.

The tank was six feet high and fifty feet in diameter. The water was murky and green. Some algae that resembled mud-colored sponges floated on the surface and clustered on the side of the tank away from the wind. A few goldfish lazily swam around. A two-by-six-foot board was fastened across the top of the edge of the tank. We sat on the board dangling our feet in the water. Then we jumped in, but we were too short to touch the bottom. The water felt deliciously cool in the hot afternoon.

We had some old inner tubes, and we sat in them and floated. MO and DA told us we were going into Lordsburg at about 3:00 P.M. to get the mail and the groceries. They said we should get out of the tank and get dressed by 2:45. We had no watches and no clock, and time just went by. Finally

MO walked partway down from the house and called to us to get out. We pretended not to hear her. She was dressed for town in her dress and good shoes and didn't want to walk through the dirt and gravel to the tank. Soon DA walked down. "Sandra, Flournoy! It is time to go. We need to leave." "No, DA. We want to stay here. We don't want to go to town today." "Girls, get out *now*. We have to leave, and we don't want you to stay here alone." "We'll be fine. Just let us stay." "Absolutely not. Get out and get yourselves dry." "No. Please, DA. We want to stay. There's nothing for us to do in town." DA walked away to the barn. We thought we were going to be allowed to stay home alone. We were wrong. Soon DA returned to the tank carrying his lariat rope. He climbed partway up the ladder. "Come on out, girls, or I'll pull you out." We laughed and said, "No, you can't. We'll duck."

He formed a loop in his lariat and circled it over his head, ready to throw it. When we thought he was going to throw it, we held our breath and ducked under the water. We stayed down as long as we could, but we had to come up for air. Thump. The rope was around Flournoy's neck, and she was quickly pulled in to the side. "Okay, DA. I'll get out, let me go. The rope hurts!" "All right. Out you go. Now, Sandra." Again I ducked, but I, too, had to come up for air. Around my neck was the rope, and I, too, was pulled to the side. "Ouch, DA. That hurts!" "Get out now and get dressed pronto. We need to get to town before the post office closes."

The fun was over for the day. Flournoy and I scurried to the house, put on dry clothes, and joined MO and DA in the Chrysler to drive to Lordsburg. Our necks were a bit red, and our egos too. We learned we couldn't always have our own way.

The trips to Lordsburg followed the same pattern each time. The first stop was the post office. Our parents leased a post office box, number GG. It was always full of mail. MO or DA would dial the combination that opened the box and then carefully extract the mail. Often the post office had additional packages and magazines for us that did not fit in the box. Our parents would mail all the letters and the out-of-town bill payments, and we would then stop at the First National Bank of Lordsburg. It was a small bank on the main street, Railroad Avenue. All the businesses were on the south side of Railroad Avenue. To the north were the Southern Pacific Railroad tracks, running east-west, the railroad roundhouse for repairs, and the little station house. North of the tracks were houses and a few small businesses occupied and used mainly by the Hispanic community.

At the bank DA would make a couple of deposits and visit for a while with the bank manager. Then we would return to the car and drive to the Up-to-Date Grocery, which was owned by a Chinese man named Fat Hoy. Fat had come to the United States in the early 1890s, when jobs building railroad lines were still available. He stayed to open a grocery store. He lived in some rooms above the store. Every year another "son" of his would arrive from China. These young men would work for Fat for a while, and then move on elsewhere to make their own fortunes.

Fat Hoy always had a smile. He would bow and say, "Hello, Missy Day. You good?" "Fine, thanks, how are you?" "Oh, belly good, belly good. What you need?" MO had a long shopping list for our house as well as the bunkhouse. She would tell Fat Hoy what she needed. He would write it down in Chinese characters, and then we would leave to do our other errands. Fat would have everything ready for us in bags and boxes when we started back to the ranch.

Next we drove to each place where DA had a bill to pay. That usually included the automotive supply store, the lumber and paint store, the veterinary supply store, and the heating oil and butane gas plant. Rather than mail his checks to these places, DA would visit each one to pay the bill, talk to the manager, and perhaps order some new supplies. Finally, in the late afternoon, we always drove to the rear of the Hidalgo Hotel and parked in the hotel parking lot. The hotel was owned and managed by Nat and Elizabeth Gammon. They lived in an apartment behind the desk at the hotel. MO and DA would go to the little bar on the mezzanine of the hotel, and we children would sit in the lobby on the big leather sofas and read or "people-watch."

In a corner office off the hotel lobby was Colonel Holt. A small, silver-haired man with a bushy mustache and a friendly manner, he wore Western-style clothes and a very large crowned Stetson cowboy hat. He was a one-man chamber of commerce for Lordsburg. His office walls were covered with photographs of prominent people he had met through the years. Our favorite was his photo of Amelia Earhart. No one knew how he'd obtained the title "Colonel," but Flournoy and I stopped in to say hello whenever we were at the hotel. He was always glad to have visitors.

Our parents enjoyed seeing their local friends: the attractive widow Faye Clayton; the lawyer Forrest Sanders and his wonderful wife, Margaret; other ranchers, such as Betty and Sherwood Culbertson and the Kipps; some mining engineers; and Mary and Dick Dockum, who owned a gasoline and fuel business. Usually several of these friends would stop by the Hidalgo, and MO and DA were always glad to see them and to visit. If we had to wait too long, MO and DA would tell us to go into the hotel restaurant and order something to eat. When they were ready to go, the last stop was at the Up-to-Date to pick up the groceries. MO and DA would talk all the way home about things they had learned from their visits in town. It would be dusk by the time we reached the ranch road—a time when the rabbits were out eating any grass they could find. We would take out the .22 rifle, load it, and call to DA to stop the car when we saw one to shoot. Six rabbits ate as much as one cow, DA said. And the rabbits multiplied quickly, so he thought we were helping Mother Nature keep the balance by eliminating a few rabbits.

Finally, we were home again. The dogs barked and jumped and were overjoyed to see us. Everyone helped unload all the groceries and supplies, and MO worked to put everything away. As soon as we had done our part unloading, we would dash to try to be the first to get the *Saturday Evening Post* or *Life* or *Time*, to read about what was going on in the world outside the Lazy B. We were all glad to be home again.

Top: *Jim at a rodeo.* PHOTOGRAPH BY DEVERE HELFRICH, FEB. 18, 1950. 81.023.0575, "JIM BRISTER CALF ROPING," DONALD C. AND ELIZABETH M. DICKINSON RESEARCH CENTER, NATIONAL COWBOY AND WESTERN HERITAGE MUSEUM, OKLAHOMA CITY

Bottom: *Jim at a team-tying competition.*

Opposite: *Jim ropes a calf.*

18.   *More About Jim*

*Some fellers just naturally create a
picture when they sit on a horse.*

R. LEWIS BOWMAN,
Bumfuzzled Too

$\mathcal{J}$IM BRISTER WAS THE TOUGHEST COWBOY WE EVER SAW AT THE Lazy B, and the best rider and roper in the Southwest. He was six foot two and 190 pounds of muscle, covered by a layer of skin that looked like rawhide pulled tighter than the stockings on the fat lady at the circus. His hair was red in his youth, but it thinned and was a balding, grayish grizzle most of his life. His nose was large, and it had been broken so often that it had various bumps and bends. He always wore Levi's, faded, dirty, and molded to his legs. His boots were never shined and showed their hard, daily use. His hat was an old, beat-up Stetson, with a dark stain around the headband where years of sweat had soaked it through. You couldn't read Jim's eyes; they didn't convey his inner thoughts. They were blue, and the whites usually showed signs of irritation by too much dust and sun.

Jim didn't talk much about his childhood in Oklahoma and Texas, but over the years bits and pieces of his early life surfaced like a five-foot rattlesnake full of venom. It was clear as the horns on a bull that he had been physically abused as a child, but whatever had happened then had forged a man of singular strength and determination, one as rare as an honest politician.

Jim had strength, agility, and coordination that would have made him a well-paid football or baseball player today. He never showed off, but he used his ability and talent to get the job done. His reputation as a first-rate rider and roper led any number of temporary roundup cowboys to try to impress Jim with their own abilities. All they ever got for their efforts was a look at Jim's back as he walked away. Every one of us would have welcomed a word of appreciation from Jim, but it seldom came.

One spring, when Alan was about fourteen, we were gathering some cattle. Alan was riding a three-year-old mare he was trying to break. Alan could ride her, but he couldn't make her turn very well. She would stiffen her neck and refuse to respond to the hackamore. Alan was sturdy, but he was not strong enough to force the mare to respond.

Jim saw what was going on; not much escaped his attention. Finally he had seen enough. He said, "Alan, I have a mare here that might suit you better than the one you're on. She's pretty and awfully gentle. Maybe you could handle her a little better. Why don't we just trade?" "Well, okay. I'll trade," said Alan. Jim reined in his mare, got off, took off his saddle, and had Alan get off his mare and pull off his saddle. Jim resaddled Alan's mare, and Alan put his own saddle on Jim's mare. Jim mounted and then reached up and grabbed the hackamore near Alan's mare's head and pulled her head down and around until her head touched Jim's knee. He held her neck bent down and put more pressure on her until he literally threw the mare to the ground. As she hit the ground, Jim stepped off as if he were stepping off his back porch. He stood and with one hand held the mare down, all nine hundred pounds of her. He put one foot on her neck and pulled her head up while she whinnied and struggled as if she were a little rabbit with a broken leg. Then he took the end of the hackamore rope and whipped the mare hard.

Alan watched with amazement. He could not even turn the mare's head, much less put her down. Alan's eyes popped and his heartbeat jumped. Jim finally released the pressure and let the mare up. He remounted her and rode her. The mare responded to the slightest touch as though she was the most sensitive horse on the ranch.

Jim's way with horses was just to be tougher than they were. He could always ride the horse all right, but when a person of lesser skill rode the horse, the horse soon learned who was in command. Sometimes the new rider would end up with a worm's view of the sky and bruises he wouldn't forget. Alan's mare, by contrast, never forgot her manners after the day Jim rode her.

Riding with Jim made us grateful to have him as one of ours. We wondered how we were so lucky. He had intuition about what cattle would do before they did it. Many times when we were gathering and moving cattle we would see Jim leave his position and head off to some unlikely place. Had he spotted a wild turkey we could have for supper? Had he seen something none of us had seen? Then, a moment or two later, the cattle would take off on a run in the same direction Jim had gone, and he would be waiting there to turn them back in the direction they belonged. We just came to expect it from Jim and to say a silent "Thank you" time after time.

If a horse one of us was riding got a burr under the saddle or was spooked by a rattlesnake or for some reason went loco, we wanted The Man at our side. Jim would be there in short order to grab the horse's reins, get him under control, and get the rider safely off. But if any of us ever complained, acted stupid, or didn't do our share of the work, we would be dead meat. Jim would see to it. When he decided to "get on someone's case," that person had better watch out. Maybe everyone has a dark side; Jim's was visible.

Bob Curtin ran away from a youth correctional facility and landed at the Lazy B as a temporary cowhand. He thought he was tough enough to be a bronc rider. He idolized Jim and tried to get Jim to let him break some horses. Jim took Bob up a mountain to cut some ocotillo to build a fence around Jim's yard. Ocotillo is a cactus that grows long, fingerlike spikes with sharp thorns all around each spike. It is wicked stuff. Rub against an ocotillo and you will have a torn shirt and bloody arms.

When they had cut a load of ocotillo branches and loaded the wagon bed with them, Jim tied them down with his rope and told Bob he should get on top of them and ride home like he would on a bucking stallion. Poor Bob said okay, and up he went. Jim whipped the team and got the wagon moving down the mountain, hitting every rock and furrow. Bob screamed for Jim to stop. Jim never slowed down. When the wagon finally came to a stop at the bottom of the mountain, Bob's backside was covered with rips, tears, and blood. We hurt just looking at him. Jim's reaction? "Bob, go sleep in the barn since you were dumb enough to ride that cart down."

One experience would have been enough for most wanna-be rodeo hands, but Bob still wanted to learn to ride the tough broncs. Jim had a mean-as-a-hornet stallion in his corral, and Bob ached to try riding him. Jim told Bob to go down to the corral and saddle the horse and he would follow along soon. Bob hustled down to the corral as pleased as if he were going to spend the night with the prom queen. Ten minutes later Jim came down to the corral and found what he expected: Bob was sitting in the branches of the hackberry tree that grew in the middle of the corral. The big bay stallion was pawing the ground under it.

Jim never told us, but we suspected he was mean to young Bob because Bob had never accepted responsibility for his wrongdoing and had escaped from his punishment in the correctional institution. In Jim's world you accepted responsibility for your actions and never complained if things didn't go your way.

The Lazy B, which was approximately one-fifth the size of the state of Rhode Island, occupied a good chunk of Greenlee County, Arizona. It was difficult to keep an eye on all of it with only a handful of people to do it. Nearly impossible, in fact. Jim and Mae lived about ten miles from the ranch headquarters. Jim was responsible for the southern and western sections of the ranch, except for the wells and windmills. He was not mechanical and never learned how to maintain them. If a windmill broke down in his area, he would ride into the headquarters and let us know about it. He would head back home immediately, before anyone could suggest that he try to repair it. When it came to the cattle and the horses, though, he was in a league of his own. He kept his horses in tip-top shape. He broke many of our horses and did most of the roping at the roundups.

One day when we were corralling some cattle at Three Mills, it looked like we had a particularly surly mess of beef. They looked like they might take off running and the hell with the cowboys. Alan was on one of his best horses, so he positioned himself near the gate with his rope down and looped, ready for anything. Jim was nearby on a good horse, as usual, but with his rope still coiled on his saddle. The cows finally moved into the corral through the gate, tossing their heads and bawling—all except one big calf that bolted off into a stand of mesquite bushes some distance off. Alan started instantly after the calf with his lariat ready and his horse running all out. Jim started after the calf a full ten seconds later. Jim reached the bushes first, jerked his rope down, and lassoed the calf before Alan even got there. That performance would have earned him first prize in any big rodeo.

Another day, at High Lonesome, we were cutting some cows out to wean their calves. We were having a lot of trouble with one cow. She would not go into the corral we wanted her to enter. She was obstinate, quick, and feisty. We tried to get her through the gate for fifteen minutes or so. Jim, on his big sorrel Jeep, rode up and bumped the cow hard with Jeep's shoulder to turn her away. Then he quickly moved to her other side and bumped her hard the other way. He kept this up a few times, until the cow would go exactly where Jim wanted, and he neatly put her through the gate. It was the best combination of horse, rider, and cow any of us ever saw.

Life on the ranch was no Sunday afternoon stroll in the park. Cowboying is the least respected and most dangerous job around. There are other equally dangerous ways to earn a dollar, but most of them—such as fire fighting, police work, and roughnecking at an oil well—get the respect and attention they deserve. And NFL football produces plenty of bruises and broken bones. Only a few men reach the top in professional football. Those that do are very well paid and have a great deal of public adulation. At the same time, the football players wear protective helmets and pads and have professional trainers to keep them in top shape. They actually play football no more than about twenty-five minutes a week. Cowboys, by contrast, wear soft hats, no padding, have no professional training, work about seventy hours a week for very little money, and at a job where painful injuries are common. It is often one man against an eight- or nine-hundred-pound animal that doesn't do what is wanted or expected. For example, while at the Lazy B, Jim broke his nose fourteen times, and broke various fingers countless times. He never went to a doctor for any of these injuries. He would set his broken finger by taping it to a stick or a nail and keep on going. He could tolerate pain better than anyone we knew. One day on a roundup he rode all day with what he called a slight pain in his neck. It turned out to be a broken collarbone. But he never missed a day of that roundup.

Once he had a sore tooth and asked Alan to look at it. Alan looked and saw a large dark hole inside the tooth. Alan described to Jim what he saw, and Jim said, "Okay, I'll take care of it." He took a fresh piece of baling wire off the roll, heated it in a fire until it was red-hot, and, with Alan guiding his hand, stuck it down the hole in his tooth. We listened to the sizzle and watched smoke come out of his mouth. Jim sat there without a word and never flinched. He is the only man we know who gave himself a "root canal" with a baling wire.

Jim would ride horseback from Willow Springs to wherever we were going to round up cattle that day. Sometimes he would have to ride eight or ten miles to meet the cowboys at daylight. He often had to leave Willow Springs by 3:00 A.M. to meet us. When we were ready to ride, he was always there. One time when we were working at Old Camp, he rode out to meet us leading an extra horse. Old Camp was probably the toughest place to ride and to round up on the ranch. There were steep canyon walls to get up and down to gather the cattle off the hillside. We worked all day rounding up, branding, and sorting the cattle. We finished about 4:00 P.M. Jim told DA he planned to ride his other horse over to Bowie to compete in the rodeo there. It was about fifteen miles. He rode to the rodeo, entered every event, then rode another seventeen miles or so to Willow Springs in time to change horses again to meet the next day's roundup. It was business as usual. "How'd you do last night, Jim?" "I won," he said, and that was that.

Sometimes Jim would enter a rodeo that was a long distance away. He would drive his pickup and trailer his horse, going straight through—

several hundred miles. He would participate in the roping and bronc-riding events and not even wait for his winnings. "Just send me the check," he'd say and head back to the ranch.

To keep up his roping skills, Jim built a roping arena in a flat area in the canyon behind his house at Willow Springs. In his horse pasture he also kept a few roping steers with horns. Jim never told DA he kept these steers. DA must have known about it, but it was never mentioned. All the cowboys knew about it, and so did Alan, Ann, and I. Sometimes we would go to Willow Springs to watch Jim and his friends practice roping. Sometimes he would invite some ropers to come for a jackpot roping. They would form into paired teams and put $500 or so per team in the jackpot. As far as we know, Jim never lost.

DA did not like roping the cattle and did not want to hire cowboys who roped cattle when it wasn't necessary. A good cowboy is at the right place at the right time to turn a cow or calf back and will not need to use a rope. Jim was always at the right place and seldom needed to use his rope. He never abused the cattle or the privilege of using his rope. When he did use it, there was none better. He could throw his loop over a head or a foot. He seldom missed.

Jim liked Alan and offered to teach him to rope and to compete in a rodeo. Alan liked to build a loop in his lariat and to throw it. Jim told Alan about how he'd taught our neighbor Phil McNeal to rope. Phil had inherited a nice ranch east of the Lazy B. Phil loved roping and couldn't get enough of it. He went to as many roping events as he could, and he neglected the ranch in the process. Finally, the debts mounted at the ranch and Phil mortgaged it. The day came when the mortgage was foreclosed and the cattle had to be gathered and sold. Jim went to Phil's ranch to help gather the cattle. He said there were about five hundred cows and only six bulls. Jim said Phil had not realized he had so few bulls. "That explains why Phil had such a small calf crop and couldn't pay his bills," said Jim.

Alan remembered that story and decided early on that he had a choice: he could be a good roper or a good rancher, but not both. Alan decided to try to be a successful rancher.

When DA took over the management of the Lazy B, there were as many as six hundred wild horses on the open range. There were stallions, mares, and foals. Occasionally, the cowboys in those days would round up some of the wild horses and take some that looked good for riding and try to make ranch horses out of them. Gathering wild horses is difficult. It takes planning, skill, and hard riding to get them corralled. The cowboys told us stories of some of Jim's favorite pastimes with the wild horses. Once the wild horses were corralled, Jim would ride into the middle of them and grab a mare's mane and jump from his horse to the mare's back. She would panic and lunge, jump, and try to buck off the unexpected weight on her back. When he tired of that mare, he would jump to another until he had enough.

Once the cowboys had selected the wild horses they wanted to keep, they would turn the others out of the corral. Jim would sometimes say, "Turn them out one at a time." There was a large flat east of the corral. When the horse came running out of the corral, Jim would be on one of his roping horses and would run up behind the wild horse and throw his lasso around its neck, then run on past the wild horse so that when the noose on the rope tightened, it would yank the wild horse backward. With its neck turned back, the horse would go flying up into the air and come down with a terrible crash. The horse would lie there stunned and shaking. Jim would ride up, release the rope, and let it go, saying, "Okay, boys, turn out another one." The wild horses had little monetary value at the time other than to produce colts. They were just playthings for Jim.

When Jim was ready to try one of the wild horses for riding, he would rope one of them in the corral and choke down on the rope until the horse would faint for lack of air. While the horse was on the ground, Jim would put a halter on its head, then tie the horse to a strong fence post. The horse, fully grown and never before touched by a human being or re-strained in any way, would pull on the rope and paw the ground in a futile effort to escape. Jim would leave the horse tied to the post all night. The next morning he would put a blindfold over the horse's eyes and then sad-dle it. It was quite a show, and all the cowboys would manage to be there to see it. Then he would get on the horse, release the blindfold and the rope, and tell the cowboys to open the gate. Out the gate the horse would go, spinning, jumping, bucking, and frantically trying to shake loose its rider. Jim would ride the horse all day. When he returned, the horse might not be fully broken, but it would be under Jim's control.

Alan asked, "Jim, you didn't even teach that horse to lead. If you had to get off to open a gate or to pee, how would you lead the horse through the gate or get back on?" "Well, I don't like to lead horses. I get on 'em to ride. It doesn't matter to me if he leads."

Jim was unconcerned about trying to make the horse gentle or able to be led. He was there to ride them, and ride them he did. That must be what is meant by "breaking" a horse. No "horse whisperer" there.

Any cowboy who says he has never been bucked off a horse is lying. Every cowboy gets bucked off sooner or later. The good ones, like Jim, just don't get bucked off very often. The only time Alan ever saw Jim bucked off was one afternoon working cattle at the headquarters. Jim was on a horse named Red Bird. He cut out a steer and was moving fast and leaning the wrong way when Red Bird started bucking and Jim went off. Jim got up, caught Red Bird by the reins, got right back on, and continued working. No one said anything about it then or later.

When Jim Brister was about sixty-seven he got the big sorrel horse he called Jeep. Jeep was about four hundred pounds heavier than any other horse we had on the ranch; he was smart, quick, fast, and mean. Jim said Jeep had been a racehorse but the owner had sold him because he bucked off all the jockeys. Jeep would behave perfectly most of the time, but occasionally he would just blow up and start bucking and looking for trouble.

Jim went to a local rodeo at Willcox with Jeep and entered the steer-roping events. Jim had thrown his loop over the last steer when Jeep began to buck. He bucked so hard he caused Jim to fly up and land hard on the saddle horn, breaking Jim's pelvis. This was the first injury Jim had that caused him to take it easy for a while. In the past, Jim had broken both legs, both arms, his collarbone, several fingers, and his nose. In each instance he just went on working as usual. Not this time. His pelvis injury left him in constant pain the rest of his life. He had trouble urinating. The doctors advised surgery, but Jim refused.

A few years later, when Jim was sixty-nine, he drove with Jeep to Salinas to a big rodeo for a team roping event. Jim and his partner had roped nine steers and they were leading in the competition when Jeep blew up and began to buck. Jim and his partner lost the event because of the time it took to deal with Jeep. Jim never complained. It was remarkable that he was still competing at sixty-nine.

Jim offered at times to let Alan ride Jeep. "No, thanks, Jim. It would be quite a ride, but no thanks."

Mae Brister, Jim's wife, was not quite five feet tall. Her skin was tan and wrinkled from constantly being out in the sun. She was pretty tough, like Jim, but she could read and write at about a third-grade level. When Mae and Jim had a few cattle of their own and sold some on occasion, Mae would try to handle the book work. She had trouble adding and subtracting and even more trouble with multiplication. If the cow buyer calculated he owed the Bristers $3,000, Mae would usually come up with an extra zero and would insist that the buyer owed them $30,000. There were sometimes battles royal when Mae was dealing with money.

Mae was exceedingly hospitable. Whenever any of us showed up at Willow Springs, she insisted that we come in and have a meal. It didn't matter whether it was 9:00 A.M. or 3:00 P.M., you could not leave until you had eaten what she prepared. Anything less was an insult. We learned not to argue with her and to try to time our visits closer to mealtimes.

One time when we were rounding up at Willow Springs, Jim failed to appear. It was particularly odd because that was the area where Jim lived. DA realized something must be wrong. He started the roundup crew on their cattle-gathering drive and rode on himself to Jim's house. When he got there, Mae said DA should come inside and look at Jim. She told DA that Jim had arisen about 3:00 A.M. to wrangle his horse and had gotten bucked off and hit his head on a rock. Somehow Mae had found him and got him back to the house. Jim was semiconscious, unable to get up, and babbling incoherently. There was a big hole in the top of his head. DA swore he could see what look like brains in the hole. "Harry, do you think I ought to take Jim to the doctor?" "Oh, my God, Mae. Yes, we have to get him to a doctor right away."

Mae and DA loaded Jim into their pickup truck and Mae drove him to Safford to a doctor. The upshot is that the next day Jim was back in the saddle and out on the roundup. He had a big bandage on top of his head, but he didn't complain, and it was work as usual.

On another occasion, Jim's horse fell with him and Jim broke his collarbone. DA was there, so he put Jim in a truck and drove him into Lordsburg to see old Dr. DeMoss, an osteopath who'd practiced for years in Lordsburg. Dr. DeMoss put a cast on Jim and said he should stay all night at the little four-bed hospital. DA said that was fine and that he would come back the next morning to get Jim.

When DA returned the next day, Jim was in his hospital bed, but there was no cast on his arm and shoulder. DA asked Jim what had happened. Jim said, "Well, the doc put that damn thing on too tight. It got to hurting in the night, so I got my pocketknife out and cut it off. I threw the blamed thing out the window." Sure enough, pieces of the cast were outside the window in the flower bed.

Dr. DeMoss came into the hospital room to see Jim. When he found out what had happened, he turned red and said angrily to DA, "Take this guy out of here and leave. I won't deal with him if he won't follow directions. Just get him out of here!"

DA had to talk to Dr. DeMoss the better part of an hour to get him to calm down and agree to put another cast on Jim. The doctor was still very angry with Jim, and he had both DA and Jim go into the surgery room with him. Dr. DeMoss then proceeded to demonstrate to DA how the bones had to fit together to heal. The doctor said, "The reason the cast is tight is because these bones have to fit right here." The doctor grabbed Jim's arm and jerked it around and said, "Now, if they're not together like this, they won't heal right." As he talked, he yanked Jim's arm back and forth and ground the broken bones together. Sweat popped out on Jim's forehead and it had to be incredibly painful, but he never said a word. After Dr.

DeMoss thought Jim had suffered enough, he put another cast on, and Jim and DA returned to the ranch.

Jim wasn't a bad horse doctor himself. He occasionally took a problem horse from someone else and tried some corrections. If the horse had a bad foot, Jim knew how to make corrective horseshoes and how to treat the wound or the condition. One time Jim accepted a nice brown horse with a foot that had been badly damaged by some wire. No one had been able to heal the hoof. Over the course of a year, Jim did a great deal of "doctoring" and made a series of corrective horseshoes. The horse, Brownie, turned out to be an excellent horse that lasted many years.

Jim had a roping partner for a while named Walt Nichols. Walt, like Jim, had never learned to read. One time Jim and Walt drove to California to participate in a team roping event at the Salinas rodeo. They drove along on a new freeway in central California, a highway Jim had not seen before. Jim had a knack for finding his way, even over long distances, despite the fact that he couldn't read the road signs. But neither Jim nor Walt had driven before on this new freeway, and neither Jim nor Walt would admit to the other that he couldn't read, although each of them suspected as much of the other. Jim was driving and told Walt to watch for the exit to Salinas. Whenever they approached an exit, Walt would be looking the other way and he would miss seeing it. Jim would say, "Walt, was that the turnoff to Salinas?" Walt would say, "I don't know, Jim, I was looking the other way when we passed it." And so it went. They wound up driving many miles past Salinas because neither would admit to the other that he couldn't read the signs.

Jim also had to fake it when he went to a restaurant. He would sit at the table and pick up a menu and pretend to read it from top to bottom. When the waitress would come to take the order, Jim would say, "Well, I guess I'll have that T-bone steak." Jim had learned that almost all the restaurants he ever used served a T-bone steak, so it was a safe selection.

It the 1970s Mae got sick. It was female problems, she said. She had several surgeries and was in and out of a few hospitals. She had a hard time walking. Alan installed an indoor toilet in the Willow Springs house to make it easier for Mae. But Mae got sick again almost the next day. She returned to the hospital and died.

Jim didn't remain a bachelor very long. He married a woman named Velma whom he had met during his rodeo career. It was soon apparent to Jim and to others that Velma had a drinking problem, and she also "popped" a lot of pills. Whenever they went to town, Velma headed right for the bar and would drink for hours. Jim would sit and wait for her, maybe having one beer to her twenty, and then take her home when she could barely walk. Shortly before Jim died he told a friend he had made a mistake getting remarried so quickly.

At seventy-five Jim was still entering some rodeos and still breaking horses. He bought a black horse that was chalk eyed, the horse's eyes looked like marbles set in his black face. Jim was teaching the horse to rope and drag cattle. One day Jim was out at Antelope Well on the black horse and was teaching the horse how to drag. Jim had his rope around a piece of pipe. The rope got under the horse's tail, and the horse began bucking violently. Jim went off and landed on his head. Jim's neck was broken, and he died instantly.

Alan was young and not yet married when Jim died, but he rode horseback with all the pallbearers from Lordsburg to Duncan, where Jim was to be buried. The trip was long, and the men started telling stories about the many good times all of them had had with Jim. They all appreciated that the times they had spent with Jim were extraordinary because of Jim and his skill and his nature. Instead of mourning, the cowboys wanted to remember the good times and the happy memories of Jim. Death is inevitable, and as far as they were concerned it is not to be feared or mourned.

Jim had a fine collection of tack—bridles, bits, spurs, and saddles he had purchased or acquired in trade or prizes over the years. He always knew the source of each piece—who'd made it, who'd used it, why Jim had wanted it, and so on. Jim also had a collection of championship belt buckles and saddles, including the 1947 World Championship saddle, all of which he'd won at various events. Jim had also taken out a $10,000 life insurance policy years before. DA helped Velma collect the insurance money. Velma stayed drunk until the money was gone. She also pawned and gave away all Jim's collection. Not a single piece remained at the Lazy B.

The Graham County Historical Society put a commemorative plaque at the place where Jim died. Jim made many friends through the years, and they all remembered him—as we did—as about the most skilled cowboy and rodeo performer they'd ever known.

Top: *Bob the bobcat, Sandra's first pet.*
Bottom: *Ann at age five and Alan at age four with the dogs.*
Opposite: *Sandra and a pet javelina.*

19. *Pets*

Animals are such agreeable friends:
they ask no questions, pass no criticism.

GEORGE ELIOT

ONE OF THE PROBLEMS OF LIVING AT THE LAZY B WAS THE AL-most constant presence of flies. The corrals, which were normally covered with horse and cow manure, were fertile breeding grounds for flies. Once we were a mile or so away from the headquarters there were fewer of them. But at our house and the bunkhouse they were ever present. MO kept a fly swatter near at hand in every room. When anyone entered the living room by the front door, MO would hover nearby with her fly swatter and urge the person at the door to hurry on inside. She would wave the fly swatter back and forth to frighten away any fly that might dare to enter with the visitor. At the bunkhouse Rastus would keep his fly swatter handy as well. When he sat on the bunkhouse porch he would swat the flies within reach and then often feed them to a lizard that frequented the porch in hopes of a meal. Lizards were a common feature of the high desert. They ate mostly insects and would capture an unsuspecting fly or ant with a sudden quick movement and a darting tongue. But Rastus's "pet" lizard could lazily accept the offer of newly killed flies on the porch with no effort at all.

At the back door of the main house we would usually find a number of cats; they would quickly gather underfoot whenever anyone entered or left the house. They were always hoping food would be put out for them, and they would meow loudly and rub against the legs of the people at the door. I was responsible for the cat population. I had a dignified old white cat named Snowball that MO allowed to enter the house. The other cats were not permitted entry. They were the product of a couple of cats brought to the ranch to live in the barn and catch mice. In time, the two produced a litter of kittens. They matured, and still more kittens were born. I would gather up the kittens and play with them and feed them near the back door. They learned quickly where to stay to be fed. DA complained aloud every time he stepped out the back door into a litter of meowing cats. Eventually, DA grew so annoyed about all the cats that he decided to get rid of them somehow. He did not want to tell me because I wanted to keep all of them. Claude suggested that they gather all of them in a gunnysack and drown them. DA didn't have the heart to do that, but he did gather up as many cats as he could find and take them around to the different tanks and windmills around the ranch. He left one or two cats at High Lonesome, at Three Mills, at Antelope, at New Well, at Robbs' Well, and at Cottonwood.

Later on, I said I hadn't seen my cats for a while. DA offered no information. In time, when I went with DA to check on the water at Robbs' Well, I spotted two of my cats there. They came to me, mewing and rubbing against my legs. "Jerry and Pug, what are you doing at Robbs' Well? DA, DA, look at this! Here are Jerry and Pug. How did they get here?" "Well, I'm not sure." "Yes you are, DA. Did you bring them here? Answer me!" Finally, DA confessed he had taken the cats to different places on the ranch because there were too many at the headquarters. When it was time to return home, I picked up the two cats and brought them back to the house. "We can't leave them at Robbs' Well, DA. They will starve. Look how thin they are." And so it was that the cat population began to increase again.

There were always a couple of dogs at the ranch. MO did not want the dogs in her house. She said it was hard enough to keep it clean without letting the dogs in. When Ann was about six years old, someone in Duncan gave her a small white female dog with short hair and a tail that curled. It looked like it had some terrier blood, and the curly tail resembled that of a chow. Whatever the mix, the little dog was smart, and Ann adored her. She named the dog Susie, and Ann begged MO to let Susie come in the house. Susie learned to sit and beg for treats, and to smile on demand. When told to smile, Susie would bare her teeth and pull the corners of her mouth back into a fine imitation of a smile, all the while wagging her curly tail. Even MO couldn't resist Susie's charm. In time Susie was allowed to come in the house, and she became a favorite family pet.

The first pet at the ranch after DA arrived to manage it was a bobcat. DA found the bobcat as a baby when DA was on a roundup near Rock Tank. The little bobcat was wandering around and mewing as though in distress. DA could find no sign of the mother. He picked up the little bobcat, put it in his jacket pocket, and brought it home. DA raised the little bobcat on cow's milk and meat, and it stayed at the ranch. Everyone called the bobcat Bob, and he behaved like a very large house cat. He would purr when contented. He enjoyed being patted and would rub against DA's legs and meow softly.

The only time Bob acted vicious was when a beef was butchered. When that happened, Bob sensed it and would arch his back and growl. When MO came to the ranch, Bob was the resident house pet. He was still there when I was born, and I treated him like an ordinary house cat once I was old enough to walk and talk. When I was about four years old, Bob disappeared. Soon after, MO and DA found a chicken had been killed and eaten in the chicken coop. It happened again every couple of nights. DA suspected it was Bob. He waited up one night and, sure enough, Bob crept into the chicken coop to make off with another chicken. DA called to Bob and rubbed him, talked to him, and brought him back to the house. Bob stayed for several more months and then disappeared for good. We like to think he found a female bobcat and lived happily ever after.

Jim Brister had a pet deer named Soupy. She was a black-tailed deer and full grown when we first saw her. Someone had given her to Jim, and he allowed her to roam around his house at Willow Springs. She was very gentle, and whenever anyone would go to Jim's house she would always come up and rub on them and beg to be petted. Occasionally she would leave Willow and wander to the headquarters of the ranch, ten miles away. Everyone was always happy to see her at the ranch because she was so friendly. MO, however, was not happy to see her because she ate all of the rosebushes. They must have been Soupy's favorite thing, and no rosebush was safe from her. After MO had raised a ruckus with everyone about her rosebushes, we would lock Soupy in the barn, knowing that Jim would miss her and come to look for her soon.

Two of the funniest and nicest pets we ever had were two baby javelinas that Cole Webb and Alan found one day with no mother. They brought these two wild pigs home and taught them to drink milk from a cup. The two little javelinas became very gentle and would jump up in your lap to be petted. They would follow Cole wherever he went. Somehow they knew which room of the house Cole was in and would always be just outside that room. The cowboys named them Sandra and Ann. The running joke around the ranch involved which one of the pigs was the nice one and which one was the ornery one. The pigs finally started leaving for a day or two at a time and then would return for a few days. Soon the times they were gone were longer than the times they would stay at the ranch, and finally they didn't come back to the ranch at all. For quite a while after they left, when Alan would see a herd of javelinas, he would wonder if Sandra and Ann were part of that group.

When Alan was twelve years old, a friend gave him a young raccoon. He named this pet Cooney. A raccoon is very smart and curious, and as this raccoon grew up, he got into everything. Nothing was safe in your pocket, because he would jump in your lap, reach into both front pockets, pull everything out to examine it, and of course put nothing back. One day DA had a pocket full of kitchen matches for the cigarettes he always smoked. Reaching into his pocket, Cooney managed to strike one of the matches. DA did quite a dance trying to get the burning matches out of his pocket and was not too happy with Cooney for his mischief. If you ever punished Cooney for something he did, he would pout and would not forget the punishment. Later, when your back was turned, he would run up and bite you to pay you back, then run and hide so as not to be punished again.

When we took our vacation to Alaska in the summer of 1950, one of the cowboys got so angry with the raccoon that he killed him. When we got home, we looked for Cooney, and he was nowhere to be found. We asked the cowboys where he was, and they said he must have gone wild, because he d just disappeared. Years later, a cowboy by the name of Vernon Perry, who had worked at the Lazy B for a short time, committed suicide. After his death, one of the other cowboys told the family that it was Vernon who had killed the coon. Not all ranch stories have a happy ending.

In the 1960s, one of the best pets we ever had at the ranch was a young sparrow hawk that Alan named Sylvester. Alan found him on the ground when he was too young to fly and could not find the nest. Alan brought the bird into the house and raised him. The bird had a funny and lively personality. He was not afraid of anything and would scold you if he disapproved of something you did, but he would praise you loudly if he approved. He had beautiful brown, gold, and blue feathers around his neck and chest and was hardly bigger than a sparrow. He learned to fly in the living room of the house, and until he became proficient would frequently crash into the sofa or onto the floor. Sylvester was never afraid to try, and he loved soaring once he had learned how. The Day children soon would take the bird outside, and he would soar high in the sky and talk to them from above. Sylvester could really convey his joy in flying.

When Alan or his wife, Barbara, would call the bird, he would come dive-bombing down from the sky and land on the top of a head or a shoulder. He would take small chunks of meat from your fingers and eat then with much relish. Alan made a perch for him on the front porch. He would be there sometimes, but most times he would be flying in the distance or perched on one of the windmills at the headquarters. It was fun to walk out on the porch with a little bit of meat and call Sylvester. He would come screeching down to get his snack and thank you for it and fly off again. He was never house-trained, so often the children would have hawk droppings on their hair or down the back of their shirts. They always thought it was a small price to pay for such a beautiful and lively pet.

Sylvester was around the ranch for many months, but he finally started going farther afield and one day never returned. We could only hope that Sylvester found a mate as beautiful and lively as he.

There was a succession of other pets that became part of the household from time to time. A desert tortoise stayed in the walled front yard for some time. It nibbled on the grass there and would eat lettuce, cabbage, and carrots. The tortoise was quite a special creature. It was about seven inches long, and its shell looked well-worn. Desert tortoises live to be forty or fifty years old, and we were never sure how old the tortoise was or whether it was a male or female. When we brought it in the house, it learned where the refrigerator was and would walk to it and wait patiently there for something to eat.

We tried keeping a baby coyote as a pet but learned that what the cowboys said was true: you cannot make a pet of a coyote. We enjoyed catching little horned toads and holding them. They were the color of dirt and hard to see. They were rather gentle and seemed to enjoy being softly stroked on their bellies. We kept a baby goat or two at different times. They were affectionate and would follow us around. The problem with the goats was that as they grew, they would eat MO's plants and flowers. They could jump over the wall easily, and we could not keep them out of the yard. MO said the goats had to go, and that was that.

Top: *Sandra and Chico.*
Bottom: *Lazy B horses.*
Opposite: *Some more Lazy B horses.*

20. *The Horses*

----

*A good rider on a good horse is as much above
himself and others as the world can make him.*

WALTER PRESCOTT WEBB
QUOTING LORD HERBERT
IN *The Great Plains*

WHEN WE WERE CHILDREN WE ALWAYS HAD SOME GOOD AND gentle horses to ride. I had a fine bay horse named Flaxy, a big white horse named Swastika, and, best of all, a little brown horse named Chico. A local man named Dick Johnson had captured Chico out of a herd of wild horses. Dick traded Chico to DA, and he was trained at the Lazy B. He never grew very big, so he was easy for children to mount and dismount. Chico enjoyed children and never bucked, jumped, ran off, or got cranky. We could ride double or triple and it was all right with Chico—bareback or with a saddle. We could get on and off on either side. If one of us fell off, Chico would stop, freeze, and not even put his hoof down until we were back on top. He would move at the pace he thought we could handle. With very small children, he would never get out of a walk. With bigger children, he would trot. With a rider big enough to know how to ride, you could do anything on Chico. He was a good cow horse and could work cattle with the best of them.

I learned to ride on Chico, and later Ann and Alan did also. Years later our own children, the grandchildren, learned to ride on him.

When Chico was about twenty-five years old he "retired." He was still in good health, and he stayed in the horse pasture. For a time, we had a pet deer at the ranch, and the deer liked to follow Chico around. They were together several years. Then our old boxer dog began to follow Chico out into the pasture. If Chico stayed out a couple of days, so did the dog. When they finally came into the headquarters, the poor dog would be so thirsty he would drink at the water trough until we thought he would be sick. But when Chico went back out to the pasture, the dog went too. Finally, the dog came in one day without Chico. We suspected then Chico had died. We saddled up and rode out into the pasture until we found his carcass. It was a sad time at the Lazy B for all of us. Chico had been an important part of all our lives.

As children, Flournoy and I would go off on Flaxy and Chico or Swastika and play imaginary games. Sometimes we were Indian girls on a hunt. Sometimes we were women ranchers doing daring deeds. We would go at a full gallop, jumping ditches, dodging cacti, and just having fun. Ann and Alan did the same when they were small, riding Chico and another little horse named Brownie. Off and away. Hair flying. The wind in our faces. A full gallop most of the time.

Alan always felt a rush of excitement and adrenaline when his horse bucked a few times but he stayed on. Ann and I, however, preferred gentle horses. We never asked to ride the broncs. Even the gentle horses would occasionally jump a few times just to prove they were not to be ignored, but then they would settle down for the day.

Ranches are sometimes defined by their horses. For example, the King Ranch in south Texas is renowned for its fine cutting horses. The old Boyce Ranch in Arizona was renowned for its bucking horses. If a cowboy didn't have a pretty deep seat and couldn't ride a bucking horse, he'd better not go to the Chiricahua, or the "Cherries," as the Boyce Ranch was known.

The Lazy B was locally known for its tough but ugly Hancock horses. Shortly after DA took over the management of the Lazy B in 1927, he gathered some six hundred horses and drove them over the mountains to the railway station at Bowie, Arizona. He sold them for a penny a pound. This reduced the horse herd to thirty or forty mares plus the horses the ranch crew rode. Then DA acquired a good Arabian stallion and put him out with the range mares. The Arabian blood produced some good colts.

About 1950 Jim Brister brought in a big blue roan Hancock stallion. The first of the Western quarter horses was a horse named Red Man, and the Hancock line of quarter horses stemmed from Red Man. They were tough horses, long-lived, with a lot of stamina and heart. Most of them worked cattle well and had what we called "cow sense." But the Hancocks looked rough and had large heads. In a few years the Arabian-Hancock genes at the Lazy B produced a number of buckskin, or dun, colts—light colored with a dark mane and tail and a dark streak down the back. They were quite good looking horses.

Next we got a blue roan stallion, a quarter horse, named Smokey. Then we began to produce strawberry roans, blue roans, and a dun roan called grulla. These horses were excellent cow horses, and they had some personality.

In the early years, when a horse was given a name there was no concern about being politically correct. The horse's color, actions, or temperament usually produced a name. A cowboy knew if he got on a horse named Runaway or Wreck he had better stay alert.

When Alan was an adult he rode a bay mare for a time that was not too big, but she was one of the toughest animals around. You could ride her all day long, and she would be as fresh or as fresh acting at the end of the day as she was at the start. This was both good and bad. She was so fresh that when you got on her, if you made any kind of a sudden move, she'd jump about twenty feet. If you weren't sitting properly on her, she'd jump right out from under you. She'd run off, too, if you started to swing on and your toe happened to touch her belly; or if your leg swung over her hip and your boot or chaps happened to touch her hip, she'd jump and run. As a consequence, we named her Idiot. But if you overlooked the silliness, what you had was a really tough good cow horse.

She loved to work cattle. She would go all day as fast as you needed to go. We always said, "When you were on Idiot you had lots of horse under you." You just couldn't wear her down.

When we were first trying to break her, one of our young cowboys rode her. It turned out he wasn't too much of a horse breaker, and she bluffed him. He rode her a few times, but all day long he'd ride along just watching her and waiting for her to jump. He was afraid to do much on her because he was apprehensive that if he really pushed her to do something she'd probably just keep on going and he wouldn't be able to stop her.

Two or three other young cowboys also tried their hand with Idiot. One of them, on a cool morning, dismounted to tie his jacket on the back of the saddle. He got one side tied on, walked around Idiot to tie the other side, and something spooked her. She jumped. The right side wasn't tied, so the coat flopped over on the left side. That really scared her. She proceeded to jerk loose and run off, right through the herd of cattle. Around the pasture she went and back around again with two cowboys chasing her. It took them about two and a half hours to catch Idiot as she ran, looking back wild-eyed at the flapping coat.

When Idiot was about four and a half years old, Alan decided that she was rather dangerous and might hurt someone. He began to ride her because he thought he could ride her without alarming her. It turned out that she and Alan were simpatico. He appreciated all her energy. She was unpredictable, but when he would sit up and act like a cowboy on her, he could do anything. He could cut cattle. He could drag calves to the branding fire. But when he was roping, he could never let a calf run behind him and get the rope behind her. If the rope ever went around behind her hips, she would go crazy. Alan was very careful how he handled the livestock when he had them tied onto a rope with Idiot. She was quite a mare.

Alan rode Idiot until she was old and ready to be retired. The only real problem he ever encountered with her happened on a day the wind was blowing hard. He hadn't trimmed her tail for a while, and it was quite long. Alan went out on the roundup to the back of the pasture, facing the wind. As the roundup crew split up and turned back to gather the cattle in the pasture, the wind was behind them. Idiot started jumping, bucking, and trying to run off. Alan got her head up, but she again spun around, jumped, and lunged. This happened several times, and Alan couldn't figure out what was wrong with her. Finally, Alan decided to get off, which was hard because every time he would start to swing off, she'd jump again. He would end up back in the saddle trying to stop her. He'd get her calmed down and start to swing off and she'd jump again. Eventually, Alan succeeded in dismounting.

Alan rubbed the back of his neck and talked to the horse. "What a true idiot you are, girl. It's just the wind. You've been in wind like this before." But as he stood back and watched her pawing the ground and snorting, her flanks damp with sweat from bucking, he realized who was the idiot. The wind was blowing her tail up between her back legs, and that was absolutely scaring her to death. So he took out his pocketknife and cut her tail off right below the bone. Idiot peered around. The offending tail lay at Alan's feet. It seemed as if she smiled at Alan. He left the discarded tail in the dust. Idiot and Alan never had another problem.

We had another bay horse called Cheyenne. He was mean. Idiot was never mean—she was just a little goosey and a little goofy—but Cheyenne was just plain mean. He would watch for his opportunity, and if he caught you leaning the wrong way and out of balance, he would buck you off. When he'd buck you off, if he had a chance, he'd kick you while you were in the air. He had several of the cowboys so intimidated that they refused to ride him.

Alan started riding Cheyenne. One day they were rounding up out of the Lordsburg Flat. A highway ran right through the middle of the flat, but they were several miles away from the highway, gathering cattle. The highway department was resurfacing the highway. On a part of the ranch several miles away, the highway crew had a hot batch plant that made the hot mix to resurface the highway. The cowboys were out well before dawn and by seven o'clock were gathering the cattle. As they crested a hill, the hot batch plant started operations. When they fired it up, a big puff of black smoke went up; no sound at all, but about three miles away, there was the gust of black smoke.

Alan was on Cheyenne. It was the kind of early morning air that makes your face tingle and your energy level increase. Cheyenne was prancing, with streams of air coming from his nose making dragonlike puffs in the air. He saw the billow of black smoke. His back quivered. Before Alan could react, Cheyenne put his head down and began to buck.

Alan stayed on, but his gloves were slick. With every jump his glove on the bridle reins would slide down a little bit farther. His hand kept getting higher and higher. Finally, his hand got to the end, and the reins slid right out of his hand. Alan leaned back to try to stay on. "Oh God," he thought, "this is what the other cowboys experienced with Cheyenne." With that, Alan went right off over the horse's hips and on the ground. One of the other cowboys had to go get the horse. Alan used his hat to dust his jeans off and help cover his embarrassment. "Darned if that wasn't pretty faint provocation for making that stupid horse buck," Alan muttered. "A puff of smoke about three miles away and he loses his head."

We had some unusual names for some of our horses. A lot of ranches would only ride neutered male horses (geldings), but we rode mares as well. When we started doing that, we would have the ones we chose to ride neutered. Otherwise, when the mare comes into heat, all the geldings will crowd around, fight, and get injured. One of the best of our mares was a brown mare. We called her Hysterectomy. She was a great horse. She would carry a cowboy all day and was a fine cow horse. Another fine mare was Scarhead, named for the big scar down her face.

We had a beautiful big white mare that was quite a problem to break. She was so difficult, the cowboys named her Hell Bitch. However, as soon as she was broken, she became one of the gentlest and best horses we ever had, and was one of the favorites on the ranch. We had another big brown horse with a gait that was quite rough. After riding him all day, you felt tired and bruised. We named him Hemorrhoid, an appropriate name for the circumstance.

Jim Brister always had more horses than anyone else on the ranch did. He rode some of his own private horses, but also had a string of Lazy B horses. Jim had two favorite names for his horses: Buck and Baldy. Any buckskin Jim had was called Buck. Jim had Little Buck and Big Buck and

Dun Buck. If the horse had any colored streaks down its face, as many horses do, Jim called the horse Baldy. Jim had several Baldy horses. We were never sure when Jim talked about his horses which Baldy or which Buck he was talking about.

One of Jim's favorites was his big sorrel Jeep. Jeep was the biggest, most powerful cow horse on the ranch. He was as big as some drafthorses were, but he was extremely quick, and for a big horse to be that quick was unusual. Usually when horses get bigger their actions are a little slower, but Jeep could turn on a dime and jump and run. He was an amazing horse. Jim could cut cows on Jeep that nobody else could have cut out of the herd. Jeep would jump over and turn the cow on a dime, then jump the other way when she turned back. He could do things that we never saw another horse do.

Alan started to break a good-looking gray mare one time. She was a beautiful mare, well formed and very intelligent. Alan was most anxious to get this mare into his string of horses, so he took special pains with her. She was a difficult mare to break, a typical Hancock. Alan called this pretty mare Candy.

In Arizona, the weather can range from darned hot to darned cold to darned windy. Some days it's just darned nice. That was the kind of day it was when one of our old cowboys, Claude, came up to Alan. He leaned against the corral fence, grinned at Alan, exposing his toothless gums, and said, "What did you name that mare?"

"Candy, 'cause she's such a sweet thing," said Alan as he glanced back at the mare. She was galloping out to the pasture to join the other horses, her tail waving silver streaks in the air as the sun shone on it. Claude pulled his sweat-stained hat lower over his head. "Well, that's a death sentence for her sure as the BLM has crazy ideas."

"What do you mean?"

"A horse can't carry a fancy name like that and you at the same time! And by you naming her that, bad luck will fall on her and she will die."

Alan took off his hat and rubbed his head. Claude has earned Alan's respect over the years for his common sense. But this idea of his about Candy's name sounded crazy. "Good Lord, Claude, I never heard that. What would you have me call her?"

"Oh," he said, "you need just a common name. You oughta call her Squaw Piss, and then she'd stay alive." He tugged at a cactus prick that had wedged itself into the leg of his jeans. Alan just laughed and shrugged it off.

Not a month later, Candy was still behaving like a bronc. She and Alan were still trying to decide who was boss. She started to try to buck and he pulled her up and started down the draw. She tried again to buck. He got her stopped. Then she put her head clear down and bucked again. "I should change your name to Stubborn Bitch," Alan yelled angrily at her.

By the time Alan and Candy were about a mile down below the ranch, Alan was sweating from the effort of trying to control her. Candy's coat glistened and dripped sweat. Her sides were heaving. They were both mad. Alan decided they needed to cool off. There was a big natural water hole in the draw not far off. It had been raining, and the water hole was full. It was about a hundred yards long and forty yards wide and quite deep. When Alan got to the water hole, he thought, "The best thing I can think of is to jump her off in there and make her swim. Maybe it will cool her off a little, and maybe it will cool me off a little too. It might just get her over this spasm that she's having." Alan got her right to the edge of the water, but she didn't want to go in. He tried several times to urge her. She just didn't want to go. Finally, Alan popped her with his rope right between the legs. She jumped out about twenty feet into the water, but to Alan's horror he discovered that Candy couldn't swim a lick.

"Swim, Candy," Alan shouted, pulling on the reins. She couldn't do it. Her eyes went white and wild. Alan had never heard of a horse that couldn't swim. If they are thrust into water, they can all swim, but Candy couldn't. Alan was there in the pond with his full cowboy regalia: chaps, spurs, and boots. Alan's eyes held some of the same terror as Candy's. He tried to stay afloat and tried to keep Candy afloat. She would go down and then come back up. She pawed with her front legs and pawed Alan with her hoofs repeatedly as she tried to get out. Alan was forced to turn loose of Candy to save his own life. He swam to the edge and got out. "Oh no, Candy," he whispered, as she went down and never came back up.

As Alan walked home, the water dripped from his clothes, leaving a trail that disappeared in a hot vapor. There was a little rowboat at the ranch headquarters. Alan loaded it onto the truck and returned to the water hole. The surface of the water carried a brown bulge. Candy had floated to the surface. Alan pulled her over to the edge. He managed to remove the saddle. To this day we have not seen another horse that could not swim. But Claude's prediction about the mare's name was prophetic. Alan hated to lose Candy. He felt sad and foolish about jumping her in the water hole. Whenever we rode past the water hole we would remember that terrible morning. Maybe Claude's theory about her name was right. In any event, we were more careful about naming our horses after that.

Alan had another big white horse, which he called Saber. Saber was raised at the Lazy B, but he didn't look like most of our other horses. He was bigger, and very athletic. He was easy to break and always seemed to just want to do things right. Saber had a wonderful sense about him, and a willingness to do what you wanted him to do. He had a fast walking gait and could cover the country quickly. Other horses would have to be in a full trot or even a slow gallop to keep up with Saber's walk. His gait was almost like that of a Tennessee walking horse, and he was a pure pleasure to ride.

Saber was not only the strongest but also the fastest horse Alan ever rode. One day he and the Lazy B cowboys were gathering cattle near High Lonesome and had just unloaded the horse trailer near the shipping pens at Summit. They had fanned out and were gathering and driving cattle toward High Lonesome when a coyote jumped up and ran in front of Alan. He did something that he had always disliked his cowboys to do: he took down his rope, left the cows he was driving, and started chasing the coyote in an attempt to rope him. DA had always said that cowboys use their ropes too much and that a good cowboy should not always be trying to rope something. Alan agreed in principle, but once in a while the temptation is too strong, the brain goes into neutral, and the rope jumps into the hand.

This was one of those occasions: that coyote looked to Alan like he had a sign on his side that said "Rope me."

Saber was quite young, but he was fully broken. When Alan turned him to chase the coyote, Saber was only too willing to play this game. The adrenaline began to surge in both of them, and the horse was running so fast that he caught the coyote quickly. Alan had his rope ready, and as they drew close, he started to swing it around his head in the way cowboys do before they throw the loop at their target. As they got close to the coyote, he leaned forward to be more ready to throw the loop. At that exact moment Saber stepped in a hole and fell down with a big crash. Alan was propelled over his head and almost landed on the coyote. It's hard to say who was most surprised of the three of them. The coyote kept running, and Alan lay there trying to catch his breath and see if he had any broken bones. Saber was surprised and frightened and immediately jumped up and ran off. He was very gentle and normally would not run off if the rider got off in the middle of a pasture, but this event frightened him, and he ran all the way across the pasture.

Alan got up and coiled his rope and had to walk after the horse for about two miles. He was only angry with himself over this incident, because he knew he shouldn't have started the chase in the first place. Saber was waiting for Alan in the far corner of the pasture, and when Alan got on, he had to backtrack and catch up with the rest of the cowboys.

The next time he chased a wild animal on Saber, it had quite a different ending. A friend called Alan one night during deer season and asked if he could come deer hunting on the ranch two days later. Alan agreed, and before hanging up, his friend said, "If you see one before I get there, kill him for me and hang him in a tree. That will save me a lot of work when I arrive."

Alan almost never carried a gun while riding. It would just get in the way. Moreover, hunting and gathering cattle usually don't mix. The next day, however, Alan carried his .30-30 rifle as he and the cowboys went to gather cattle. Riding Saber, he was scouting for cattle on a rocky creosote-covered mesa when he heard a noise and a running sound to his right. He wheeled around and saw a huge buck deer crashing through the creosotes. He gave chase, and Saber quickly caught up with the deer. Alan got his gun out and prepared to shoot at the buck without dismounting. When he got close enough he stopped Saber and attempted to aim, but the horse was panting, and Alan couldn't hold the gun still enough to shoot. In disgust, he spurred Saber to catch the deer again. Saber ran about another half mile and caught the buck again. This time Alan stopped the horse and jumped off and shot a couple of times at the buck. He missed both times and was thoroughly disgusted with himself.

The luxury of having such a strong horse is that no matter where you want to go, you know you still have enough horse under you. With all the other horses on the ranch, if they had gone this far they would've been completely exhausted. Alan mounted again and, with a guilty conscience, asked Saber to catch the deer one more time. The horse was willing, even though he was panting hard and sweating a lot. By this time the deer was running parallel to a deep sand wash, and when they caught him, he turned left and jumped off a bank about eight feet high into the wash. When the deer landed, he fell down, and when Alan jumped off to look over the edge, he was still struggling to get up and run some more. Alan was so close to the deer when he shot him that he felt more like an executioner than a hunter. He and Saber dragged him out of the wash and hung him up in a tree.

After he had finished the day's work of cowboying, Alan went back with a pickup to haul the buck home. The animal was so big that when Alan slid him in the eight-foot bed of the pickup, he had to fold his head back to close the tailgate. Alan was—and still is—amazed at Saber's ability not only to catch the deer but to do it two more times. He said that being on Saber was like driving a Ferrari after driving an old jeep.

When Saber got near a bunch of cattle, he would get intense. He wanted to work them. He knew what you wanted him to do before you knew you wanted him to do it. One time, when he was in his prime, we were working cattle down below the corral in the lower dry lot. Alan finished lunch early and went to the barn, saddled up, and went back out to the herd. He was the first one out there. The other cowboys were slowly going to the barn to saddle up after lunch. Alan picked a big half-Brahma cow that looked pretty athletic and decided to turn Saber loose on her. Alan had always held him back a little and had never really let him loose on a cow to run her and turn her back because he was so powerful and so fast. Alan always wanted to throttle him back a little. This time, just for fun, Alan turned the old cow up the fence. Then he gave Saber the signal to run past her and turn her back along the fence. He let the reins go slack and thought, "Well, let's see what happens here."

The cow made a run up the fence. She was a big, long-legged cow in good shape. She was really running. Saber ran past her and just ducked in front of her. She turned back, and he turned back with her. He turned back so fast that he got clear down on his side with the turn, churning dust in the air. He was like a water-skier leaning way over to make a sharp turn. The ground was pretty soft, and Saber's hooves slid clear out from under him. The cow turned back. Saber was faced back by this time the way the cow was, but with all four of his feet out from under him. Alan was still sitting in the saddle with one leg underneath as they slowly slid under the fence. All four of Saber's legs ended up under the barbed-wire fence. Alan was still sitting in the saddle with one leg underneath the horse.

Saber lay there for a moment, and Alan could see his mind work. He looked at Alan as if to say, "Well, cowboy, what do I do now?" Alan saw that they were pretty much in a wreck. If the horse started struggling he would get tangled up in the barbed-wire fence and probably get hurt seriously. So Alan started talking to him. Rubbing him on the neck, Alan murmured softly, "Saber, you did a good job. You did just what I asked you to do." Saber raised his head slightly, as if taking in what Alan was saying. "It isn't your fault that your feet went out from under you. Everything's all right. Lay real still." And Saber didn't move. The sound of Alan's voice soothed him. He knew not to move. He lay right there.

It seemed at least an hour, but in reality it was only a few minutes before one of the cowboys came along. When he saw what had happened, he rode up and pitched his saddle rope down. Alan put the rope on his saddle horn. Then the cowboy pulled Alan and Saber out from under the fence. "Sorry I missed the action, boss," the cowboy said with a grin. "Must have been quite a wind that came up and blew you two under that fence."

Saber and Alan became quite close. But maybe Saber's name, like Candy's name, was too heroic for the horse. He was doomed. Traveling to headquarters on the ranch road at dusk can be tiring, not only because of the distance from the main road, eight long, dusty miles, but also because of the irritant of the sun being right in the driver's eyes. MO was returning home from town at twilight one evening. Saber stepped out in front of her car. She couldn't see him because of the sun in her eyes. There was a terrible thud and a high shriek. His leg was broken. MO drove on to the ranch and told Alan and DA what had happened. They drove back to the injured horse. The horse whinnied in pain. Alan stroked Saber's head and said, tears in his eyes, "Good-bye, old friend." Then Alan used his .22 Hornet to put a bullet in Saber's brain. Even in death, Saber seemed to understand.

Top: *Saddling up at the barn.*
Bottom: *A Lazy B windmill.*
Opposite: *Sandra on Flaxy.*

21. *Just Another Day*

When most all the other girls her age
Were learning how to dance,
She was out there with her dad,
Just helping out on the ranch.

BOB E. LEWIS,
"THE COWGIRL AND
HER HORSE"

I WAS LYING ON THE HALL COUCH READING A BOOK. IT WAS A Nancy Drew mystery, and I was totally absorbed in the story. DA came in and said, "Sandra you'd better get your nose out of that book and come with me. I want to show you something." "Oh, DA, can't it wait? I am at a very exciting part. Let's go later." "No. Now. Come on." "Please!" "No. Right now." "Well, okay. Let's not be gone too long."

DA drove the Chevy pickup out of the area around the headquarters and into the East Pasture. After a few miles on the dirt road, he left the road and drove across country. A few vultures circled overhead. He slowed down and said, "Here we are." In front of the pickup lay a small calf, no more than a few days old. Its rear end and haunch were mostly gone, leaving a bloody, grisly mess. The calf was still alive, breathing and trying to bawl for its mother. The vultures overhead had been feeding on the calf and had flown up when the pickup approached.

"What happened, DA? What can we do?"

"The calf was attacked by a coyote—probably when its mother left to get water. The coyote started eating the calf in its hindquarters." "Let's help it." "We can't help this calf. It's too late. It will die soon. The best thing we can do is put it out of its misery."

"Oh, don't shoot it, DA. We can do something. Let's take it back to the ranch."

DA shook his head and took out his rifle, which was in the holder behind the pickup seat. He aimed between the calf's eyes and fired. The calf's head jerked and it was still.

"DA, how could you?"

"It was the only kind thing we could do. The calf was too far gone to live. Now we have to send Rastus out to find the mother cow."

In the late afternoon, when Rastus returned from his day's ride, DA told him about the calf and suggested that Rastus might want to find the calf's mother and bring her in to see if she would let one of the dogie calves in the corral suckle her. Rastus agreed to go out for the cow the next day.

Normally a cow will not allow another calf to suckle. She knows her own calf, largely by smell, and will not "adopt" a strange calf. But sometimes, with frequent exposure in a corral, a cow who has lost her calf will allow another calf to suckle.

It was a dry summer, and there were six or seven dogie calves in the corral that we were trying to raise. When they are very young, that requires rigging up a bottle and a rubber nipple and feeding the calves with milk from the milk cow. If we allowed the dogie calves to suckle the milk cow, we would have no milk left for our own use.

Rastus rode out to the pasture the next day and found the calf's carcass. He used his pocketknife to remove most of the hide of the dead calf. The mother cow was not far off. She was bawling for her calf, and her udder had already started to swell with the unused milk. He drove the cow back to the headquarters and into the corral.

Once in the corral, Rastus selected the youngest dogie calf and tied the dead calf's hide over the dogie calf's back. He then put the cow and the dogie calf together in a small holding pen. The calf bawled and tried to suckle the cow. The cow kicked the calf away, but then sniffed at it suspiciously. After an hour or so, the cow decided the calf could suckle. She was apparently reassured by the smell of her own calf's hide. Rastus was pleased to report what had happened to DA, and I walked down to the small corral to see how the adoption was progressing. The dogie was able to suckle for a few minutes, and it appeared he might have found a new mother.

I spotted Chico coming into the headquarters for some water. After he'd had his fill, I got his bridle out of the barn and slipped it over his head and got the bit in his mouth. Chico switched his tail back and forth to get rid of some flies and shook his head to clear the flies from his eyes, then stood by the barn while I got my saddle and the saddle blanket. I rubbed Chico's back and brushed off a few cockleburs. "You want to go out, Chico? Let's go back in the horse pasture, okay?"

I put the saddle blanket on his back, then the saddle, and tightened the cinch. "See you later, DA." "All right. Keep your eyes open."

It felt good to sit on the horse and to be so high off the ground. Chico felt warm and strong. Indeed, no other relationship between humans and animals is as close as when one is riding a horse. We moved together. I felt the horse's every move. I was aware of his breath, his sweat. When he stopped to pee, the strong smell of urine enveloped us, and drops of liquid splattered my boots. When he expelled gas, I heard and felt it. I often talked to my horse while riding.

I rode north that day along the trail leading from the ranch building out to the horse pasture. The trail led up a steep bluff. From the top of the bluff I could see all the ranch buildings, the corrals, and the windmills. It was late afternoon and there was only a hint of wind and the mills turned slowly into the wind. I could see Rastus limping up to the bunkhouse from the corrals. I gave Chico a little kick to get him moving out into the horse pasture. His hooves made a crunchy sound in the rocky soil. A red-tailed hawk circled overhead, riding the updrafts of air with its outstretched wings. It could stay up and circle for long intervals without flapping its wings. How wonderful it would be to be able to float above the ground like that!

There was a sudden rustling and quick movement from the greasewood bush to my right. It startled me for a moment, until I realized it was only a big jackrabbit that had been disturbed by my presence nearby. The rabbit loped off about twenty-five yards and stopped, listening with its enormous ears to decide if it was safe to stay.

After a couple of miles Chico perked up his ears and held his head high. He sensed the presence of some other horses. Sure enough, down in a grassy draw there were four other horses grazing. They stopped and held their heads up and neighed a little to let Chico know they had seen him. We moved closer to the other horses, and they moved off in hopes of being able to stay out in the pasture. They didn't want to have to go to the corrals.

"Well, Chico, let's leave your pals alone and head back." I turned Chico's head back toward the ranch, and no kick was needed to encourage him to move quickly this time. Once we started to the barn, no urging was necessary.

We neared the draw and went into an area next to a rocky hill. The trail led around the hill and into another narrower draw. As we went around the hill I heard the dry hissing sound of a rattlesnake's rattles. Almost simultaneously Chico jumped to the side and I almost fell off. My heart pounded and I felt terrified. Where Chico had been on the rocky trail was a diamondback rattler coiled and ready to strike. Its tail was raised, and the rattles continued to sound their warning. I urged Chico off to the side of the hill and away from the snake. Rattlesnakes were often seen on the Lazy B, and I never stopped being frightened by their presence. Occasionally a horse would be bitten in the nose, or a dog would be bitten. The results were serious and sometimes fatal. The rattlers were not aggressive: if you stayed out of their way, they did not pursue. But it was not always easy to see the snake until you were practically on top of it. I felt lucky this time, but my heart didn't stop pounding until we were back at the headquarters.

When we got back, I dismounted and opened the gate for the corral next to the barn to let Chico in. He stood patiently by the barn door until I loosened the cinch and removed the saddle and blanket, then the bridle. I put the saddle on a sawhorse in the dark barn and hung the bridle on its hook along the wall. The barn had no windows. There were rows of sawhorses with various saddles on them, with the blankets on top. There were hooks all along the walls for bridles and lariat ropes. I went in the adjacent area of the barn, where the hay was stacked, and got a wedge of hay to give Chico as a reward. He ate contentedly, then got water from the trough. I went up to the house.

DA was sitting at his desk in his office, pecking at the typewriter to produce a letter. "Hi, DA. I'm back. How about some gin rummy?" "I have a few letters to get out and some checks to write, but then I'll join you. Are you ready to lose?" "Not a chance. I'm feeling lucky today."

I returned to the hall couch and my book. DA tapped and pecked at his typewriter. MO worked in the kitchen on some supper, which she planned to serve about 6:30. Finally DA got up from his desk and said, "Deal the cards. Let's see if you can play this game."

I ran into the living room and took out a deck of cards and a pad of paper and pencil. The card table was up and ready, as it often was. I shuffled the cards and DA said, "Cut for deal." Under our "house rules" for gin rummy, the low card gave the deal to the person turning it up. I won the deal and dealt out ten cards to each of us. DA picked each card up as it was dealt and arranged his hand according to potential matches for groups or runs. I turned the next card faceup beside the stack of remaining cards. It was a three. DA played cards the way he carried out his business—with caution. He couldn't resist taking the low card and discarding a high-counting face card. As in life generally, DA's children were inclined to take more risks than he. I picked up the discarded face card and completed a group of three of a kind, then discarded. DA refused my discard and drew the next card. He bent up the front edge to see what it was rather than just taking the whole card from the deck. Again, a cautious approach. "Hah!" he said, and took the card into his hand. This went on a few more times, and then DA said, "What is the name of this game?" "Oh dear, DA. You didn't 'gin,' did you?" "That's right," said DA. "Give up now?"

MO came in from the kitchen to kibitz. "Who's winning?" she asked. "Now, who do you think?" said DA. "Just you wait, DA. I've got you now," I said. "Well, dinner is ready," said MO. "Why don't you finish later?"

"We'll be along pretty soon," said DA. "I'll polish Sandra off in just a few minutes here."

This scene was played out many times at the ranch. Alan and Ann learned to play card games when they were eight or nine, and we would play hearts, canasta, bridge, and gin rummy whenever we could get DA or MO to sit down for a while. DA liked to win and would rub it in when he did. We three children became quite competitive, as a result, much to MO's dismay. That competitive spirit has stayed with all three of us ever since.

With the card game over, we all went to the small dining room and sat around the table for the meal MO had prepared. More often than not we had a roast beef, roasted covered in the oven with potatoes, onions, and carrots, or meat loaf, or some other dish using ground beef, such as tamale pie. Beef was the staple and was always available. DA liked cucumbers sliced thin and sprinkled with salt, pepper, and cider vinegar. We often had sliced tomatoes with a cooked sour-cream dressing made from DA's mother's recipe. Often MO would make a cake or pie or custard for dessert. It was not the kind of diet recommended today by the National Institutes of Health, but we survived.

During dinner we had lively discussions about politics, world events, economics, or current ranch problems. Everyone joined in. After dinner, Ann and I helped MO wash the dishes and put them away. Then all of us sat in the living room reading and talking until time for bed. Before going to bed, all of us walked outside to look at the sky. That night, it was clear and no moon was up. The stars were so bright and so numerous that we stood in silent awe. The universe appeared overhead, and we were bit players indeed—small specks of life on a small planet circling the sun. Our concerns seemed less important somehow.

"Good night, MO. Good night, DA. What are you going to do tomorrow?" "Good night, Sandra, I'll see. I need to fix a coupling on the windmill at High Lonesome. Maybe you'd better come along."

Top: *Ira Johnson and Sandra at lunchtime.*
Bottom: *Branding.*
Opposite: *Sandra, age sixteen.*

22. Bug's Stand-In

A job doesn't get done when it's started
with a promise and finished with an alibi.

R. LEWIS BOWMAN,
Bumfuzzled Too

*I*N JULY 1945, I WAS HOME FROM EL PASO, WHERE I WOULD BE A senior in high school in the fall. When the spring roundup had ended, in May, some of the calves had been too small to brand, and DA thought they had missed quite a few cows when they'd gathered the cattle at Antelope. The country around Antelope Well is particularly hilly and rugged. The basalt rocks are large and numerous, and the hills are covered with juniper, catclaw, and mesquite. It is easy to miss seeing some of the cattle there. DA decided to spend a few days gathering all the cows with unbranded calves, along with any cows suffering from pinkeye that required treatment. Bug Quinn was up in the Coronado National Forest working with the Forest Service for the summer. MO said she would prepare the lunches for the crew for those few days, and I volunteered to take the lunches out to meet the roundup crew each day.

"Where will you be today, DA, when you are ready for lunch?" "We'll head for Antelope Well, by the water tank there. Can you find it?" "I think so. I go up to Robbs' Well and go right, to the west, along the canyon." "That's right. When the road forks, take the one to the left." "What time should I be there?" "Oh, I don't know. It could be anywhere from nine-thirty to eleven-thirty when we get there with the cattle."

That night MO and I put a large pot roast in a heavy deep pot with a lid. We sprinkled plenty of salt and pepper on the meat, then added some chopped onions and some green chili. We set it in the oven at about 200 degrees and left it cooking slowly from 10:00 P.M. until 5:00 A.M. We got up about the time DA, Alan, Ann, and the cowboys left to start the day's roundup. It was an hour or so before daylight. MO and I made some coleslaw, cooked some scalloped potatoes and some green beans, and made an applesauce sheet cake. We loaded the chuck-wagon box in the bed of the pickup truck, along with the food we had prepared and a large thermos of iced tea, some ground coffee, and the old metal coffeepot. The chuck-wagon box had all the tin plates, tin cups, forks, spoons, and knives, as well as salt, pepper, sugar, and matches.

MO asked, "Sandra, are you going to be all right? DA won't want you to be late. It will take you about two and a half hours to get there, so you should leave about seven A.M." "I'll be fine. I'll get started pretty soon."

I started the pickup. It was a Chevy, several years old. It had never been washed since the day it was purchased. The pickup, like all the motor vehicles at the Lazy B, was just parked in the open area near the bunkhouse. The keys were always left in the ignition, ready to go. I checked the gas; it was half full. I started the engine and drove out of the ranch compound onto the dirt road. At the top of the hill I turned off on the smaller dirt road to Robbs' Well. I had to stop and open two different gates, then close them again, to keep the cattle in the two large pastures between the house and Robbs' Well. The sun was up, and it was getting hot. I rolled both windows down for air. I had to drive slowly on the rough dirt road—it was more a track than a road—and the dust boiled up behind the pickup as I drove along. The truck began to feel a bit wobbly and heavy. It did not steer quite right. I stopped the truck, put on the brake, and got out to see what was wrong. It didn't take long to find out: the left rear tire was flat. "Just on one side," as DA would say. There was no going on or back until the tire was changed. I looked in the back of the pickup. On one side, under a metal cover, was a spare tire. I rummaged around and found a jack. I knew no one would be coming along the road either way to help. If the tire was to be changed, I had to do it. I put large rocks behind the two front wheels so the truck would not move when I jacked it up. Then I put the jack under the axle on the left side and put the lug-wrench handle in the slot and started pumping it. It was easy until the weight of the truck was on the jack. Then I pushed with all my strength and got the tire off the ground. I took the lug wrench out of the jack and fitted it over one of the nuts on the bolts on the tire and tried to turn it. The tire rotated, and I could get no purchase on the nut. Finally, I decided I would have to let the truck back down until the tire rested on the ground again so that I could loosen the lug nuts before jacking it up again. It was harder to let the truck down than to jack it up, but I got it down. The lug nuts were too tightly attached to move. Probably the tire had not been changed for a couple of years. I pushed with all my might, but the lug nuts would not loosen. Finally, I stood on the lug wrench and tried to jump a little on it to create more force. Joy! It worked. There was a bit of movement. Working one at a time, I finally got all five nuts off the bolts. Then I jacked the truck up again so I could lift the tire off the wheel. At last it was off. I was soaked with perspiration and red faced. The sun was overhead, and the temperature was soaring. I got the spare tire out and rolled it over to the bare wheel. I managed to lift it up and fit it onto the posts. Then I started to screw on the lug nuts using my fingers alone, screwing them down as tightly as I could. Once that was done, I lowered the jack again until the tire rested on the ground. I then used the lug wrench to tighten the lug nuts as best I could. The flat tire and the jack were stowed in the bed of the pickup, and I started the engine and continued on.

It was late. The tire problem had taken more than an hour to solve. I followed the track past Robbs' Well and took the left track leading to Antelope. The track crossed a rocky canyon several times. I had to put the pickup in low gear and maneuver it around the worst of the rocks. The track was barely visible in many places. It was close to 11:00 A.M. when I reached Antelope Well. I could see the cattle and the cowboys already there. There was dust boiling. The cows and calves were bawling, and the men yelled as they tried to keep the cattle encircled. A branding fire was burning, and the men had started to brand the calves.

I parked and got out. I could see DA, but he didn't acknowledge my presence. The crew continued to work the cattle. I knew it would be a couple of hours or more before they finished. I also knew they liked to eat lunch as soon as they arrived with the cattle and before they had to brand and work on them. Tempers would be short today, I thought. "This wouldn't have happened if Bug had been here," they would think.

I scouted around for some mesquite wood to build a fire. I found a little dry grass and some weeds to get a flame going. I piled the wood up in a cone around the little fire to get the wood burning too. I got the old metal coffeepot out and filled it from the pipe that conveyed water from the well to the water tank. When the fire was going well, I found some flat rocks to put around it and placed the coffeepot over the fire, resting on the rocks. Bug always dumped a quantity of coffee grounds directly in the pot. There was no coffee strainer or percolating device. I dumped the coffee grounds in and put on the lid. Then I got the chuck wagon open at the end of the bed of the truck. I got the food out and some big serving spoons, along with the thermos of tea and some plastic glasses. The coffee came to a boil, and I moved it to the side to steep. I took a raw egg, cracked it, and threw the whole thing, shells and all, into the coffeepot. Bug said that settled the grounds and cleared the coffee. Then I waited. There was still no sign or word from DA.

The dust boiled up where the cattle were running around. The noise of the cattle bawling was constant—the cows bawling for their calves, and the calves bawling from the burn of the branding iron and the cut of the knife. The smell of burning hair and hide as the calves were branded filled my nostrils. No wonder they like to eat first, I thought. Jim threw his lariat, caught another calf, and dragged it to the branding fire. Claude grabbed the calf by one front leg and one back leg and threw it down on its side, bawling and kicking. Claude quickly tied three of the calf's legs together with the pigging string, the short piece of rope used for that purpose. He turned the helpless calf over so that the left hip was exposed for the brand. Jim rode near, flicked off his lariat, and gathered it in loops to make his next catch. DA took a red-hot branding iron and stamped the Lazy B brand on the calf's left hip. The calf kicked and bawled as his hide was singed. Rastus used his pocketknife—razor sharp, as always—to flick off the tip of each ear to complete the earmark. Then he just as quickly reached between the calf's hind legs and castrated him. Ira vaccinated the calf and untied the pigging string. "Yo-ah!" he yelled as he shoved the calf to get him to stand up and stagger off to find his mother. Jim was already back with another calf, which was struggling to get free of the encircling rope. And so it went for a couple of hours. When the last calf was branded, and the last cow with symptoms of pinkeye had been treated with medication on her eyes, DA said, "Well, that's about it. Let's go get some lunch."

It was close to 1:30 P.M. The crew looked dusty, dirty, and exhausted. There were no jokes or remarks. They just headed for the water and the iced tea. The tea by then was barely cool, but it was still wet. They sat down in the dirt near the pickup and rested. It had been a long, hard day.

"You're late," said DA. "I know," I said. "I had a flat tire the other side of Robbs' Well and had to change it." "You should have started earlier," said DA. "Sorry, DA, I didn't expect a flat." "You need to expect anything out here." "DA, how about some lunch? I'll get you a plate." "No. I'm too tired to eat now."

I had expected a word of praise for changing the tire. But, to the contrary, I realized that only one thing was expected: an on-time lunch. No excuses accepted.

The rest of the crew ate, and all the food disappeared in short order. "So, Tanny. Had a flat, did you?" said Rastus. "Yes—at least it was flat on one side." "Did you find the spare okay?" "Oh, yes. It was there." "Probably picked up a nail over at Old Camp. We were doing some work over there and had the pickup." "Yeah. Might have been."

In thirty minutes or so everyone had eaten, and they headed back to sort out some of the cows to be moved to a different pasture. They collected the branding equipment and put it in the pickup. I gathered up all the dirty dishes and the pots, pans, and bowls and loaded everything in the bed of the truck. "I'll be off now," I said to no one in particular. And I sure hope I don't have another flat on the way home, I thought.

When I got back to the ranch at about 4:00 P.M., MO was at the front door looking anxious. "You're late," she said. "Yes. Had a flat tire this morning." "Oh, no. What did you do?" "Oh, I changed it." "Good for you. Everything okay?" "Yes. Sure. But DA wasn't very happy about how late I was." "I know," said MO. "He gets that way."

A couple of days later, on July 16, DA was gathering the cattle in the big pasture near the headquarters. Because it was near and the horses were there, he decided they didn't need to leave the corral until about 6:00 A.M. I decided to ride that day, and Ann, Alan, and I got up at 4:00 A.M. to get ready and have breakfast. We were still in the kitchen at 5:30, rinsing off the breakfast dishes. The sink was below a kitchen window looking out to the northeast; there was a little light in the sky where the sun would soon rise in the east. DA and I were standing in front of the sink when we saw an enormous flash of intense light to the northeast. It looked like an enormous ball of fire in the distance. There was no sound. A dark cloud formed where the light had been, and then the cloud rose in the sky. "What do you suppose that is?" said DA. "I don't know. It looked like an explosion. How far away is it?" "Pretty far. I didn't hear anything. It must have been a munitions dump or a big chemical explosion somewhere. Hard to tell."

It was several weeks later that we read in some of our weekly mail about the first atomic-bomb test at Alamogordo, New Mexico. The Day family at the Lazy B was astounded to learn they had witnessed that ominous and historic event some 180 miles distant. In the land of cactus and cattle, scientists had unleashed the most stupendous force in the universe. The world we knew was changed forever.

Top: *DA sits atop a calf.*

Bottom: *Starting a cattle drive.*

Opposite: *A cattle drive; DA is in the foreground.*

23. *A Steady Hand*

Someday this'll all be over
just the prairie, grass and wind,
I hope He'll let me pass this way
When it's time for headin in.

ROD NICHOLS,
"HEADIN IN"

*I*T WAS JULY AND IT WAS HOT. THE SUMMER RAINS HAD NOT YET fallen to cool things down and settle the dust. Dust boiled up with every step. The cattle were thin. The windmills were breaking down, one after another. Times like these defined how we could survive. Every animal was important to us, and we tried to keep them alive and well.

Rastus gathered the thinnest cows and brought them into the corrals at the ranch. We then fed them high-protein hay and some grain. Some of them were so weak that they could not get up on their feet once they lay down. When that happened, the cowboys had to go to the corrals three times a day and literally help the thin cows up and make them walk around for a while. The cowboy term for this procedure is "tailing up" the cow. It took three men to accomplish it. One man would stand at the cow's rear end, bend down, and wrap her tail around his shoulders and neck, then stand up to lift the cow's hindquarters. The two men in front of the cow would then slip a rope under the cow's belly toward the front legs, and they would lift up her front end. The cow would wobble a bit, but usually she could stand for a time and walk around. The man who had to wrap the tail around his shoulders usually had a ring of cow manure on his shirt as evidence of his efforts.

Rastus had more patience than most of us with the thin, sick cows. He would get some hay in his hands, put a little grain on it, and then offer it to a recalcitrant cow, saying, "Come on, Bessie. Have a little bite. It'll make you feel better." He would bring a bucket of water to a cow too weak to walk to the water trough. That July there was a thin cow that was particularly weak. She had not improved with the hay and grain. As soon as the men would tail her up, she would fall down again. Finally, Rastus, who had helped tail her up dozens of times, just walked away saying, "By God, she's sick." He was right. She died a day later.

In midafternoon, when the heat was the worst, Ann, Alan, and I would sometimes go to the bunkhouse. The cowboys, if they were not out on the range somewhere, would take an afternoon break there to get some shade. There was always a pan of biscuits sitting on the stove, and a bowl of cooked apricots in the refrigerator. We would get a biscuit, break it open, fill it with a couple of apricots, and enjoy a snack.

"Rastus, how about playing some poker?" "Okay. Sure. Get some matches for chips." I got a handful of wooden matches from the box by the stove. "Here we are. We can each take twenty." "Let's cut for deal." "There. You're high, Rastus. You deal."

The old, worn-out cards were too limp to shuffle. Rastus just mixed them up a bit and dealt five cards facedown for each player. "Ready? Put down your bet." I put down five matches. Rastus matched it. "Okay. Hit me." Rastus dealt the next card to me faceup. "Again," I said. "Okay. I'll stand on this." Then Rastus dealt himself two more cards. Seven in all. "Well, what do you have?" "A pair of kings." "I guess that beats my eights. You win." The matches were scooped up, and I got the deal. An hour passed with the poker hands keeping us occupied.

Alan opened the screen door and entered the bunkhouse. Alan was ten years old. He had learned to drive the pickup truck and enjoyed any excuse to drive it. It was time to put some feed out for the weaned heifers in the big pasture. "Rastus, would you go with me to put the feed out?" "Sure. I'll go with you." He gathered up the cards and put them in their carton and got his hat from the peg on the wall. Then he got his .22 rifle from his bedroom, and Alan and Rastus put the cottonseed meal in the pickup to feed the heifers.

Alan drove and Rastus opened and closed the pasture gates when they crossed the fences. As they drove along they saw an occasional jackrabbit. Alan would stop and Rastus would take careful aim and shoot the rabbit. He seldom missed.

At the end of July, after the rains began and the grass started to turn green and grow, DA announced it was time to gather some old cows and some old bulls to sell at the auction in Bowie. We rounded up the cattle in the Big Pasture first, then those in the Black Hills. With each drive, once the cattle were gathered, it was necessary to "cut" them—to remove from the large herd those specific cows and bulls that DA thought should be sold. Cutting cattle out of a large herd is the ultimate test of a good cowboy. There are many categories of cattle within the herd. Sometimes it is necessary to cut out the mother cows with calves that will be sold. But the cows with heifer calves that are to be kept as replacement cows will not be cut out. Or perhaps only certain older cows and bulls will be cut out. In a milling herd of cattle, cattle that are bred to look alike, it is difficult to know which calf belongs to which cow. Sometimes they are close together and it is clear you're looking at a mother cow and her calf. Sometimes they become separated and it is hard to know which calf belongs to which cow. Rastus had an uncanny ability to identify a particular cow and her calf. He could identify small physical characteristics that distinguished one from another, characteristics that the rest of us could not see.

Alan, DA, Rastus, Jim, Claude, and Cole were the crew the day in July when they rounded up the cattle in Big Pasture. The cattle were bunched up in a herd and Claude, Cole, and Alan rode around the outside to keep them circling and together. DA, Rastus, and Jim rode inside among the cattle to identify and cut out the ones to be sold. The calves tended to be skittish and tried to run off. Jim always tried to keep the mother cow between him and the calf so the calf would feel more protected and not be as apt to run off. The men riding on the outside had to remain constantly alert and try to be in the right place at the right time to turn the other cattle back but still make an opening for the cow being cut out to move out of the herd. Alan was on the outside when Rastus was moving fast on his horse to chase out of the herd one of the old cows DA wanted sold. Alan was a bit slow making room for the charging cow to run out of the herd. It was too late, and the old cow ran back into the middle of the herd. Rastus was angry. He thought Alan had not been paying close attention. "By God, boy, didn't you see what I was bringing out?" he shouted. Alan said, "Yes, but I didn't know what to do about it."

Rastus didn't care about Alan's response. He wanted and expected a good performance from everyone on the crew. Everyone in turn respected Rastus and wanted to look good in his eyes. And in Rastus's view, things were only black or white, good or bad, truth or a lie.

Rastus went back in the center of the herd to find another target. He identified a cow and a calf as being ones that should be cut out. He worked the two of them to the edge of the herd and then ran them out to be held for the cut. DA rode up to Rastus and said, "Hell, Rastus, that is not a pair you just cut out. That calf belongs to another cow." Rastus looked shocked. "Well, then you run the outfit. I'm through." Rastus rode out of the herd and back to the ranch. "I quit," he said. Rastus's pride was such that he would defer to no one else when it came to identifying the cattle. His honor was at stake. Rastus packed up his trunk, took his saddle and bridle, and asked Claude to drive him into Duncan that night. "I'm through here," he said.

We were stunned and heartsick. Rastus was part of the family. A week passed, then another, then another. We heard nothing from Rastus. Finally, DA drove to Duncan and asked around at the Duncan Mercantile, the barbershop, and the Bonnie Heather about Rastus. He found Rastus finally and apologized for questioning his judgment. DA asked Rastus to please return to the Lazy B because he was needed there and he was missed. Rastus thought it over and decided to return. None of us questioned Rastus's judgment about the identification of a particular cow and calf ever again.

Rastus rode almost daily to different areas of the ranch. He always carried his .22 rifle with him in a scabbard. Shooting rabbits and coyotes was a favorite pastime for Rastus. One of his horses was a big sorrel named Major. Major also enjoyed hunting, and he learned to spot jackrabbits for Rastus. When Rastus rode Major, Major would stop and turn occasionally, looking straight at a jackrabbit. Rastus would pull his gun out of the scabbard, take aim, and fire. The rabbit would drop, and Rastus and Major would move on.

When we were in between roundups, Bug Quinn would go back to Duncan, and Rastus, Claude, and an extra cowboy would live in the bunkhouse. Rastus did most of the cooking. Every other day Rastus would make a pan of biscuits. His method was always the same. He filled a large stainless steel bowl half full with flour and added about a teaspoon of salt, measured only in his cupped hand, and about a tablespoon of baking powder, measured the same way. Then he put in a large mixing spoon's worth of white lard, which he would cut fine with a wire pastry cutter and mix with the flour, salt, and baking powder. Next, he made a hole in the center of the bowl and added milk. He would stir from the center, incorporating a little more flour into the dough with each stir. When all the flour was incorporated and the dough more or less held together in a mass, he dumped it out on a floured board and patted it into a round an inch or so thick. He used a round tin biscuit cutter to cut the biscuits, then put each one in a buttered old metal pan. The pan went in the oven until the biscuits were brown.

DA once asked Rastus why he didn't make just half a pan of biscuits when there were so few people there to eat them. "I don't know how to do that," said Rastus. The dogs hanging around the bunkhouse were happy that Rastus never learned to make half a pan, because they got all the ones he threw out.

One of Rastus's horses was a dark brown gelding named Scorpion. Rastus liked to ride Scorpion because he had a very fast walking gait and could cover many miles quickly. Rastus never waited for anyone riding with him to catch up. The unspoken code of conduct required people riding together to ride abreast rather than following one after another.

Horses usually prefer to follow, but cowboys prefer to stay abreast. When I went with Rastus, I was constantly falling behind and having to gallop my horse to catch up. When Alan returned to the ranch after college, he particularly enjoyed riding his horse Saber. Saber had a natural easy fast walk, almost like a Tennessee walking horse. One day Alan was riding with Rastus. They rode into the Black Hills, with Rastus in the lead, as usual. When they got out of the hills, into the flat country, Alan eased up on Saber and let him go at his own natural pace. Saber could walk considerably faster than Scorpion in the flats. Just to pay Rastus back for all the times through the years he was in the lead, Alan kept Saber a little ahead, but kept reining him in to make it appear that Saber was going at as fast a walk as he could. Rastus would spur Scorpion to get him to move faster. When he did, Alan would let Saber walk a bit faster. After a few miles of this, Rastus became very annoyed—not with Alan, but with Scorpion. He thought Scorpion was just being lazy. Alan secretly chuckled that he finally had a horse that could get ahead of Rastus.

As Rastus grew older, he slowed down a little. DA told him he should just work when he felt like it. He said the ranch was Rastus's home, and if he never worked again it was all right. But Rastus never really stopped helping. He usually did the chores—milking the milk cow, feeding the dogie calves in the corral, wrangling the horses.

When Rastus was seventy-five, he felt quite feeble. He had developed tuberculosis when he was drafted in World War I, and his respiratory system never quite recovered. MO asked him if he wanted her to take him to the veterans hospital at Fort Baird, near Silver City, to get some medical treatment. He agreed and packed a few things to go to the hospital. The hospital staff treated Rastus kindly and kept him several months. We went to see him every few weeks, but he did not get better. Rastus told MO he didn't want his money and stocks to go to all his relatives when he died. "There are a couple of them who are all right. And I'd like to give a little to Sandra's, Ann's, and Alan's children." MO said she would get a lawyer to prepare a will, and she did. Alan went to see him one day a month or so later and asked Rastus how he felt. "Not good," he said. "I expect I don't have long to live. But it is all right. I'm ready."

Rastus died the next day. None of us were with him when he passed away, which made us especially sad. We got his good suit, which had been made in El Paso in 1945 and had never been worn. Rastus was buried in the cemetery in Duncan in his gray suit. His grave is near the ranch, which had been his home and his life for most of his seventy-five years. The cemetery is rather rocky and barren, but there is a quiet dignity about it nonetheless. Somehow it is the proper resting place for Rastus. Nearby are the graves of our grandmother Mamie Scott Wilkey and her parents, Andrew and Evelyn Scott—all of them hardworking, good people, weathered by the sun and shaped, like Rastus, by their understanding of life in that dry and harsh land.

Top: *Lazy B cattle.* PHOTOGRAPH
© 1990 TOSHI KAZAMA

Bottom: *DA and Boo Allen with a range-management tour.*

Opposite: *MO and DA in the 1940s.*

24. Government Action

Nowhere else on earth has the conflict between
the old Lockean faith in free property as
the guarantor of free men and the new faith
in collective ownership as the promise of a
secure society been so fiercely drawn.

DONALD WORSTER,
Under Western Skies

$\mathcal{U}$NTIL THE PASSAGE OF THE TAYLOR GRAZING ACT, IN 1934, THE federal land in Arizona and New Mexico was open for grazing by anyone without payment of a fee and without supervision. Great stretches of the western lands were still not populated, and there was little thought given in Congress or the Department of Interior in the years before the Depression to the need for legislation. Almost every family in the Southwest owned some horses and cattle. These animals roamed free wherever their owners turned them out to graze. Some people acquired large numbers of cattle, and everyone competed for the use of any green grass wherever and whenever it appeared. The result was severe overgrazing of the public lands by the 1930s.

There was also a serious erosion problem. The highways and the railroads that were built across the area of the Gadsden Purchase ran generally in the lower elevations, where rainwater would accumulate in the rainy season. The roads and railroads were built with virtually no planning for flood control, and no effort to avoid soil erosion from the occasional rains.

The Lazy B was in the drainage basin of the Gila River. The major valley on the ranch leading into the Gila was Railroad Draw. The Southern Pacific Railroad went through the Lazy B for eighteen miles, much of it along Railroad Draw. In an effort to keep floodwater away from the railroad tracks, the railroad company built levees and diversions to channel the water out from the rail bed. In time these efforts led to massive erosion, cutting a channel in the draw as deep as fourteen feet in places. Where formerly the rainwater had spread out over wide areas of the draw and produced thick grass in the rainy seasons, after the levee and diversion work, gullies formed, which in turn developed into steep defined canyons. Because the floodwater would find these defined channels, it could no longer spread out widely to produce grass. The combined effect of soil erosion and overgrazing was to leave the land along Railroad Draw much less productive of forage than before the railroad and the ranchers.

Nothing was done to correct the problem until the summer of 1950. Heat waves rose from the flat hardpan surfaces of the desert. An occasional dust devil spiraled up in the distance. Alan was toying with a lariat one of the cowboys had given him, and MO and DA were having a glass of iced tea and discussing some of the things that should be done at the ranch. When he saw the telltale dust trail of a car approaching on the ranch road, DA stopped his long tirade about the problems with one of the windmills and watched. A car arrived and stopped in front of the house. DA got up and opened the squeaky screen door. "Come on in, Boo. It's cooler in the shade, and the iced tea is all right." Boo Allen, the chief of the Safford Grazing District, was a frequent visitor to the largest ranch in his district. A large man with a big smile, he usually moved slowly, but on this particular day he almost bounded into the house. He took the glass of iced tea without seeming to notice it and said, "I've got an idea that will surprise you. I've been working on a plan for some time now for flood control and irrigation. The Lazy B fits perfectly into my plan."

Boo's idea was simply to slow down and delay the rainwater runoff and spread the water out so it could soak into the ground and produce more grass and other plants. It was a difficult task because the ranch went from an elevation of 6,200 feet above sea level at the top of the Peloncillo Mountains to 3,400 feet at the Gila River—a drop of some 2,800 feet over approximately sixteen miles.

Boo proposed that DA build a series of large dams along the Railroad Wash and the other major canyons. Below the dams the captured water would be released slowly and would spread out over as much land as possible to irrigate the vegetation. Nothing like it had been tried on BLM territory, and Boo wanted to start it on the Lazy B. He thought twelve major dams would be needed and several hundred small diversion spreaders below the major dams. Boo said he wanted to propose that the BLM would provide most of the initial construction cost but the Lazy B should put up 15 percent of the cost and agree to maintain all of it thereafter. DA listened intently and questioned the proposals. He could see the possibilities, but the ranch had been hard put to pay for all of the fencing and cross-fencing, the improvement of the breeding herd, and the maintenance and improvement of the wells and cattle troughs. He needed to keep a tight rein on his expenses to make ends meet. Finally, DA said, "Boo, it just might work. But I don't know how I can come up with the money."

MO had listened quietly. She loved DA and loved the ranch. She said she would contribute her own money toward Boo's plan. She thought the ranch would benefit greatly from the flood control. Abashed by MO's offer, DA then agreed that Lazy B would put up its share of the costs. He said later that "MO may look like a frail, little middle-aged wife, but those looks are deceiving."

Boo had to sell his concept both to the federal agency in Washington, D.C., and to the ranchers in his area. It is hard to say which was the harder sell—the BLM brass or the local ranchers. The end result on the Lazy B in time produced dramatic results. The dams built across the normally dry canyons and washes had large pipes to permit the water behind the dams to drain out in a slow, controlled manner. Small flood spreaders below the dams continued to distribute the water slowly to wide areas. The construction work on the Lazy B took five or six years to complete. After completion, constant maintenance was needed to keep the system working properly. Some spreaders needed to be made larger, some needed repair. But in a few years the results were impressive. Wide stands of thick, healthy grass replaced barren rocky ground. Every rainy season produced areas of good grazing for the livestock. The Lazy B became a showcase site for the soil conservationists. The State Department sent various visitors from arid lands around the world to visit it and see what could be done in areas of limited rainfall. DA enjoyed showing the visitors around. He began to claim that the idea was his, and he thought the problems of reduced grazing areas were over.

In 1959 DA attended a United Nations–sponsored meeting in Safford on watershed protection and flood control. Nineteen nations were represented, and there were interpreters for several languages. The meeting lasted two days. DA said the representatives asked many pertinent questions about the cost, and the benefits, in economic and other terms. They asked how it was financed, and whether the groundwater levels were recharged. DA enjoyed his conversations with the committee enormously and came away even more convinced that the flood-control work on the Lazy B was useful.

As Alan became more involved in management of the ranch he decided that, although providing slower and better irrigation of the grass was important, it was equally important to provide periods of rest when no grazing of the grass would be allowed. He thought that the long-term health of the grass and vegetation required intervals of rest, or "timed" grazing. The primary advocate of rest/rotation grazing was a Rhodesian immigrant named Alan Savory. He argued that proper grazing of grasslands is better for the land than no grazing at all. The hoof action on the land and natural fertilizers and grazing at intervals seem to produce more and better vegetation than no grazing at all. Alan began implementing these concepts at the Lazy B, again with dramatic results. The range became far more productive than it had ever been in DA's lifetime. The average weight of the calves increased by more than one hundred pounds. The range improved to the extent that bighorn sheep and some antelope were reintroduced on the ranch.

All the progress had both a monetary and a human price tag. Every time a new range conservationist was assigned to the Safford Grazing District, we had a new education cycle. Most of the new conservationists arrived with the notion that grazing cattle were bad for the water and the soil. We had to show them that good grazing practices could be good for the land.

Part of the education process happened in the saddle. After the conservation project got under way, we would invite the rookie range conservationist to saddle up and ride with us on part of a roundup. Teaching the newcomer how to find his way and how to stay out of trouble was also a lesson in patience for our cowboys. But the cowboys knew it was part of the job.

After work we would share a few beers and tell some tall tales. The camaraderie on the bunkhouse porch probably did more good than days of looking at the grass and explaining the flood spreading and the range rotation.

Sometimes a district ranger would get some ideas that tested the tolerance of all of us. A new ranger named Frank decided we should move all the cattle out of the big East Pasture to the area called High Lonesome. It was midsummer and hot. There were about three hundred cows, many with small calves only a few weeks old. DA told Alan to handle it.

Alan explained to Frank, "You need to be aware that this is the hottest time of the year. The small calves don't move very well, especially in this heat. Cowboys are willing to do a lot of tough things, but we shouldn't force this on them either. It could be disastrous for all of us."

Frank crossed his arms over his chest and said, adamantly, "I'm the conservationist here. Move the cattle."

Alan considered his options; he shoved his hands in his back pockets and remembered the old adage Experience is the name we give to our mistakes. Alan guessed Frank needed some experience. "Frank, why don't you come along with us, then, and help us move the cattle?" Frank agreed, and the next morning we saddled up early. There was an uneasy quiet that morning. There was none of the usual cowboy banter. Even the horses were quiet and didn't do their usual early-morning prancing and snorting. We fanned out in the East Pasture, gathering the cows and calves as we moved along. By 10:00 A.M., it was 100 degrees and climbing. The little calves started to quit. They wouldn't move. A layer of fine dirt covered all of us completely. There had been no summer rain as yet. By noon, the cows just balked. They would go no farther.

Some of our cowhands that day were local teenage boys on summer break from school. Even they were weary, too. The cows settled in groups near any kind of bush for a bit of shade on the heated ground.

Finally, we spotted a dust cloud moving along. It was Bug Quinn, our cook, with the lunch. Cold drinks were on the way! Everyone was so hot, tired, and cranky that all we wanted was some cool water and shade. The crew shared a bit of shade under the chuck wagon. "Let's just rest a while," Alan said. "Maybe we can get the cattle moving again after an hour or two."

Time dragged. We didn't even have the energy to swat the flies that found us. Finally, the teenagers started poking each other and whispering about some girls in town. It was time to get moving. We mounted the horses, and with much shouting and waving of hats we got the cattle moving slowly along toward High Lonesome, still some five miles away. Some of the small calves were carried by the crew across their saddles. Most of the cattle made it, but Frank's mistake became his experience. Never again did he order a sudden move of the cattle at a time when it wouldn't work out.

Over time, the Bureau of Land Management increased its staff and the number of paper-pushing bureaucrats. Development of new rules and regulations became the top priority instead of on-site range improvements. At the same time, the ability of the rancher to produce a profit declined. The increase in grazing fees and monthly expenses more than offset the improvements in the land and the grass. The Lazy B was designated for "stewardship" because of the demonstrated improvement in the condition of the range. No more than eleven stewardship designations were ever made by the BLM. There were too few Boo Allens and Harry

Days in the western rangelands. The outlook in general for the ranchers was not bright. And the bureau was reluctant to reward the best and most creative of the private ranches. Time, the federal bureaucracy, and public sentiment about grazing on public lands combined to make ranching on those lands an increasingly difficult and risky business.

Alan with the horses. PHOTOGRAPH © 1990 TOSHI KAZAMA

Opposite: *Alan with MO and DA in 1981.*

25. *Midlife Concerns*

When I am able to do a job and do it right
and accomplish something I get some satisfac
tion out of it, but when I am unable to accomplish the job it leaves me feeling thwarted. I
have decided that the responsibilities of running this ranch are too much for me at my age
and my physical condition.

LETTER FROM DA TO SANDRA IN 1955

$\mathcal{A}$FTER ALAN GRADUATED FROM THE UNIVERSITY OF ARIZONA, he married Barbara Mellick, whom he had met at the university. Alan and Baa, as she was called, came back to the Lazy B. MO was exceedingly happy to have Alan back at the ranch. They were always close, and it meant a great deal to MO to have Alan and his family there.

For DA, Alan's return was a mixed blessing. DA was getting older. He'd developed an ulcer and some back problems, which he called "lumbago." These health problems slowed DA's activities, and he felt less able to do all that he was accustomed to doing. He needed Alan's help with the roundups and dealing with the hard physical labor. At the same time, DA found it very difficult to share management decisions with Alan. DA was accustomed to making all the decisions, and it was not easy for him to accept other views from his young son. He was also obsessed with keeping expenses low, and Alan's easygoing ways were a source of great irritation. Alan thought that if certain equipment was needed, the ranch should buy it.

DA had spent his years at the ranch building up the Hereford breed of polled cattle. They were a handsome red color with white faces. But the years of inbreeding had started to produce some dwarfs. Alan decided to buy some Angus bulls, and later he bought a new breed developed in the

Southwest called Barzona. Barzonas are a solid red color. The breed is a mixture of Hereford, Angus, Santa Gertrudis, and others. DA resisted these changes and complained about the cost of the new bulls and the uncertainty of the future. Alan was young, inexperienced, but eager to try new ways of doing things and new ways to expand the business of the Lazy B. He wanted a better financial prospect than DA had achieved. The conflict between father and son was foreseeable and understandable. But it was also real and painful to watch. As early as 1959 DA wrote to me, "It is impossible for Alan and me to work together. I suppose it is probably the father and son complex at our ages."

In the years from 1959 to the late 1970s Alan and DA continued to feel the unhappiness and tension from both sides. DA often would be moody and unhappy. More often than not MO would bear the brunt of his unhappiness. He would return to the house hot and dirty from working on a windmill somewhere and then say that MO had "slugged him with a new taste thrill," and that MO then was in a "bad humor because I wouldn't eat her food and ate canned beans instead." MO would explain, "It is delicious—Sandra gave me the recipe." In a letter to me DA urged, "In the future please be careful about putting these ridiculous ideas about cooking in her head."

DA was inclined to view the future with pessimism and to worry about every conceivable problem and calamity. In the ranching business there were always many obstacles that could occur. The rancher had no control over the weather, the price of cattle, or the price of the commodities that had to be purchased. His only control was over how many employees to hire, when to buy the necessities, and how best to use the available pasture. In 1976 DA wrote, "The future of Lazy B Ranch looks very bleak to me. I don't see how it is going to be able to operate at a profit for the next few years. BLM cutting our numbers hurts. They have greatly increased the grazing fee. . . . In addition the State leases amount to a good deal and our property taxes go up every year. We have too many built-in expenses—gasoline . . . telephone bill . . . butane gas . . . electricity . . . regular labor . . . insurance. . . . I guess I am a pessimist but I can't be optimistic with all these expenses facing us."

Beginning in 1957, some grandchildren were born. John and I had three sons, Scott, Brian, and Jay. Ann and her husband, Gene, had two sons and a daughter, Curtis, Barry, and Jill. Alan and Baa had a son and a daughter, Alan Jr. and Marina. MO and DA loved their grandchildren and welcomed them at the ranch with open arms. Alan Jr. and Marina lived there and were part of the daily life at the ranch until they left for college. The others spent as much time there as possible during summer vacations and at Christmas. DA was never at rest unless all of his children and grandchildren were under his roof.

As Alan and DA each grew older, the tensions between them eased somewhat. For one thing, DA was no longer able to ride horseback after a hip replacement, and he was forced to rely more on Alan's day-to-day management. Alan, in turn, grew less confrontational on many of the business decisions. The coming and going of the grandchildren also provided diversion and interest to both MO and DA by the early 1960s. Each grandchild learned from DA the same respect for people of every walk of life, and for hard work and careful use of resources that his children had learned a generation earlier.

Top: *Lunch at the chuck wagon. Ada Mae, pregnant with Sandra, stands in background.* Bottom: *Branding.* Opposite: *The Bonnie Heather Inn.* COURTESY OF J. A. JOHNSON

26. *Off Duty*

If yer gonna drink, gamble, and chase girls,
be sure ya do 'em one at a time.

R. LEWIS BOWMAN,
Bumfuzzled Too

*T*HE OLD COWBOY SONGS HAD IT ABOUT RIGHT. THE LIFE OF A cowboy was a lot of hard work, low pay, few female companions, but a great deal of loyalty and pride in the craft and skill. Most of the time the work went on seven days a week. Every few weeks one of the men would decide to go to town. Rastus, who didn't drive, and anyone else who didn't have a truck or car would usually go along. The first stop in Duncan was at one of the two bars, the Bonnie Heather or the Snakepit. There wasn't much difference between them. The smell was the same: stale cigarette and cigar smoke, stale beer, and dusty, dank leather.

The sawdust on the floor of both bars was changed only about once a month. All the spilled drinks and wads of chewing tobacco just stayed there until the monthly cleanup. Both places had old-fashioned long wooden bars that showed their hard use through the years.

For years the local status symbol for the cowboys at the Bonnie Heather was how deep they could put their teeth marks into the bar. After enough liquor was consumed, the men would try to take a bite out of the rounded front edge of the bar. Usually, the best they could do was to leave a few scrape marks.

The partying usually started at the Bonnie Heather, and if things were lively it would continue there. If things fizzled out or got dull, the cowboys would wander across the railroad tracks to see what was happening at the Snakepit.

One year when a Gila River flood hit Duncan, the water reached about four feet on Main Street. The Bonnie Heather was built on about a two-foot-high concrete slab, and the water inside the place only came up about two feet inside. The flood marks are still there on the old wood bar. The Snakepit was completely washed away in the flood, but it was rebuilt about a block away, and the old wooden bar was saved.

There was a musty little dance floor in the back of the Bonnie for an occasional Saturday-night dance. A shuffleboard game was against the wall, and there were dice cups on the bar. Many an hour was whiled away throwing the dice in the game ship, captain, and crew. The main room had a pool table. The price of a game was usually just the quarter on the rail to challenge the winner. Often a game would be played for a beer. There were not many hotshot pool players in Duncan, but the cowboy games could be pretty competitive.

The town drunks could be found at their regular bar stools every afternoon. Most of the clientele were the "regulars" and the occasional cowboys and miners from the outlying areas. The cowboys took comfort in the fact that they could be at the ranch a month or more and then get to town and walk into one of the two bars, sit down, and continue a conversation with one of the regulars that had started the last time they were there. Sometimes a few women would visit the bars—an occasional wife of a male customer and, sometimes, a single woman. When a Duncan couple divorced, it was not unusual for the divorced wife to tend bar for a while at one of the two bars. A fresh female face at the bar would create a stir and increase the adrenaline and the hormone count. One or more of the cowboys would try to match up with the new woman. The competition could get vigorous.

The talk in the bars was usually of local events—who did what to whom and when and where it had rained. A fight would break out now and then over some real or imagined slight, but most were soon over. The Lazy B had a cowboy for a time named Dane. He loved a good fight and would provoke one if he had a chance. He gave the ranch a bad name for a while, and it got a little dangerous for a Lazy B cowboy to be there at all. We finally had to let Dane go to keep our crew in one piece.

Alan invited a Phoenix lawyer friend to come to the ranch for part of a roundup. The friend liked to ride and wanted to make a hand. One night, after a good many days of riding, they decided to go into the Bonnie Heather for a few beers. The bartender asked Alan's friend what he did. The visitor said, "Oh, I'm a Harvard Law School graduate." The bartender looked puzzled and said, "What's that?" The bartender also asked him what he wanted. Alan's guest said, "Cutty and water." The bartender looked blank and said again, "What do you want to drink?" "Well, what kinds of Scotch do you have?" The bartender said, "Mister, we have whiskey and beer. Which do you want?"

Jim said he had never had a drink in his life until he was over forty. He said his first drink was during a blizzard; one of the other cowboys had a half-pint of whiskey in his pocket and said, "Jim, here. Have a drink of this. It'll warm you up." He said it did, but the most we ever saw Jim drink was an occasional beer.

One time Rastus was in Duncan at the Bonnie Heather and got pretty drunk. That didn't happen often with Rastus. Jim happened to be in town and said he would bring Rastus home. Jim sat patiently in the bar waiting for Rastus. There was a young cowboy Jim didn't know bragging about how he could ride anything and could rope whatever moved. He said he was riding the rough string out at the Lazy B, which of course Jim knew was not true. The young cowpoke went on and on, even though everyone in the bar knew Jim, Rastus, and the Lazy B. They just let him continue. Finally, the young cowpoke turned to Jim and said, "You look like a cowboy. What do you do? Where do you work?" Jim quietly answered, "Well, I ride the rough string out at the Lazy B." That was the end of the storytelling that day, at least in Duncan.

One afternoon in April in the 1970s, some of the cowboys had gone to Duncan. Alan went along. After the haircuts and the shopping, they gathered at the Bonnie Heather for a few beers before going back to the ranch. The conversation ranged from the weather to the roundup just ended, and then to Hard Rock, a local character who frequented the bars. If Hard Rock had a last name, no one knew it. He was an old bachelor who'd acquired his name by working in the local mines in his younger days, drilling through the hard rock in the mine shafts. He'd eventually decided cowboying was more to his liking than mining. He ended up working for a neighboring rancher, Elmer Stevens. Hard Rock had a tough life both in his chosen work and in the troubles he brought on himself.

Hard Rock's biggest trouble was that he could not pass a bar without visiting it. Anytime he had cash in his pocket, it was soon spent in the nearest bar. He tended bar from the customer's side quite often. Over the years, he had lost all his teeth. He went to a dentist who told him, "Yes, I can fit you with false teeth. But it will cost you several hundred dollars." The price was more than Hard Rock could scrape up. He always said he was going to save enough to get some false teeth; the problem was that all his cash was spent at the bars.

Hard Rock was well known in Duncan for two events there. One summer Hard Rock was gathering cattle on Elmer Stevens's ranch with the rest of the roundup crew. They came across a pickup truck in the middle of the pasture. There was a dead man inside it. Apparently, the man had driven out in the pasture and just died sitting in his truck. At that time, most ranches didn't have a telephone. The cowboys all leaned on their saddle horns and looked concerned. Finally, Hard Rock spoke up. "Well, if he has false teeth, they're mine. I want 'em." That story went around Duncan with some chuckles.

The second event, which ended Hard Rock's life, was also often discussed. Hard Rock was sitting in the Bonnie Heather in 1978. Word had come to Duncan that a major flood was coming down the Gila River. The whole town was preparing and bracing for the flood. Every able-bodied person was filling sandbags, placing them along doorways and plate-glass windows, and was helping store owners put all the merchandise on higher shelves.

The Bonnie Heather was on a foundation about two feet above street level. To enter the bar, one had to climb several steps. Hard Rock was sitting on a bar stool drinking beer out of the bottle. Everyone in the bar said, "Well, it's time to leave. The flood's almost here. Let's get going. Come on, Hard Rock." "Hell, I've lived here all my life. Water has never gotten up here in the Bonnie Heather. You go on. I'm gonna stay right here and drink. Let the flood come if it chooses. I ain't going to get out of this here bar." The waitress made a looping sign with her finger next to her head, signifying that she thought Hard Rock was crazy. "If that's your choice, stay here then. But we're leaving," she said.

Everyone left to seek higher ground. Hard Rock stayed, sucking happily on his beer. The flood soon swept right down Duncan's main street. It filled the bus station. Then the gasoline station. Then Lehman's Dry Goods. Then the Up-to-Date Grocery, the Art Gallery Drug, and the movie theater. Still the brown foamy water came, higher and higher. Soon it came up the steps and into the Bonnie Heather. It was ankle-deep when Hard Rock decided to get out. The problem was there was no place to go. He waded out the front door and down the steps to street level and was swept off his feet by the swift current and carried down and across the street. He grabbed the branches of a big cottonwood tree as he was floating downstream. He held on and climbed up the tree to a limb he could sit on above the raging floodwaters.

The water receded some by morning. At nightfall both the tree and Hard Rock were still there. The Army Corps of Engineers had sent some people to Duncan to monitor the flood and rescue people if necessary. The corps decided it should use its helicopter to pluck Hard Rock out of the cottonwood tree. The helicopter hovered over the tree and lowered someone down on a sling to get Hard Rock on it. He was able to get into the sling. The helicopter lifted up and flew across the flooded river, with most of the town watching in fascination. In a hayfield on the north side, the helicopter lowered the sling to the ground. When the crew went to the sling to help Hard Rock out, they found him dead. He had died of a heart attack while he was being rescued. That story, too, was a topic of conversation in the Bonnie Heather for years after.

Top: *Our wedding reception at the ranch, December 20, 1952. Left to right: Ann, John's sister, DA, Sandra, John, John's father, Alan, John's mother, and MO.* Center: *The ranch house at sundown.* PHOTOGRAPH © 1990 TOSHI KAZAMA Bottom: *MO and DA in front of the ranch house, 1950.* Opposite: *A close-up of our wedding picture.*

27. *A Wedding*

To get the full value of joy
you must have someone to divide it with.

R. LEWIS BOWMAN,
Bumfuzzled Too

$\mathcal{I}$N 1946 I ENTERED STANFORD UNIVERSITY AS A FRESHMAN. MO and DA drove me to Palo Alto to get me settled. I was sixteen, and I felt poorly prepared compared to the other freshmen I met. I returned to the Lazy B at Christmastime and for summer vacation. There were heated discussions at the dinner table with DA. The Keynesian economic theories I was learning at Stanford were not consistent with DA's pay-as-you-go economic theories.

In my third year at Stanford, I took an undergraduate class taught by one of the law school professors. I loved the class and decided to enter law school at Stanford for my fourth year as an undergraduate, if I could be accepted for early admission. MO and DA said they would pay the cost of any graduate education and that law school was all right as far as they were concerned. DA said he wouldn't mind having a lawyer in the family whom he could consult. Stanford Law School accepted me, and I began the studies that would shape my life.

The summer before I started law school, I persuaded Forrest Sanders to let me work in his law office in Lordsburg as a secretary and receptionist, a job I would also continue the following summer. Forrest had a small-town general practice. He represented defendants in some of the major criminal cases in the county. His clients also included the owner of one of the local bars who ran an illegal gambling operation in the back room and a woman whom Forrest said ran the largest house of prostitution in the country. He had some less colorful clients who just needed wills written or contracts prepared. I saw a side of Lordsburg I had not known existed.

For years MO and DA and other local citizens managed to attend at least part of the most dramatic criminal trials when Forrest was defending. It made for good theater and Forrest usually talked the jury into a defense verdict.

During the spring break at Stanford, my first year in law school, I brought three of my Stanford women friends to the ranch for part of the roundup. DA was apprehensive and said he didn't know how they could take care of my friends and also do the work that needed doing. But Beatrice Laws, Barbara Finn, and Calista Farrell proved to be great company and good sports. DA talked nonstop, telling our visitors all about the ranch. Even the cowboys liked Beatsie, Barbara, and Calista and were sorry to see them leave.

The following spring, I brought John O'Connor, a fellow law student, to the ranch to meet my family. John and I had been assigned to edit and cite-check a law-review article at the law school, and John had suggested we finish the project by having a beer at a local pub in Palo Alto. That had led to a series of dates for the next forty nights in a row. Things had begun to look "serious."

John had grown up in San Francisco and knew nothing of ranch life. I was concerned that MO and DA might not approve of my beau. John and I drove to the ranch from Palo Alto and arrived at the headquarters in midafternoon. DA, the cowboys, and Alan and Ann were all in the corrals doing some branding. John and I went to the house to greet MO. MO was very happy to see us and suggested that we go on down to the corral to see DA. We walked to the corrals and let ourselves in by a gate, then walked across the first corral to the second one, where a branding fire was burning. The branding irons were heating in the fire, and the crew were putting the calves through the branding chute one at a time. DA was branding them. Alan was vaccinating. Claude and Rastus were castrating the steers and earmarking the calves.

DA was aware that we were there, but he did not stop the work to say hello. He nodded at us briefly but continued to use the branding irons. Finally, he motioned John and me over and said, "Hello. Glad to see you. This must be John. We're a little busy right now, John. We'll be through after a while." Then DA went to the corral fence and took down a piece of baling wire that was hanging there. He straightened it out and reached into a dirty-looking bucket and pulled out a couple of bloody testicles that Rastus had tossed in there after castrating some calves. DA trimmed them a bit with his pocketknife, then put them on the baling wire and placed them in the branding fire, where the "mountain oysters," as we called them, sizzled and cooked. DA turned them to cook all sides, then brought the baling-wire skewer over to John and said, "Here, John, try some of these." John gulped a bit and said, "Sure, Mr. Day." He plucked one of the "oysters" off the wire and popped it in his mouth. "Umm, pretty good," he said.

Welcome to the Lazy B, I thought. There is nothing like a gracious introduction to ranch life.

We spent the next few days riding on the roundup and letting John get acquainted with everyone at the ranch. John had a ready Irish wit and made everyone laugh, so the visit was a success. In summer, John and I announced our engagement and broke the news to John's parents and to MO and DA. The wedding date was set for December 20, 1952, at the Lazy B. I had graduated from law school the preceding June. I'd stayed some weeks in California trying, without success, to find a job as a lawyer and also studying and taking the California state bar exam. John's law school graduation was not until June 1953. After the bar exam, I returned to the ranch to help plan the wedding.

DA was building a new barn near one of the windmills. MO decided they could use it for the wedding reception before anything else was put into the barn. DA agreed to butcher a beef and prepare it in a pit barbecue for the wedding dinner. The local cowboy band was hired, and invitations were sent. MO, DA, Ann, Alan, and I went to the mountains near Silver City a few days before the wedding and cut a number of piñon pine trees, many pine boughs, and some mistletoe to decorate the barn. The piñon pines' fragrance perfumed the whole barn. MO put some hay bales around and covered them with canvas for extra seating. DA and the cowboys dug a pit about five feet square and brought in a pile of mesquite wood. They butchered a Lazy B yearling and boned most of the meat. They seasoned it with season salt, pepper, some chopped onion, and green chiles and wrapped the beef in aluminum-foil packets of several pounds each. The foil packets were then wrapped in wet burlap. The day before the wedding they built a mesquite fire in the pit and let it burn down to hot coals. A thin layer of dirt was shoveled over the coals, then the meat packets were laid in the pit, and more dirt was shoveled over the top. The beef cooked in the low radiant heat until midday of the wedding, when the dirt was removed and the meat packages carefully extracted.

John's parents came to the wedding, and John's father, Dr. Jay O'Connor, served as the best man. The rector of All Saints Episcopal Church in El Paso performed the wedding ceremony. Many of the neighboring ranchers and friends drove long distances to the Lazy B for the wedding, and most brought salads and casseroles to contribute to the meal. The men wore their fancy boots and best Stetsons. Grandmother Wilkey attended, along with other Wilkey and Day relatives. All the cowboys were present, and one of them even danced with John's mother. The band played country music, including old favorites like "Put Your Little Foot" and "The Virginia Reel." Some of the grizzled old ranchers told John "that he'd better be good to Sandra or he would have to answer to them." The dust didn't settle on the ranch road for days after the wedding.

Time to saddle up.

Opposite: *The Duncan Mercantile Store.*

COURTESY OF J. A. JOHNSON

28. The Race

> *When I bestride him, I soar, I am a hawk;*
> *he trots the air; the earth sings when*
> *he touches it.*

SHAKESPEARE, *Henry V*

$\mathcal{I}$T WAS A THURSDAY IN MAY IN THE 1960S. THE SPRING ROUNDUP was over, and several of the cowboys had gone into Duncan and were at the Snakepit for a beer. Willie Babers, a local rancher, was there talking about his rope horse. "I'll tell you boys, my rope horse not only is the best rope horse around here, he's also the fastest." He pushed back his hat and exposed some of his red hair. The Lazy B cowboys looked surprised. One spoke up: "Hell, that horse isn't all that fast. There are plenty of faster horses around here."

Alan couldn't keep quiet. He knew Willie's horse and knew his sire, a big gray named Bimbo. Bimbo was also still in the Duncan Valley and owned by a fellow named Robert Johns. Alan said, "Hell, Willie, your horse can't even outrun his daddy."

An argument ensued. Willie finally said, "Well, put your money up. We'll have a race."

A few more beers and considerable negotiation resulted in a wager. Contingent upon Alan getting the consent of Robert Johns to race Bimbo, it was agreed that Alan and Willie would each put up $1,000. The race would be at the Duncan Fairgrounds in thirty days, for a distance of one-half mile, winner take all. That was pretty big for Duncan.

Alan was a bit chagrined the next day. He wasn't sure he could borrow Bimbo, and he wasn't certain all the cash would really be put up. But he drove out to Robert Johns's place. Robert was sitting on his porch steps picking at the rough wood that the weather had dried out. "Alan, I think you're right. Bimbo can outrun his progeny. In fact, I'm so sure, I want half the bet."

Alan was only too glad to assign half his bet to Robert, and Robert agreed that Alan could take Bimbo out to the Lazy B for the thirty days to train him with a jockey. Robert and Alan shook hands. Alan returned later in the day with his pickup and horse trailer. Bimbo loaded easily, and Alan took him to the Lazy B.

By that time Alan's son, Alan Jr., was nine years old and was a good rider. He weighed about ninety pounds, a good weight for a jockey. Every day after school for the next thirty days, Alan Jr. would saddle up Bimbo and "breeze" him. To "breeze" a horse is to get the horse in a gallop and run a number of short distances until the horse is working and breathing hard. Alan Jr. did some distance training with Bimbo, but mostly speed-work. Alan bought some high-powered grain, and they fed Bimbo well. Bimbo began to shine and look strong—probably better than he'd ever looked.

Finally the big race day rolled around. All of Duncan had heard about the bet, and at least half of the inhabitants showed up at the fairgrounds. Alan decided the occasion called for beer, so he drove into town and bought a keg of beer and some plastic cups.

The bet was on a race of half a mile—the distance of once around the race track. Many of the people around the track were busy making side bets on the race. Willie was there with his horse, and he had decided to ride his own horse. About 3:00 P.M. they decided it was time to get started. Willie and Alan Jr. lined up and were jockeying for the better starting position. Willie was crowding a bit, but Alan told Alan Jr. not to worry because Bimbo was faster.

Alan and Willie had agreed on who should be the starter. The start on a cowboy horse race consists of having a man on the ground just take off his hat and drop it on the ground. When the hat hits the ground, the race is on.

The hat dropped. The horses jumped out in a run. The crowd roared. The race was on. It was over all too soon. Bimbo was in great shape, and Alan Jr. was not very heavy. Bimbo won the race by fifty yards. It wasn't even close. But everyone had a great time. Willie was a good sport. The people there decided cowboy horse racing on a Sunday afternoon was something they would like to see more often. A few came up to Alan and said, "I have a pretty good horse. How about another challenge?"

In a week or so we arranged another race with the challenger. Alan Jr. continued to train and ride Bimbo, and they won the next race handily. Robert was pretty excited about how easily his horse Bimbo had won the two races. Robert matched another race with a fellow from out of town who was going to bring his horse into Duncan for the race. Alan smelled a ringer and told Robert he had planned a week in California with his family and couldn't be there with Alan Jr. for the third race. "Not to worry," said Robert. "I'll handle it."

Alan and his family left for the week in California. The challenger brought in a sure enough ringer, as Alan had suspected, and won the third race easily. Alan and Alan Jr. were happy their racing career had ended with two wins and no losses.

Top: *Alan with Round Mountain in the background.*

Bottom: *Alan and the Lazy B cattle.* PHOTOGRAPH © 1990

TOSHI KAZAMA

Opposite: *Ann, Alan, and Sandra.*

29. Round Mountain

A ranchman's life is certainly a very pleasant
one, albeit generally varied with plenty of
hardship and anxiety.

THEODORE ROOSEVELT,
Ranch Life and the Hunting-Trail

*T*HE YEARS PASSED QUICKLY. JOHN AND I LIVED AND WORKED IN Phoenix. We built an adobe house that we enjoyed with our three sons. Trips to the ranch were scheduled several times a year. It took almost five hours to drive there from our house. Our children looked forward to going as much as we did. We usually went for Thanksgiving and, every other year or so, for Christmas as well. We sometimes went for a long weekend during the fall and spring roundups. And we went to the ranch in the summer to leave one or two of our sons there for a more extended visit. Ann and her family also made frequent trips to the Lazy B from Tucson, where they lived.

The Lazy B was always a welcoming place. As we turned off the highway onto the ranch road, our hearts would beat a little faster. There was always a contest for who could see the windmills first. As we drove up near the house, MO and DA would come outside to greet us. The dogs would bark. Alan and his family would come out. The conversations would begin immediately, and DA would still be talking as we drove away a few days later.

It was a secure sanctuary. It was much too remote for a casual visitor. There were always recent events at the ranch that DA and MO wanted to describe in detail. There were current events in the larger world they wanted to discuss. There were drives to take, sunsets to see, DA's pheasants to observe, cowboys to visit with, horses to ride. The Day family felt lucky to have such a place in our lives—a never-changing anchor in a world of uncertainties.

DA suffered various complaints as he grew older. A hip was painful, and he finally had a hip replacement. It was only partially successful. He began to be short of breath and was diagnosed as having emphysema—scarcely surprising after his many years of heavy smoking. His eyesight grew worse. In time, he had to wear an oxygen inhaler and walk around with a tank of oxygen attached to a tube.

MO, like her mother, began to have a faulty memory. She remained physically fit and active, however. She still loved to go on walks with Alan. DA's mind was as sharp as ever, so he would tell MO what to do, and since she was physically able to do things he would remind her to do them. They were a pretty good team.

DA continued to express worry and concern about his children and grandchildren. "You never stop worrying about your children," he said. "I am only content when all of you are here at the ranch under my roof."

DA was no longer able to ride horseback, so he had no occasion to disagree with the hundreds of small decisions Alan made each day concerning the cattle. Alan's attempt to establish a cattle feedlot on the Lazy B farm at Virden, New Mexico, was unsuccessful financially and was terminated. Alan had also promoted the acquisition by Lazy B of some adjacent land as it became available. Some of these additions required additional work.

Rastus, Claude, and Jim Brister passed away. For some years a man named Cole Webb worked at the ranch and became the de facto foreman. He had a wife, Malynda, and five children, four of whom lived for a time at the ranch. The Webbs occupied a small frame house about two hundred yards west of the windmills. The Webb children were all helpful and very nice youngsters. They attended school in Duncan along with Alan's two children. Malynda worked for the school district and drove the children to and from school. The Webb children and Alan's children often rode horseback on the weekends and during school breaks to help with ranch work.

In the summer of 1981 life changed dramatically for me and my family. President Reagan announced my nomination as a justice of the Supreme Court of the United States. It did not seem possible that a ranch girl would grow up to serve on our nation's highest court. The announcement produced an avalanche of telephone calls, letters, and even visits to my parents. Everyone they had ever known wanted to contact them and say how pleased they were. The ranch, which had always been a quiet backwater, suddenly became the focus of national attention.

MO and DA responded to all the calls and letters. *People* magazine sent photographers, who photographed MO and DA just as they were, day in and day out. They traveled to Washington, D.C., to see me take my oath of office. That terse ceremony brought tears to my eyes as I looked down from the elevated bench in the courtroom to see my husband, our three sons, MO and DA, Alan, Ann, and President and Mrs. Reagan seated and watching the proceedings. It was a moment suspended in time, bridging the life in the harsh desert terrain of the Lazy B and the fast-paced, sophisticated life in Washington, D.C.

After a few days in our national's capital, MO and DA returned to the Lazy B and their regular routine. DA said he was glad he didn't have to live in Washington, D.C., and MO said she was sure she had seen President Reagan somewhere before. We assured her that she had—on the evening news on television.

I made several trips to the ranch in the years from 1981 to 1984. I spoke to MO and DA on the telephone at least once a week. During one telephone conversation with DA in 1984 he said there had been a "catastrophe" at the ranch that day. "What was it, DA?" "Your mother is out of cigarettes. I wanted to go with her in the car to the Franklin Store, but when I went out to the car without my oxygen I couldn't make it. So we can't go to the store." He laughed about the "crisis" and said MO finally had him on a short leash.

Despite his declining health, DA wanted to know what was going on with the ranch operation, and he insisted that the ranch office be kept in his house. Even though we had kept books by a computer program for several years, he insisted on keeping a parallel set of books by hand in his old manner, which took much time and effort. He had been strongly opposed to the genetic changes in the breeding herd that Alan had initiated some years back. He still insisted that the Herefords he had been so proud of were the best possible cattle for the ranch.

DA particularly enjoyed spring at the ranch. If there had been rain or a little snow during the winter, the desert would come into full bloom in the spring. It is not only beautiful but very nutritious for the cattle. The cows get fat and the baby calves receive a lot of milk from their mothers and grow fat and healthy. It brought DA and all of us much pleasure to see the new calves run and play. By March the California poppies would bloom and the hills would be golden. Poppies were DA's favorite flower.

In years with good grass from the previous fall we would keep many of the calves that were by that time six or eight months old and weaned from their mothers, and we would sell them the following spring. In years with less grass we would sell the calves in the fall. In the spring of 1983 we had kept about a thousand calves after weaning in hopes that we would have a wet winter followed by a green and beautiful spring to fatten the calves, and our hopes had been realized. The cows were fat, the baby calves were happy and sleek, and the yearling calves we had held over were very fat and beautiful. The roundup crew was assembled to start the spring roundup. Everyone was looking forward to it.

Alan started the spring roundup on April 9, 1984. They branded sixty-five new calves that day and gathered about a hundred weaned calves to keep in a holding pasture until their sale later in the month. These weaned calves were still in the corral and Alan was walking through the corral when an inner voice told him to show DA the calves. Alan argued with himself: "I'm too busy, and he is not feeling well." But again some inner voice told Alan to get DA to the corral to see the calves. Alan called to the cowboys who were waiting for him and told them to go have a cup of coffee while he did something he needed to do. When Alan entered

DA's living room, DA was feeling well and did not even have his oxygen supply attached. He was glad to have Alan put him in the car and drive him to the corral to see the calves.

DA asked Alan to drive him among all the calves again and again. They had gained so much weight through the winter that they now weighed about six hundred pounds each. He was amazed by how fine they looked and commented again and again about it. When they finally left the corral and drove the short distance to the house, DA said, "Alan, this is the finest set of steers that has ever been raised on the Lazy B Ranch."

DA and MO ate supper that evening and DA went to his desk in the office and began typing a letter to an old acquaintance. He went to bed at about 9:30 and never awakened. MO awakened at about 7:00 A.M. and discovered DA's body next to her in their bed. No one else was in the house. Alan and the roundup crew had gotten up early that morning and had left before dawn to go to the Gruell area of the ranch to gather more cattle. MO put on a housecoat and walked to the small house near the far windmill, which was occupied by Chad Moore, one of the cowboys, and his wife, Glenda. Glenda was there and offered to find Alan and the cowboys. At about 9:30 A.M., when Alan and his crew were about to corral the cattle they had found, Glenda drove up in her pickup to report DA's death.

Alan immediately returned to the headquarters and called Dr. Lovett, the local osteopath in Duncan who had been treating DA. The doctor said he would fill out the death certificate. Alan called the mortuary in Safford, which sent an ambulance to pick up DA's body. Then Alan called me and Ann to tell us the sad news.

We decided to have a memorial service for DA at the ranch. Old friends, present and former cowboys, and all the family gathered in the front yard of the house. We had baskets of poppies next to a photo of DA, and each of his children spoke. One or two of the grandsons also spoke. The memories were strong and fresh. His imprint was all around us in everything we could see, and touch, and feel.

The next day Alan, Ann, and I and our spouses and children, as well as our cousin Flournoy, took the box with DA's ashes and hiked up to the top of Round Mountain. It is rather steep and very rocky. We dodged several rattlesnakes along the way. They are always present on Round Mountain—perhaps because of the dark, volcanic rocks, which provide some warmth for them during the day. We knew the rattlers would guard DA's remains. On the top we looked around to see most of the land that comprised the Lazy B. There, around us, lay the site of DA's life for most of his eighty-six years. We put his ashes in a rock cairn that we piled up to hold them. We joined hands and recited the Lord's Prayer, and shed some tears for the great loss each of us felt. But we also knew that DA was where he wanted to be—a place where all the ranch could be seen, a place where the wind always blows, the sky forms a dome overhead, and the clouds make changing patterns against the blue, and where the stars at night are brilliant and constant, a place to see the sunrise and the sunset, and always to be reminded how small we are in the universe but, even so, how one small voice can make a difference.

Top: *DA and MO, September 25,
1981.* Center: *At the Supreme
Court, September 25, 1981.*
Bottom: *In front of the Supreme
Court building, September 25,
1981.* Opposite: *Alan in a
pasture.*

30. Nothing Is Forever

For almost everyone who has come into this
country in modern times the land of the West
has jolted the mind and tried the body. Very
little of it has seemed designed for human
ease. . . . Everywhere in the region there is so
much space—so much amplitude of rugged
rock, soil, climate, and vista—that the landscape, like the gods of old, can leave men
and women feeling humbled or diminished,
exhilarated or threatened.

DONALD WORSTER,
Under Western Skies

*A*LAN HAD BEEN THE MANAGER FOR SOME YEARS BEFORE DA passed away, but DA had remained very active in ranch business throughout. He didn't like all the changes in the government policies regarding land management, and he grumbled a lot about all the new young "wet-behind-the-ears" government employees who were running around on the land. He had delegated all of the responsibility of dealing with the government agencies to Alan soon after Boo Allen had retired as head of the local BLM office.

Dealing with the administrative work with federal and state regulatory agencies took much of Alan's time. Alan took the responsibility of ranching on government land seriously and participated in many meetings and seminars on the subject. He served on, and as president of, the local grazing advisory board of the BLM. He was active in public-land issues with the state and national cattlemen's associations. He applied for and was granted the designation of stewardship from the BLM. This was an acknowledgment from the government agency of his dedication to good land management. He attempted to help other local and statewide ranchers in their dealings with government agencies.

Alan's intense involvement in the issues of public-land management eventually made him somewhat discouraged about the future of cattle grazing on public land. Day by day it was becoming more difficult because new rules and regulations seemed to be adopted frequently. The number of employees in the Safford BLM office went from 4 people to 115 during the time Alan was managing the ranch. Those employees all needed something to do. Implementing all of the new regulations and ideas kept them busy. Of course, some of the rules made sense, but others appeared to the ranchers to have been dreamed up by people who had no experience "on the ground." Problems that could have been resolved out in the field would be referred instead to the state office and then to Washington, D.C. Decisions would be made by people who had never been in the area where the problem arose and sometimes were lacking in common sense.

A humorous example of bureaucratic overkill occurred one day when four trucks stirred the dust up on the ranch road and arrived at the head-quarters with eight people on board and various funny-looking things loaded in the back. Alan asked what was going on, and the BLM employees replied that they were going out to select sites on the ranch to build hawk nests. Alan asked why new, artificial hawk nests were needed. The reply was that someone in the local office had developed the idea and hoped to get a good write-up in his personnel file when it was installed. Alan asked if hawk numbers were declining, and the reply was that they didn't know. Alan asked if they had done a census of hawks to see how many there were. Again the answer was no. "Well," he said, "how do you know that the hawks will like these nests?"

"We don't know, but it seems like a good idea."

It took the eight men six days to install the six hawk nests they had constructed in their shop. They were essentially just large birdhouses on fifteen-foot poles. The BLM set these poles in concrete, and the nests are still there years later. No one has ever yet seen a hawk on, in, or near any of the nests.

Some of the decisions regarding grazing were more serious. The numbers of cattle the ranchers were allowed to run on the ranches were reduced in many cases, and reduced again and again. In the northern part of Greenlee County, the county where the Lazy B was located, the Forest

Service reduced numbers on all the ranches to such low levels that no one could make a living on any ranch in the area. Since then, ranching has ceased in that part of Greenlee County.

Alan had read about the Savory "rest/rotation" grazing plan and embraced the idea of resting areas to let the grass regenerate. But many ranchers did not like this rest/rotation system of grazing, and when the government insisted that they implement it, some ranchers resisted vigorously. Instead of trying to persuade the ranchers that this was a good system, the BLM just announced that the ranchers had to comply. One neighbor, a man ranching south of the Lazy B, told the BLM to "go fly a kite" and to stay off of his ranch. The BLM officials went out to his ranch and counted more cattle than he was allowed to have on his ranch. One day Alan and two cowboys were going to High Lonesome to work on the well and found the county road blocked by armed officers. Alan asked what was going on and was told to turn around and go back because the BLM was gathering all of the neighbor's cattle from his ranch. It took twenty armed men, ten cowboys, and one helicopter to gather approximately a hundred cattle from that ranch. The cattle were impounded and sold at auction, and all the expense of gathering them was deducted from the proceeds. By the time the fine for overgrazing and the cost of gathering and selling the cattle were deducted, there was no money left for the rancher. Although Alan never condoned overgrazing, he was unhappy about the heavy-handed, costly handling of the problem. All of these concerns over grazing on federal lands caused a good many sleepless nights and much discussion with neighbors and family.

The Lazy B was the largest BLM permit holder in Arizona. At one time this might have been something to be proud of, but because grazing had fallen so much out of favor and was being attacked from all sides, Alan thought that having the largest permit merely made the Lazy B a bigger target. There were even some members of Congress who expressed their opposition to all public-land grazing permits. And the federal government was not the only opponent of grazing on public land: several private organizations were spending considerable time and money trying to persuade the public that grazing by cattle was damaging all of the public lands and that the only way to save the West and preserve it in a pristine manner would be to remove all the cattle.

The three Day children had all married and had families by the 1980s. MO and DA's grandchildren loved to come to the ranch, and they all spent time there each summer. DA and Alan both hoped that one of the grandchildren would express an interest in running the ranch. All of the grandchildren were bright and energetic, but none chose to make the ranch their lifework. It was a sad realization that the next generation would not maintain the ranch.

MO continued to live at the ranch as before. Alan checked on her several times a day and took her for walks as often as she wanted to go. We were fortunate to employ three kind women from the area to take three-day shifts to stay with MO. Over a period of time her memory grew steadily worse and she was less active. She never failed, however, to be gracious with everyone. In March 1989, MO passed away. Like DA, she was able to remain at the ranch until her death and avoided any hospitalization. Again the family held a memorial service at the ranch that was attended by all the family, neighbors, and friends. And again the family carried MO's ashes to the top of Round Mountain to be placed in the rock cairn with DA's ashes. They belonged together at that special place.

In 1986, after much soul-searching and with a great deal of unhappiness, Alan called a meeting of the stockholders of the Lazy B—himself, Ann, our cousin Donald Mason, and me. After a good lunch and pleasant conversation he got down to business. The future of Lazy B did not look good: with no family member after Alan interested in making the ranch his or her home and with the future of public-land grazing very much in doubt, it seemed an appropriate time to sell the old ranch. Ranch prices had declined in the few years prior to this decision—no doubt because of problems with government leasing—but the old place was still worth something. After much discussion we ultimately decided to sell the Lazy B. Because of its large size, there was no ready market.

Alan decided to sell it in smaller units. It was divided into five units, and each of them was sold separately to different buyers. The sales covered a period of seven years. It was a heart-wrenching time for all the family. The Round Mountain section was the last one sold, and that was after MO's death. Alan was the last of the family to leave after the sale closed. He took some family pictures, albums, and mementos but left everything else in place—the tools, vehicles, and equipment, the contents of the bunkhouse and barn, and even furniture in the house. As Alan drove away on the ranch road in 1993 he knew he left behind 113 years of family knowledge and memories, cattle, horses, and a way of life. He also left behind the remains of our parents, forever part of that desolate place they'd made their home, and the way of life for their children, their grandchildren, and the people who worked there and also made it their home for more than a century. The world will not be a better place if ranching ceases on the public lands of this nation. But the era of ranching as we knew it at the Lazy B is surely gone forever. The remaining ranches are smaller and probably less likely to survive. The fragile Southwest high desert lands comprise a region of arid beauty and diversity of plant, animal, and insect life. It is exceedingly important that they be preserved. The area is far too large to be able to be preserved by stationing rangers on it, as in a national park or monument. The law governing its use allows multiple uses of the land by many people for recreation as well as grazing. The best way to preserve these vast acreages of public lands in the Southwest necessarily calls for responsible use of those lands by people who care about both those lands and their own survival. MO and DA accomplished that in their years at the Lazy B, as have many other capable and sensible ranchers.

Leaving the Lazy B. PHOTOGRAPH © 1990 TOSHI KAZAMA

Opposite: *A desert view.* PHOTOGRAPH © 1990 TOSHI KAZAMA

Epilogue

An inhumane and limited code, the value
system of a life more limited and cruder
than in fact ours was. We got most of it by
inheritance from the harsher frontiers that
preceded ours . . . mainly from our contacts
with what was left of the cattle industry.

WALLACE STEGNER,
Wolf Willow

*T*HE POWER OF THE MEMORIES OF LIFE ON THE LAZY B IS STRONG. It surges through my mind and my heart often. Alan and Ann say the same. We know that our characters were shaped by our experiences there as surely as Arturo Gonzales shaped his clay sculptures in art class at Radford School. The value system we learned was simple and unsophisticated and the product of necessity. What counted was competence and the ability to do whatever was required to maintain the ranch operation in good working order—the livestock, the equipment, the buildings, wells, fences, and vehicles. Verbal skills were less important than the ability to know and understand how things work in the physical world. Personal qualities of honesty, dependability, competence, and good humor were valued most. These qualities were evident in most of the people who lived and worked at the Lazy B through the years.

A basic instinct in both animals and humans is that of territoriality. We want to belong to a place familiar to us. If we have such a place, we are part of it and it is part of us. Intruders and outsiders are tolerated but not welcomed. We knew the ranch, its hills, its mesas, its canyons, its rocks, its soil, its climate, and the life it sustained. We knew the vastness of the sky and our total dependence on the weather. We knew well our family, the men who worked there, and their families. We belonged to the Lazy B, and it belonged to each of us. We thought it would always be there, that our children and our children's children would know it as we did. We knew that no matter how far we had traveled, we were still welcome there.

As the years went by, Ann and her family, and John and I and our children, lived lives far removed from the Lazy B. We were concerned and involved with state government, with the practice of law, with child care. When we returned to the ranch for visits, the years and our own personal concerns melted away immediately. Within minutes it would be as though we had never left. The immediate needs and problems of ranch life became the topic of conversation: the cattle, the rainfall and grass conditions, the condition of the various wells and fences, the cowboys, and the equipment. Deference to DA permeated the atmosphere, and MO spread her blanket of welcome and affection over all of us.

The decision to sell, to let the ranch go, was so difficult that I still avoid confronting it directly. I fear returning to the ranch and seeing it in other hands and with all its changes. Alan has returned several times. He reports that one of the two huge windmills at the headquarters was removed but later restored, that the ranch buildings show changes and some decay, that the cattle are no longer uniform in quality and appearance. These are things I do not want to see for myself.

Alan, Ann, and I worry about the future of the federal and state lands in the greater Southwest. We agree on one thing: the land is better protected from destruction by off-road vehicles and people out for target shooting when it is occupied by responsible ranchers. James Galvin described it well in his novel *Fencing the Sky*:

> The American West had two things to lose: its distinctive horse-based, non-progress-oriented culture, and its natural environment. . . . They aren't two things but one. You lose either, you lose it all. What we want is the land and the wildlife itself, and a culture based on stewardship and care.
>
> Stockmen and environmentalists have long been at odds. They demonize each other out of fear. Both groups are afraid of

losing what they value most. They burn up bushels of rhetoric over issues like grazing fees and wolves. But really, both embattled camps have more in common than they have to disagree about.

They both love the land. . . . They are both idealists. Nobody gets rich ranching, and nobody gets rich being an eco-warrior. No environmentalist ever put a ranch out of business. And if you can face up to the present and stop clinging to obsolete stereotypes, no rancher worth his salt is going to destroy the land that is his livelihood.

The little towns we knew Lordsburg, New Mexico, and Duncan, Arizona—have both shrunk and changed. The interstate freeway bypassed Lordsburg, leaving it on the sidelines to shrivel and decline in population. The old Hidalgo Hotel has long since closed, along with several other businesses. Fat Hoy and Colonel Holt have passed away. The little hospital is closed. There is no longer an active mining business nearby, and the ranchers have cut back in many ways. Duncan was flooded several times by the Gila River, and the buildings along the main street are largely closed or gone. A few farms remain. The Art Gallery Drug is a piece of history.

Wallace Stegner wrote in *Wolf Willow* that "frontiers, like wars, are said to break down established civilizing restraints and to encourage demoralization. They are also sometimes said to engender in people, by freeing them from artificial restraints and throwing them into contact with clean nature, a generosity, openness, independence, and courage unknown to the over-civilized."

So, which was it? Were we demoralized, or did our ranch life make us more generous, open, and independent than we otherwise would be? We like to think we benefited in many ways from our ranching experiences, that openness, generosity, and independence were ingrained in each of us. If so, it is due to the life created for us by our parents on that inland island called the Lazy B, and to the men and families who lived and worked there in the twentieth century. The land is still there, but not its former inhabitants. We suspect that the land will remain more or less as it is over the twenty-first century as well. The area is not likely to be developed or to attract a greater population. We are not so sure that it will be peopled by those who will give the land and its limited resources the same care and attention as those described in this memoir. But, as with life and death on the Lazy B, that's the way it is.

ACKNOWLEDGMENTS

Remembering the past is treacherous.
We tend to remember the good things and
bury the bad. In order to try to re-create
on paper the life we lived at the Lazy B,
we received needed help and encouragement
from our sister, Ann, from the letters written
long ago by our parents, from Alan Day Jr.,
Gil Alexander, Phil Martinetti, Suzanne
Tucker, James Shaw, and Craig Joyce, and
from our editor, Kate Medina. We also are
indebted to Linda Neary for transcribing our
writing and putting it on a computer disk.
In a few instances names have been
changed to protect surviving relatives
of those mentioned.